MENU
PRICING &
STRATEGY
SECOND EDITION

MENU
PRICING &
STRATEGY

SECOND EDITION

JACK E. MILLER

VNR VAN NOSTRAND REINHOLD
New York

*The second edition of this book
is dedicated to my wife, Anita,
as my thanks to her for
encouragement and help in
writing it.*

Copyright © 1987, 1980 by Van Nostrand Reinhold

Library of Congress Catalog Card Number 86-28127
ISBN O-442-26442-9

Printed in the United States of America

DESIGNED BY BARBARA MARKS

Van Nostrand Reinhold
115 Fifth Avenue
New York, New York 10003

Van Nostrand Reinhold International Company Limited
11 New Fetter Lane
London EC4P 4EE, England

Van Nostrand Reinhold
480 La Trobe Street
Melbourne, Victoria 3000, Australia

Macmillan of Canada
Division of Canada Publishing Corporation
164 Commander Boulevard
Agincourt, Ontario M1S 3C7, Canada

16 15 14 13 12 11 10 9 8 7 6 5 4 3

Library of Congress Cataloging-in-Publication Data
Miller, Jack E., 1930-
  Menu pricing and strategy.
  Bibliography: p.
  Includes index.
  1. Restaurants, lunch rooms, etc.—Prices.
2. Food service—Prices. I. Title.
TX911.3.P7M55 1987   647'.95'0681   86-28127
ISBN 0-442-26442-9

CONTENTS

PREFACE TO THE SECOND EDITION

This book is about the development and pricing of menus—the basis of profit in any restaurant operation. The book's primary purpose is therefore to provide both the student and the restaurant owner/operator with a body of basic information that addresses marketing strategies, menu development, and pricing methods. The book does not offer set rules, but rather, it provides alternatives, concepts, and principles by which the student can learn and the owner or manager can develop profit concepts.

The book is structured for both teaching and learning; it is organized in units from concept to reevaluation of present systems. If you are a student, the book will help you devise strategies for pricing and development of menus. If you are an owner/operator, the book will help you improve sales and marketing of your operation.

Every chapter of the book takes economic, marketing, and advertising strategies and gives them a practical application in menu planning. There are solutions for owners who want to control cost without decreasing quality standards. Both student and owner can develop a menu philosophy based on sound mathematical and economic principles and so make decisions that will result in a quality, profit-making operation. In this revised edition, my obligation to you, the reader, is to give you a choice of various alternatives and let you make the decisions. This book will provide the means, methods, and systems to achieve successful marketing and profit in any foodservice operation.

ACKNOWLEDGMENTS

A text of this nature is the result of the involvement of many people. Without the contributions of owners and managers of restaurants throughout the country—who permitted their menus to be a part of this book and who gave me permission to comment on their menus—a major part of this book would not have been possible. I am grateful that they were willing to do this. My thanks to: Vincent Bommarito, *Tony's*, St. Louis; Richard Turner, *Bordello*, Hannibal, Missouri; Sally Hopkins, Hallmark Cards, Kansas City, Missouri; David Flavan, *Noah's Ark*, St. Charles, Missouri; Helmut Steiner, *Das Stein Haus*, Jefferson City, Missouri; Pete Nikolaisen, *Nikolaisen's*, Sunset Hills, Missouri; Herb Traub, *Pirates' House*, Savannah, Georgia; Ray Jacobi, *Sheraton St. Louis Hotel*, St. Louis; David Slay, *La Veranda*, St. Louis; Arthur B. Schneithorst, Jr., *Hofamberg Inn*, St. Louis; Mike Saracino, *Bartolino's South*, St. Louis; Steve Gorczyca, *Hullings Cafeteria*, St. Louis; Dorothy Lee, St. Luke's Hospital, Chesterfield, Missouri; Dan Cusanelli, *Cusanelli's*, St. Louis; Bill Federhofer, *J. R. Federhofer's*, St. Louis; Tom Scheffer, *Zeno's*, Rolla, Missouri; *John Clancy's Restaurant*, New York City; John Kawa, *Johnny's Cafe*, Omaha; Ralph Brennan, *Mr. B's*, New Orleans; Richard Perry, *Richard Perry's Restaurant*, St. Louis; Francis Haussner, *Haussner's Restaurant*, Baltimore; and James Furry, *Buffalo Chips*, Santa Monica, California.

I also wish to acknowledge the Restaurant Associations of California and New York, which permitted me to use the accuracy-in-menu materials that they developed as guides for their memberships. The statistical data provided by the National Restaurant Association have been invaluable for outlining marketing, feasibility, and customer characteristics for the marketing strategies discussed in this text.

I also want to acknowledge all of the students who have challenged my theories in cost control and menu planning courses. Students have required me to improve my teaching methodology and to show them the best and most current systems to prepare them for careers in the hospitality field. I especially want to acknowledge the students in these two courses in the spring of 1985 who suffered through the tape recording of the principal text of this revision.

I also want to give credit to my wife, Anita, who struggled through my handwriting, misspelled words, and long tape recordings—all while trying to master a new computer and prepare the manuscript for this revision.

I believe that a book is the result of contributions from many people, and I am grateful to all those who have contributed to what I believe will be a useful text for menu strategies.

CHAPTER ONE

MENU
DEVELOPMENT

PHASES OF MENU DEVELOPMENT

The menu is the ultimate profit center and theme control of a restaurant. Regardless of the status of your restaurant, there must be a menu. If your operation is only in your head or on the drawing board; if your restaurant is ongoing; if your profits are declining; if your restaurant is in transition from one type of operation to another—your menu always is the focal point. It is essential to examine and understand the menu's critical role in each of these four phases.

The Conceptual Stage

If your restaurant is in the conceptual stage, a proposed menu will help you determine what kind of establishment it will be. The image of your foodservice operation will be defined by that menu, so it is an all-important tool. An appropriate menu is essential for conveying your concept effectively.

What does the menu tell about a restaurant? It reveals something about the intended clientele, because it is written to attract specific types of people. It also dictates the purchase of certain equipment, because specialized items may be necessary for preparing dishes on the menu. Space requirements and conditions also are affected by the menu. If everything is made on the premises, for example, then a large preparation kitchen will be necessary. If, however, the restaurant will rely on ready-made or convenience foods, then a large storage area will be needed.

The menu will also provide a general guide to the type of personnel needed. Will the restaurant require experienced staff or can employees be trained on-site? A fast-food operation, for example, does not need experienced personnel; employees can be trained in a short time to attain an acceptable performance level. The skill requirements of food preparation and restaurant service increase as the complexity of the operation increases.

The menu also has an impact on the restaurant's decor. The food that is offered must be compatible with the decor. As the menu develops, you can begin to visualize colors, wall art, and the general ambiance of the dining area(s). The decor will reflect the personality and taste of the individual who is planning it.

The Operational Stage

If you surveyed a number of restaurants in your area, you probably would find that the most successful ones are those that keep up with the current food trends and public eating habits. Every restaurant that opens includes menu items that are popular—at the time. Many restaurants, however, open, become established, and never change their menu. Customer count may then decline because the restaurant has not stayed abreast of the food that its customers want.

Monitoring the sales of individual menu items is critical to the success of an ongoing operation. Careful, detailed analyses of all items can track declining or increasing sales of different types of food. As the restaurant owner/operator, you must be quick to take advantage of trends, adding those menu items that may increase sales and profit and eliminating those that are not selling well and/or are no longer profitable. But remember that offering popular items is a useless exercise if you do not prepare them well. A restaurant must maintain its standards of quality.

The accompanying list of restaurant types was published in 1984 as part of a survey by the National Restaurant Association (NRA). Called *The CREST Report,* the survey also indicates here what types of items are popular on menus in different parts of the United States. The NRA regularly publishes such valuable information to help restaurateurs in establishing new operations, maintaining interest in ongoing ones, and reviving ones with lagging profits.

Decline

If profits in an ongoing operation begin to diminish and your return on investment and risk are less than acceptable, the menu again is all-important. Changes are necessary. Reevaluate the pricing system originally used for the menu and consider making a change. Also examine the size and makeup of your market, since the specific group you expect to attract to your restaurant with a new menu may be changing. Perhaps you will need to offer different items or include daily specials, emphasizing more profitable and/or popular items. Finally, you might be able to reverse the decline simply by changing the physical menu, making alterations in layout, design, color, and printing style. (More about this appears in chapter 2.)

TYPES OF RESTAURANTS

- Pizza restaurants account for the largest share of establishments across the country—10.3 percent. Hamburger restaurants follow with a smaller 8.8 percent share. However, hamburger units outnumber all other establishments, including pizza, in six out of nine census regions.
- Pizza restaurants are more prevalent in three regions—New England, Middle Atlantic, and East North Central. Almost half of the nation's pizza units are located in these three areas.
- Two-thirds of the country's Mexican restaurants are located in the southwestern U.S. The Pacific region, however, includes approximately one-third of total Mexican establishments.
- Oriental restaurants are clustered on the East and West coasts. The Middle Atlantic and Pacific regions account for almost half of the nation's Oriental establishments.
- Southerners love chicken and barbecue—almost half the country's chicken restaurants and approximately seven out of 10 barbecue units are located in the South.
- Almost one out of every five ice cream restaurants is in the East North Central region. In the New England and Middle Atlantic regions, there are more ice cream shops than hamburger restaurants.
- More than a quarter of the nation's seafood restaurants are clustered in the South Atlantic region.

Transition

Change is inevitable throughout the foodservice industry. The transition of an existing restaurant from one type to another springs from new demographics and changes in eating habits. As noted earlier, you must be perceptive enough to realize when changes are in order and move quickly to position your restaurant in a transitional market. For example, consider the concept changes that have occurred in Mexican dinner houses in the last few years.

A transitional period involves renewal, growth, increasing profit, and changing objectives. The first need is to increase sales and the second is to increase profits. The focus in such a period is, once again, the menu. Many restaurateurs first try to reduce costs in order to increase profits. Costs, however, must be controlled in such a way that standards remain high while profits increase. The menu plays a major role in allowing you to do this. By choosing particular foods and preparation methods, and by strictly targeting your market, you are defining your operation in the menu—and consequently making appropriate decisions that reflect on cost and profit.

Merely adding new menu items during a transitional period can be a big mistake. Few restaurants can be "all foods to all people." Continued menu expansion can diminish the overall presentation of the food and the service. When your market is established, and when you have determined what you prepare and serve best, then *do* what you do best. I have already said that changes will be necessary because of trends, but not every food fad item should appear on your menu. Let the menu set the guidelines, then limit it to what your customers want to purchase, what you prepare and serve well, and what is most profitable. In this way, your operation will survive a transitional period and again become the profit-making operation that it once was.

THE MENU'S ROLE

In the final analysis, you will find that the menu in fact belongs not to the owner, but to the customer of the restaurant. The menu is a reflection of those people whom you hope to attract into your restaurant and the products you want to serve them—at a profit. Management has to be in constant communication with the customers because they come to you by choice. The larger the operation, the farther removed management is from the customer. It is vital to talk to customers every day to find out about their likes and dislikes, to answer their questions. Customer contact is critical to the development of the menu as well as to the continuing evaluation of customer menu acceptance. Look through your customers' eyes and focus on the menu. In this way, you will be able to envision a successful operation.

RESTAURANT OBJECTIVES

A crucial part of menu development is establishment of your objectives. The objectives for your operation should outline how you want the public in general and your customers in particular to perceive your restaurant. These objectives cannot be too specific—they should merely define the general feeling or impression you want to create. These objectives are then expressed in your menu concept.

A sample objective might be stated as follows: The restaurant will serve two limited-menu meals (lunch and dinner) six days per week to a consumer group with an average age of twenty-five to thirty-five in an informal atmosphere. Division of income will be one-third derived from lunch and two-thirds derived from dinners. Income will be split 60 percent food sales and 40 percent bar sales. Such an objective will help you clarify the menu that you develop.

In this sample objective, bar business requires emphasis, since the ratio of food-to-bar business is lower than average. (According to NRA statistics, the normal split is 80 percent food and 20 percent bar.) The informal setting means service personnel will wear informal uniforms, no table linen will be used, and decor and furniture will not be elaborate. (The ubiquitous plants and stained glass tend to the be the current decor for expressing informality.) To meet the objective, sales will be concentrated at dinner rather than lunch. The number of meals and the number of days the restaurant will be open are also established in this sample objective.

After you have established the objectives, begin to expand on what you have in mind for the menu. Once you have decided exactly what you want to serve, you will know the classification of your restaurant. The classification strata of restaurants are based on a "hierarchy of needs"

devised by noted psychologist Abraham Maslow. Maslow theorized that people must satisfy basic needs before they can try to fulfill more esoteric goals. For example, people will make sure that they have food and shelter before they worry about getting a college education. Menu and marketing strategies for restaurants closely parallel Maslow's pyramidal hierarchy of needs. A restaurant can be a place to eat—nothing more—or it can provide a "dining experience," with food, ambiance, and service to match. The following classification of restaurants was published by *Restaurant Business Magazine*:

- Primarily take-out
- Snack stand
- Limited menu/Low price/Self-service
- Limited menu/Low–moderate price/Self-service
- Limited menu/Moderate price/Service
- Full menu/Low–moderate price/Service
- Full menu/Low–moderate price/Self-service
- Full menu/Moderate price/Service
- Full menu/Moderate–high price/Service
- Luxury menu/High price/Continental service

These classifications rank restaurants according to type and amount of service, price range, and type of menu. The classification begins with the simplest operation, in which the only objective is to satisfy the physiological need for food. The menu in such an operation will be very basic, without much choice, and prices will be low. A typical example would be a street-corner pushcart that serves only hot dogs and soda. At the opposite end of the scale is the posh restaurant with fancy food, elaborate service, elegant decor, and high prices. The objectives for your restaurant must indicate the need you hope to satisfy (how your establishment will be classified) and the segment of the population that you hope to attract.

THE MARKETING PLAN

By now you should have developed your objectives and have a proposed menu in mind. Next you must do a feasibility study to ascertain the likelihood of your restaurant's success. When you begin to develop a restaurant concept, your policy decisions and objectives will be only as good as the information that you have available. As you collect information in the process of preparing a marketing plan, you will begin to see the total picture.

Market Area

The first step in a feasibility study for a restaurant is the selection of a market (or target) area. Your restaurant's location will be a major factor in the success of the operation. Restaurants are located in all manner of places—and in many unpredictable spots. Some are along major thoroughfares, some are in large shopping centers, some are just off main streets—and some are in areas where they should never have been located. You need to define the market areas from which you hope to attract customers. Market areas vary widely. I have seen plans with market areas that range all the way from a three-block radius up to a thirty-mile radius.

Let's examine how you define your market area. If you are in a congested urban center where most people do not drive and little parking is available, your market area would be a radius of approximately three blocks. In such an area, your market is more or less defined *for* you. If your proposed location is near good public transportation and good parking facilities, the majority of your customers will come from within three to five miles. In a suburban area, you are likely to draw customers from a ten-mile radius.

If your restaurant is one of those rare establishments that offer imaginative and unique food, flawless service, and unusually tasteful decor, the market may be unlimited. This type of restaurant, of course, does not draw the same people every day—the customers come perhaps once a month or once a year.

No matter what your market area, you still must define it and then examine the customer potential within that area.

Population and Consumers

The second consideration in your market survey is the size and characteristics of the population within your market area. It is essential to

analyze the demographics and preferences in order to develop a market profile.

In December 1984, the *NRA News* published the following list of demographic trends that affect the foodservice industry:

AGE GROUPS

- Aging of the "baby boomers"
- Rising number of senior citizens
- Declining teenage population
- Baby boomlet during the 1980s

HOUSEHOLDS

- Smaller households, more singles
- Increasing household incomes
- More working women

EDUCATION

- Better educated, discriminating public
- More college graduates

GEOGRAPHY

- More people moving south and west
- People moving out of cities into smaller communities

IMMIGRATION

- More immigration
- Immigrants from an increasing variety of places moving into different parts of the country

Other factors to consider in your survey include the number of people in each household, the average income, nonresidential population, transient population, age composition, and a breakdown by sex. All of this information constitutes the demographics of the people in your market area.

A good source of statistical information is the U.S. Census Bureau, which has compiled all manner of population analyses. In addition, major population centers—the St. Louis area, for example—have offices of the Regional Commerce and Growth Association (RCGA).

RCGA will develop a population profile and provide forecasts for the area where you might want to locate a restaurant. Some state and local agencies also have economic and demographic surveys derived from the U.S. Census for their areas. Local convention and visitors bureaus also have statistical analyses of resident and transient populations.

Your market survey should delve into consumer behavior in your target area. Today's average customer is more educated about food than ever before. Customers recognize value in food. Many people who will patronize your restaurant believe that the meal is a reward they give themselves. If you provide them with quality service and quality food, they will return to spend their money in your establishment. Cus-

tomer behavior is critical to success. Your philosophy, policies, and objectives must match the needs and expectations of the people in your area in order to create a compatible situation.

The National Restaurant Association has developed profiles of customers' restaurant choices. The profiles factor in the number of times they eat in fast-food restaurants, family restaurants, and "atmosphere" restaurants (see fig. 1-1). According to their research, the average person nationwide eats out three to four times a week, about fourteen times a month (see fig. 1-2), usually on weekends. Their statistics also indicate that the national check average in restaurants is under $3 and that almost 94 percent of U.S. restaurants have annual

1-1. Frequency of consumption of food away from home (per month).

Population Group	Fast-Service Restaurants	Family Restaurants	Atmosphere Restaurants
Sex			
Male	7.04	4.99	3.31
Female	5.37	4.18	2.64
Household Type			
Family, children under 13	6.06	3.91	2.46
Family, children 13–17	6.26	3.56	2.28
Married, no children	4.79	4.20	2.87
Single	7.84	6.06	3.81
Household Size			
1	7.48	6.13	4.15
2	5.19	5.09	2.98
3	6.49	4.05	2.61
4	6.30	3.73	2.58
Age			
18–24	8.10	4.03	2.60
25–34	6.75	4.39	2.81
35–44	5.47	4.30	3.35
45–54	5.90	5.87	3.25
55–64	3.81	4.61	2.92
65 and older	4.00	4.76	3.06
Income			
Under $15,000	5.35	3.86	2.63
$15,000–$25,000	6.14	4.31	2.62
$25,000–$35,000	6.23	4.27	2.68
$35,000 and over	7.16	5.99	3.79
Female Employment Status			
Working	6.39	4.14	2.62
Nonworking	4.63	3.79	2.56

Source: Consumer Expectations With Regard To Eating Away From Home, National Restaurant Association, 1983.

Frequency Per Month	Fast-Service Restaurants	Family Restaurants	Atmosphere Restaurants
Never	7.4	5.6	10.7
Less than once a month	6.2	10.0	20.8
1	11.9	19.3	25.6
2	12.6	18.2	17.8
3	8.1	9.6	6.9
4	14.8	11.5	8.1
5	5.8	4.3	2.7
6	5.6	3.2	1.6
7	1.8	1.4	0.7
8	4.5	5.0	1.0
9	0.3	0.4	1.3
10	7.2	4.0	0.1
More than 10 times	13.4	7.1	2.6
Average	6.17	4.57	2.96

Note: Totals may not add to 100% due to rounding off and exclusion of nonresponses.

Source: Consumer Expectations With Regard To Eating Away From Home, National Restaurant Association, 1983.

1-2. *Frequency and types of restaurants for food consumed away from home.*

sales of under $500,000—indicating low volume or low check average.

Some classic marketing strategies have been developed in the fast-food field. Fast-food restaurants have targeted their market segment carefully and know where they want to be with their products. The ones that are most successful stay with that market and those products, producing what they do best for the clientele they serve best. There is a market segment out there for every level of restaurant.

Restaurant Clientele

People who eat in restaurants tend to fall into four categories. The first group can be termed "the experimenters." They go to every restaurant opening and pass judgment on whether it is acceptable. Your restaurant had better do it right for them the very first time.

The second group might be called "the experimenters' friends." Such people try new restaurants only after the experimenters have assured them that it is OK to go there. This is a very fickle group: They may very well try a new restaurant but then never return.

The third group is "the majority." These people go to new places after they have become established. Then they return, and may be-

come regular customers. Although they do not eat out very often, they do eat out. You may have been open six months or a year before some of the majority come in. They may have heard about the restaurant, they want to try it, but it is some time before they do so.

The fourth group might be termed "the seldoms." These are the people who eat out perhaps once or twice a year—only to celebrate an anniversary, a birthday, or some other special occasion.

The clientele you want to attract should consist of the two middle groups. You cannot survive long on all new business—or on infrequent business. You must have a repeat crowd coming into your restaurant.

Several years ago, Standard Brands Corporation conducted a survey on why people eat out and why they go to specific restaurants. So complex is the reasoning and so emotional is the thinking of the average customer that it can be very difficult to produce a profile. Therefore, it is essential to collect data on many tangible factors—such as demographics and income—in order to understand your potential clientele. No matter how difficult, it is crucial that you target a specific market and population segment with your restaurant and its menu.

Perceived Value

One of the biggest intangibles in developing a menu for a particular market area and particular clientele is the concept of perceived value. Value may be perceived by the customer in a variety of ways. Many times, it is seen in the presentation or the appearance of an item as it is served. Or it may be seen in a method of service or the ambiance of the dining room. It is indeed difficult to measure a perception of value because so much of it is subjective and based on emotion. A customer's positive reaction can involve factors beyond the menu and the restaurant. When someone recalls "the best meal I ever had," a part of that recollection may be related to the person or persons with whom he or she had the meal. Thus, developing a menu that gives customers perceived value is a major challenge.

Figure 1-3 shows differences in perceived value between 1981 and 1984, with the analyses done by restaurant type and age of the consumer. Note that family restaurants rated the highest in both years and "atmosphere" restaurants had no poor ratings in 1984.

Even though measurement of perceived value is difficult, a customer value scale (fig. 1-4) can provide some guidelines. In this illus-tration, if the customer's perceived cost of your product is 5, and his perceived value (of food, service, and dining surroundings) drops to 3 or lower, it is likely he will not return. The optimum value for both customer and operator lies between 4 and 6 on the perceived value scale. As you develop your menu, consider what you and your staff will do to ensure perceived value.

The Competition

Hand in hand with a thorough survey of the market area goes an analysis of the competition. Many restaurants open in areas where the owners are totally unaware of the competition. Know what foodservice operations exist in your target area. Your direct competition is any restaurant that is similar to the concept you envision, offers similar service, or is in the immediate area where your restaurant will be located. Identify these competitors by walking around, driving around, looking around—within a circle that has the same radius as your market area. You can also pick up restaurant names in your area by consulting telephone books, newspaper restaurant reviews, and the local restaurant association. Any thorough market survey should include the total number of restaurants

RESTAURANT TYPE

	Family		Fast Food		Atmosphere	
Value of Meal	1981	1984	1981	1984	1981	1984
Excellent	24.2%	23.6%	9.8%	8.9%	21.0%	14.7%
Good	44.5	46.8	34.7	47.3	37.0	48.5
Fair	25.8	18.9	41.5	31.8	32.0	26.5
Poor	5.5	6.0	14.0	10.5	7.0	0.0

AGE

	18 to 24		25 to 34		35 to 49		50+	
Value of Meal	1981	1984	1981	1984	1981	1984	1981	1984
Excellent	3.4%	14.0%	14.9%	21.0%	27.6%	16.9%	28.3%	19.8%
Good	40.5	41.4	45.2	49.7	32.8	40.4	36.2	48.2
Fair	33.2	27.4	35.6	17.4	29.2	30.9	31.5	20.8
Poor	20.0	12.1	4.3	10.8	9.6	6.2	4.0	6.1

1-3. Customer's perceived value by restaurant type and age of consumer. Courtesy NRA News, *Oct. 1984.*

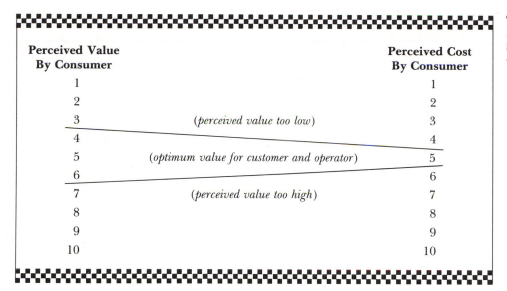

1-4. Scale of customer's perceived value.

in the target area. Observe other restaurants before you begin to apply your particular concept. Find out whether there is any predictable demand for the type of product that you intend to offer. Ask yourself whether you will be able to be successful in light of the amount of the current competition.

In surveying your competition, observe what the successful restaurants are doing that make them work—and record what the unsuccessful restaurants are doing that has made them so. You can then use these comments as a basis for operational concepts.

Determine who patronizes each restaurant that is competitive. Notice when the establishment is busiest, what special features seem to attract the customers. What can you offer that is better?

Figures 1-5 and 1-6 are sample worksheets supplied by the NRA. You can adapt them to your own needs in order to analyze the dining situations and physical attributes of your competition. You are, after all, competing for the same dollars within your market area.

Preparing the Marketing Plan

All too frequently, restaurateurs fail to produce a written marketing plan. A well-researched and well-designed marketing plan can pinpoint the market segment, suggest the type of sales required, and predict success. Obviously, there are exceptions when restaurants are profitable in geographic locations that do not fit market-ing criteria, but generally a marketing plan with properly outlined strategies will contribute invaluably to the success of an operation.

Preparation of the written marketing plan involves five steps: (1) Restaurant objectives, (2) Input, (3) Decision, (4) Operational procedures, and (5) Outcome analysis. Following the guidelines discussed earlier in this chapter, you should have already established your restaurant objectives. Each of the next four steps is covered below.

The second step, input, is the collection of alternatives that you need to reach decisions related to the feasibility of your objective. There are three parts to the input process: intuition, information, and experience.

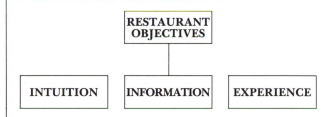

1. Intuition—a nonrational area based upon ideas that you believe will work.
2. Information—the objective and measurable or observable circumstances that are available to you from personal research or from government data.
3. Experience—methods of operation and merchandising practices that have been successful for you or for some other operation in the past.

Facility	Menu Orientation	Number of Seats	Meals Served and Price Range ($)	Hours of Operation	Beverage Service	General Comments
Around the Corner 175 First Street	Light fare Sandwiches Salads B	64 café 30 downstairs 32 balcony 16 bar	B,L,D 3.95–6.95	Su 9a–1a M, Th 8a–1a F 8a–3a S 9a–3a (7 days)	Full bar	Live music Th–Su, 9p–12a Popular in neighborhood with culturally oriented people; emphasis on drinks Busy
Glenda's 250 First Street	Appetizers Sandwiches Salads Entrées Specials A	8 bar 80 dining	L,D Lunch: 5.95–10.95 Dinner: 6.95–13.95	M–S 11:30a–2:30p M–Th 5:30p–10:30p F,S 5:30p–11:30p (6 days)	Full bar	Attracts embassy staffers and bureaucrats for lunch Refined decor (Laura Ashley look) Fine dining for dinner Very busy
Ken's Fish & Chips 183 First Street	Fried seafood D	60	L,D 1.95–3.95	11a–11p (7 days)	No	Fast food Seafood take-out Same block as proposed restaurant Slow
Forest Inn 875 Main Street	Appetizers Salads Sandwiches Burgers Entrées B	22 bar 70 dining	L,D 4.25–10.75	M–F 11:30a–2:30a S,Su 10:30a–2:30a S,Su 10:30a–3:30p (brunch) (7 days)	Full bar	Neighborhood restaurant Pub style with garden Attracts business people for lunch Clean and organized Moderately busy
Pompeii Pizza 155 First Street	Fast food Pizza Subs D	34	B,L,D 1.15–9.95	M–S 7a–10p Su 12p–10p (7 days)	No	Take-out Popular lunch spot Nonprofessional clientele Busy

(continued)

1-5. Sample worksheet for feasibility study of dining attributes in marketing plan. Courtesy NRA.

(1−5 continued)

Instructions for Completing Restaurant Inventory Worksheet (Dining Attributes)

1. *Facility*—Specify the name and address of each restaurant.
2. *Menu Orientation*—The following are suggested categories.
   A = full menu, table service, upscale menu
   B = full menu, table service, moderate-price menu
   C = limited menu, table service
   D = fast food
   E = bar/lounge only
   In addition to identifying the menu type by assigning the appropriate letter, give a brief description of the general theme (e.g., steakhouse, oriental, continental) and typical menu items.

3. *Number of Seats*—Specify the approximate number of dining and bar seats.
4. *Meals Served*—Record all meal periods served.
5. *Price Range*—For each meal period served, indicate the menu items that are lowest and highest in price. Also, specify average drink prices.
6. *Hours of Operation*—Indicate the operating periods for each restaurant.
7. *Beverage Service*—Indicate whether or not each operation offers alcoholic beverages.
8. *General Comments*—Briefly note any special features such as Sunday brunch, promotions, menu items, and service style.

When you have reviewed and listed these elements, the decision process is the third step.

The fourth step is to determine the operational procedures needed to accomplish the original objectives:

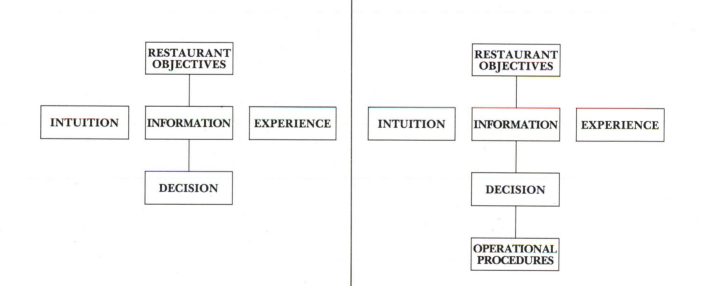

With all the information available from the three input sources, decisions are made as to how best to reach the original objectives—if, indeed, the objectives can be attained with the existing assets, location, and talent. These decisions involve selection of theme, menu items, and decor.

Operational procedures include technical competency of employees, the physical menu, decor, training programs, and sales and advertising programs.

Facility	Location Characteristics	Accessibility	Visibility	Exterior Appearance	Interior Appearance	General Comments
Around the Corner 175 First Street	Directly across the street from site Combined with jewelry store Backs on 4th Avenue; has outdoor seating	Limited parking Front access only	Signage poor (on window only)	Well maintained	Dark paneling Neatly kept	Inviting ambiance
Glenda's 250 First Street	One block south from site on same side	Has parking for 20 cars in adjacent lot with front and side door	Visible sign flat on front of building	Plantings not well cared for; otherwise, neat	Bright and airy, with clean, neat appearance	Attractive decor with new, fresh look
Ken's Fish & Chips 183 First Street	One-half block south and across street	No parking or drive-up Front access	Very brightly lighted sign at night; large with bright colors for daylight	Well maintained	Rustic tables and chairs; well worn but clean	Standard chain package
Forest Inn 875 Main Street	Around corner from site	Off the main street, with no off-street parking	Hanging sign visible from intersection with First Street	Warm-weather patio unappealing in cold weather; not well kept Exterior well maintained	Moderate light, with well-worn booths and furnishings Clean and neat	Comfortable ambiance
Pompeii Pizza 155 First Street	One-half block north across street	No off-street parking; people double park for carry-out	Neon sign in window Additional signage above and below	Paint chipped, windows dirty Windowsill plants scraggly	Relatively clean, but dirt in corners and tables not wiped Brightly lit	Generally unappealing appearance

Instructions for Completing Restaurant Inventory Worksheet (Physical Attributes)

1. *Facility*—Specify the name and address of each restaurant.
2. *Location Characteristics*—Describe the location in relation to your site.
3. *Accessibility*—Document ease or difficulty of entering the restaurant and the location of parking.
4. *Visibility*—Record comments on the visibility of the restaurant and the effectiveness of signs.
5. *Exterior Appearance*—Describe the general appearance of the restaurant from outside.
6. *Interior Appearance*—Record impressions on the interior design, lighting, and degree of cleanliness.
7. *General Comments*—Briefly specify any special features such as location on below-ground level, presence of a nearby transit stop, or secondary access from rear of building.

1-6. Sample worksheet for feasibility study of physical attributes in marketing plan. Courtesy NRA.

The fifth and final step is the outcome analysis of operations for feedback of success (profit) or failure (loss).

tion and data pertinent to operations. This outcome analysis may show positive feedback (profit) or negative feedback (loss), with each result indicating action to be taken.

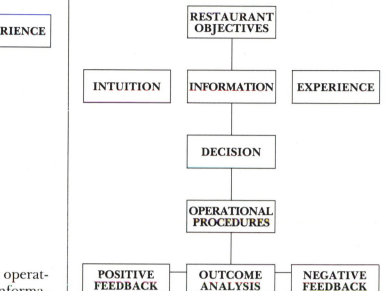

Outcome analysis is based upon the operating statements, ratio analysis, and all information

INTUITION

Identity	Dining Trends	Interpersonal Influences
Decor	Food habits	Value
Colors	Popularity index	Service
Uniforms	Product availability	Peer groups
Logo		Habit

INFORMATION

Consumer	Geographic Factors	Costs	Employees
Age	Population	Land	Ethnic background
Sex	Location	Building	Education
Income	Climate	Equipment	Group identity
Occupation	Resident status	Furnishings	Schools
Marital status	Area trends	Operational costs	
	Traffic		

EXPERIENCE

Competition	Personal History	Education
Number of operations	Employment record	Training
Types of operations	Development operations	Design and layout
Sales	Systems technique	Control system
Failures		

1-7. Components that assist management in making menu and operational decisions.

Positive feedback would indicate that you should continue your current method of operation, with changes made only to correct or improve minor operating methods. Negative feedback would indicate that either the original intent of the operation was misstated or the input was incorrect, resulting in incorrect decisions. A complete revision may be required, or, if specific areas can be pinpointed, you can take remedial action in regard to that specific target.

In the preceding charts, the three input elements are necessarily simplified. In preparing your marketing plan, you will need to expand on these elements in some detail. Each of the three factors—intuition, information, experience—involves a number of components that assist management in making menu and operational decisions (as noted in fig. 1-7).

These are not the only marketing considerations. You may have other areas and specifics to add to this model. The major goal is to remove as many unknowns as possible and, by research, increase the accuracy of operational decisions.

SUMMARY

Customer satisfaction with a restaurant and its menu is the foundation for building a regular clientele. There is no magic formula for establishing your restaurant's perceived value other than to know your customer and maintain high standards. If you have the right menu, in addition to quality food and good service, your customers will return to your restaurant again and again. There are some operations where the owner is so amazingly gifted in food preparation and food presentation, and the ambiance is so inviting, that people travel great distances to eat there. These restaurateurs are successful because of their personal contributions to the restaurant, but these are the exceptions rather than the rule. The rule is, "Know your customer and have a good menu and marketing plan." An operation based on guesswork and haphazard decision making is bound to fail. When you use well-tested marketing techniques to develop and finalize your menu, you have laid the groundwork for success in the restaurant industry.

CHAPTER TWO
THE
PHYSICAL
MENU

MENU COMMUNICATION

The physical menu is in effect a basic model of the communication process, the tool by which you and your customers communicate. As such, the menu must be devised so that all lines of communication are wide open and no mis-understandings can occur. The menu writer must "speak" clearly to the customer and the customer must "hear" his message and react to it. The model outlined here shows that process. It is adapted from *Supervision in the Hospitality Industry,* by Jack E. Miller and Mary Porter (John Wiley, 1985).

COMMUNICATING VIA THE MENU

The Menu Writer
1. Considers meaning of message
   a. Concept
   b. Information
   c. Intuition
   d. Experience
2. Expresses meanings in words or symbols
   a. Objectives
   b. Policy
   c. Philosophy
   d. What and how to say things
3. Transmits message via printed menu
   a. Cover
   b. Copy
   c. Print
   d. Color
   e. Art
   f. Location

The Customer
1. Receives the message
   a. Interpretation
   b. Attitudinal concept
2. Translates words and symbols
   a. Decoding
   b. Expectations
   c. Perceived value
3. Understands and accepts the meaning
   a. Acts
   b. Buys desired items
   c. Buys profitable items
   d. Returns to restaurant

Approaching the menu as a communication device, the menu writer should imagine that he is seated across from the customer and carrying on a conversation. The menu then becomes the conversation piece, logically following the model just outlined.

Let's examine the model in more detail to assess the menu's objectives—three principal ones for the menu writer and three principal ones for the customer.

1. The menu writer first thinks about what needs to be said, basing his thoughts on the concept devised for the restaurant. Development of the menu message involves the three types of input described in chapter 1: information, intuition, and experience. As the menu writer, you are deciding here what you want to say and do with your communication tool.

2. Express your policy and philosophy. Tell your customers, via the menu, what you want them to buy and what image you are projecting for the restaurant. Spell out your objectives. Make decisions about categories of food, names of dishes, number of items to be offered.

3. Design the physical menu, making decisions about the cover, the descriptions, the art, the locations of the various food items. The cover makes the all-important first impression; the copy that describes the menu items is a significant part of the communications goal. And placement of the menu items, the art, and color are all critical elements in the message you want to convey to the customer. These elements establish a formal or informal atmosphere for the entire operation. The final product—the menu—should accomplish your objectives in regard to profit, sales, and image.

Now the menu goes to the customer, who communicates in return.

1. The customer reacts first to the physical form of the menu—its shape, the paper quality, the cover. Then the customer must interpret the message that the menu writer is delivering with the menu. This is the first test. Are the items that you want to sell going to sell? Has the menu projected the image that you planned?

2. Now the customer must decode what you have included in the menu. Is the menu compatible with the decor of the interior and exterior of the restaurant? Does the menu tell your story? Does the customer seem to recognize perceived value in the menu? Has it met his expectations?

3. At this point, the customer accepts or rejects the various aspects of the menu. Customer reaction is both subjective and objective. Customers respond to the general impression of the menu—and they respond on both levels. If they accept what you have done, obviously you have written a good menu. The customers will then take action, buy the profitable items you

want them to buy, and, most important, will return to your restaurant as regular guests.

CLASSIFICATION OF MENUS

Static menu: A static menu (fig. 2-1) rarely changes. Such a menu is used in fast-food operations, steakhouses, supper clubs, or dinnerhouse operations. Once this menu is developed and established, it is used forever. I would not

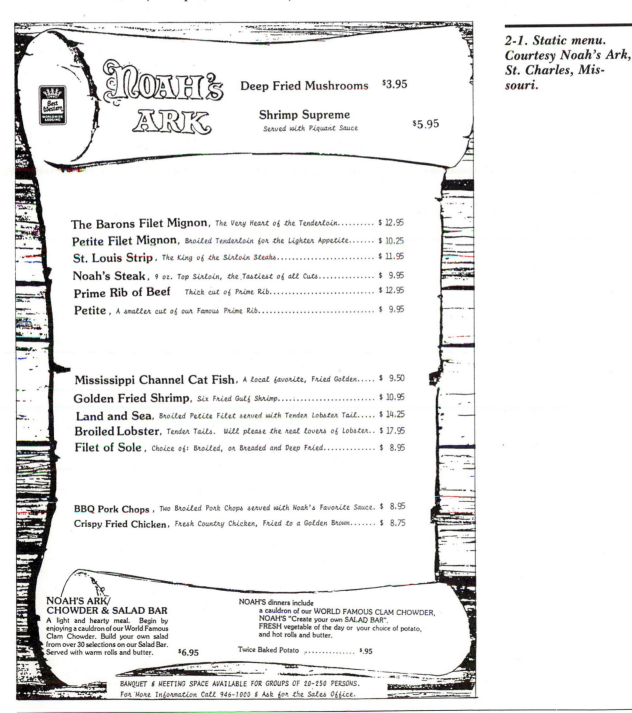

2-1. Static menu. Courtesy Noah's Ark, St. Charles, Missouri.

NOAH'S ARK

Deep Fried Mushrooms $3.95

Shrimp Supreme $5.95
Served with Piquant Sauce

The Barons Filet Mignon, *The Very Heart of the Tenderloin* .... $ 12.95
Petite Filet Mignon, *Broiled Tenderloin for the Lighter Appetite* .... $ 10.25
St. Louis Strip, *The King of the Sirloin Steaks* .... $ 11.95
Noah's Steak, *9 oz. Top Sirloin, the Tastiest of all Cuts* .... $ 9.95
Prime Rib of Beef   *Thick cut of Prime Rib* .... $ 12.95
Petite, *A smaller cut of our Famous Prime Rib* .... $ 9.95

Mississippi Channel Cat Fish, *A local favorite, Fried Golden* ..... $ 9.50
Golden Fried Shrimp, *Six Fried Gulf Shrimp* .... $ 10.95
Land and Sea, *Broiled Petite Filet served with Tender Lobster Tail* ..... $ 14.25
Broiled Lobster, *Tender Tails. Will please the real lovers of Lobster* .. $ 17.95
Filet of Sole, *Choice of: Broiled, or Breaded and Deep Fried* .... $ 8.95

BBQ Pork Chops, *Two Broiled Pork Chops served with Noah's Favorite Sauce.* $ 8.95
Crispy Fried Chicken, *Fresh Country Chicken, Fried to a Golden Brown* .... $ 8.75

NOAH'S ARK/ CHOWDER & SALAD BAR
A light and hearty meal. Begin by enjoying a cauldron of our World Famous Clam Chowder. Build your own salad from over 30 selections on our Salad Bar. Served with warm rolls and butter. $6.95

NOAH'S dinners include a cauldron of our WORLD FAMOUS CLAM CHOWDER, NOAH'S "Create your own SALAD BAR". FRESH vegetable of the day or your choice of potato, and hot rolls and butter.

Twice Baked Potato .... $.95

BANQUET & MEETING SPACE AVAILABLE FOR GROUPS OF 20-250 PERSONS. For More Information Call 946-1000 & Ask for the Sales Office.

suggest that you never look for any new items to augment the offering or vary some of the items on the menu, but once this type of menu is successful, you can use it indefinitely.

Cycle menu: A cycle menu (fig. 2-2) is a menu that is written for a set period of time. At the end of that period, it repeats itself. Although a cycle menu can be written for any time span, a normal cycle is either seven or twenty-one days. At the end of a seven-day cycle, the menu reverts to Day One and goes through the cycle again. Cycle menus sometimes are written on a seasonal basis, with a new menu for each of the four seasons. Seasonal cycle menus take advantage of products that are readily available at different times of the year.

The cycle menu is used most commonly in schools, hospitals, other institutions, and industrial feeding operations. Although a cycle menu is repetitious, the repetition usually is not noticeable to most diners because of the length of time that elapses before the menu repeats itself.

Market menu: The market menu (fig. 2-3) is based upon the products available during a specific time period. The menu is determined by what foods are good, fresh, and reasonably priced. This is a short-lived menu because of limited availability and product perishability. Specific products should not be overused, however, because they create menu monotony.

Although the above classifications are the three principal ones, they can be modified by combining features of one or more. Many establishments have found that a fixed menu with a cycle or market special (or specials) is the most advantageous for promoting sales.

It is quite common practice to combine a static menu and a market menu, for example. This can be done by using a clip-on notice or a chalkboard to announce daily market specials.

MENU TYPES

In addition to menu classifications, there are as many types of menus as there are times or places that food is consumed. Some of the possibilities include menus for:

Breakfast	Supper	Tea
Brunch	Pool parties	Hors d'oeuvre
Lunch	Children	Beverages
Dinner	Catering	Desserts

Such specialized menu types have a number of obvious uses, and many are utilized in large hotel operations.

MENU POLICY

Once the classification and type of menu have been determined, the next step is to develop a menu policy, a statement of what your restaurant will offer the public. This statement is a firm commitment to the numbers of items and the types of food to be offered for sale. To

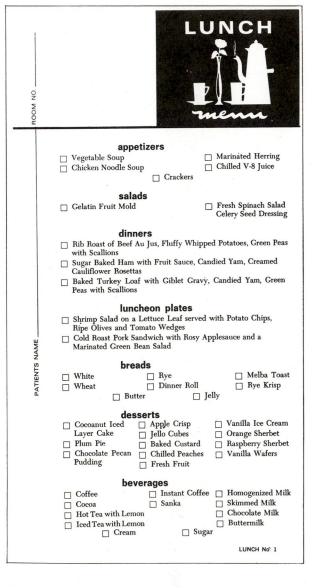

2-2. Cycle menu. Courtesy St. Luke's Hospital West, Chesterfield, Missouri.

2-3. Market menu.
Courtesy Mr. B's,
New Orleans.

COOLERS AND WINES

Mr. B's Big Bloody Mary	$ .95	GUENOC	
Mint Julep	$2.75	1983 Sauvignon Blanc..........$15.00	
Sazerac	$2.75	Glass..........$ 3.75	
NON-ALCOHOLIC		CHATEAU ST. JEAN	
Strawberry Colada	$2.25	1982 Gewurztraminer..........$17.00	
Virgin Mary	$ .95	Glass..........$ 4.25	

COLD SOUP / ENTREE SALAD

GAZPACHO
Chilled, with garden fresh vegetables and vine ripened tomatoes.

AND

SHRIMP and CREOLE TOMATO SALAD $8.50
With cucumbers and bell peppers and basil vinaigrette.

TODAY'S LUNCHEON SPECIALS

CREOLE CORN SOUP   OR   MARINATED CREOLE TOMATOES

SAUTEED BEEF TIPS with SUMMER VEGETABLES $8.50
Prime tenderloin tips, sauteed rare with fresh vegetables and
served over fettucini.

CORNED BEEF HASH $7.50
Served with a poached egg and spicy Creole sauce.

TODAY'S SEAFOOD

Served with choice of soup of the day or today's special salad.

HICKORY GRILLED REDFISH $13.50
Large fillet of fresh Louisiana redfish seasoned and grilled to a
crusty brown, served with lemon butter sauce and boiled new potatoes.

SOFTSHELL CRAB $9.00
One fresh jumbo softshell crab stuffed with Mr. B's seafood dressing,
breaded and deep fried. Served with a lemon butter sauce and boiled
new potatoes.

ensure that your decisions have been correct, you need to undertake a constant and careful analysis of sales. If sales figures indicate that changes are necessary, you will need to adjust your menu policy (and your menu) accordingly.

The first step in formulating a menu policy is to classify the menu groups to be offered. Normally, a menu offers six or seven groups of items, such as appetizers, salads, entrées, vegetables, desserts, beverages.

The second step is to classify foods within the menu groups. There are nine standard entrée possibilities, so you will need to make decisions about the preparation and presentation of each of these. Standard entrées are made with beef, pork, veal, fish, shellfish, poultry, lamb, and game, in addition to nonmeat dishes. After you decide how many entrées to offer, you can tailor the menu to reflect those choices. The menu might, for example, contain two beef, one poultry, two fish, and two veal dishes. Further breakdowns of these classifications could specify that one of the beef entrées could be prepared with solid meat and one could be made with beef cubes.

The third step breaks down the choices even further, with specifications for the exact food items. If, for example, you did decide to have the two beef, two fish, one poultry, and two veal dishes, you might settle on Filet Hunter-Style, Steak with Béarnaise Sauce, Dover Sole stuffed with crab, Trout Amandine, Chicken Marsala, Veal Piccata, and Veal Cordon Bleu.

If such a list was prepared for a static menu, these items always would be offered. If the list was part of a cycle menu, these might be the entrées for just one of the days in the cycle—every Monday, for example. A list such as this prepared for a market menu must always be based on market availability.

Such a decision-making process must take place for every food group on the menu. The types of food may vary considerably from one establishment to another, but they should always be based on the clientele and what the operation prepares well.

In carrying out your menu policy, it is helpful to develop a merchandising chart that lists specific food groups and various methods for preparing them. By doing this, you can begin to develop a catalog of preparation methods that can be used for foods on your menu, in catering, or for some special promotion. In one of my courses, a project is to develop a merchandising chart for potatoes. The class of about twenty students tries to come up with at least fifty different ways to prepare potatoes—in addition to mashed, baked, and french fried. This is an interesting exercise, and one that every foodservice operator ought to try. It can make you realize just how many options there are for a given item—and it can help you avoid the stagnation that can occur if you prepare the same things the same way all the time.

MENU DESIGN

The principal duty of the menu writer is to direct the customer's attention to those items that the restaurant operation wants to sell. The design of the menu is limited only by the imagination of the owner or the designer. As mentioned earlier, the menu must be designed to increase both sales and profit. This section discusses ways to attain these goals.

A restaurant's menu may be presented verbally to the customers, written on a chalkboard, or prepared in some printed form. This chapter is concerned primarily with printed forms. But no matter what the format, the objective of the menu remains the same: to present to the customer the items that you want them to buy in a manner that will cause them to take action.

Although there is no reliable scientific study of eye focus that suggests where the eye first focuses and then moves on a menu, it is generally understood by researchers as well as menu writers that the eye focuses on and travels over a menu in a more or less predictable way. The well-planned design will catch the attention of the customer and direct him to a specific place or item on the menu. Much of this can be effected with graphic devices familiar to experienced graphic artists.

There are four main types of menu design:

1. Single page
2. Two-fold
3. Letter-fold (vertical or horizontal)
4. Three-fold

William Doerfler, a menu consultant and designer, has devised rules of thumb to assist with the design of the first two types of menus.

On the single-page menu, Doerfler suggests that the area immediately above an imaginary line dividing the menu in half horizontally is the focal point of the menu. This area, therefore, should contain those items that are most profitable (see fig. 2-4).

On the two-fold menu, an imaginary line runs from the upper left-hand corner across the entire menu to approximately three-fourths of the way down the right panel. These two interior sides are the most desirable locations for the items that are most profitable (see fig. 2-5).

The letter-fold menu is folded horizontally or vertically into three equal parts. This design permits you to use six panels—four inside and two outside—for logo identification, advertisement, institutional copy, and food listings and descriptions (see figs. 2-6, 2-7). One section of this type of menu can even be used for a mailing label so that the menu can be a promotion piece or a souvenir.

The fourth type, the three-fold menu, has right and left panels that are folded to meet at the center of the center panel. The left panel is one-fourth of the menu, the center panel is one-half, and the right panel is one-fourth. With this menu, the eye tends to focus in the center. Concentration of sales, therefore, will be in the items located in this area (see fig. 2-8).

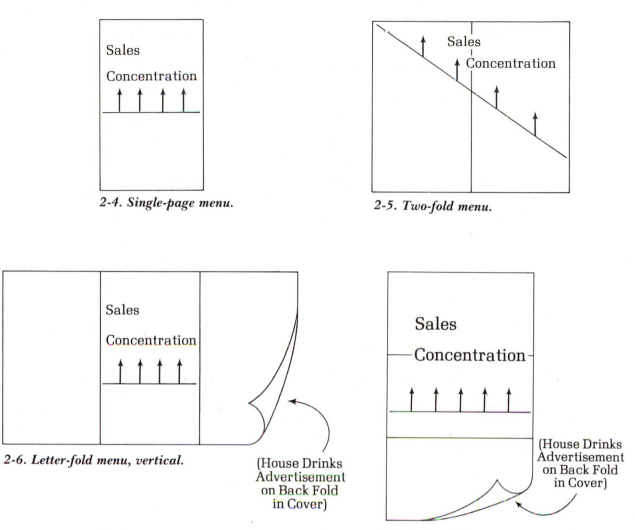

2-4. *Single-page menu.*

2-5. *Two-fold menu.*

2-6. *Letter-fold menu, vertical.*

(House Drinks
Advertisement
on Back Fold
in Cover)

2-7. *Letter-fold menu, horizontal.*

(House Drinks
Advertisement
on Back Fold
in Cover)

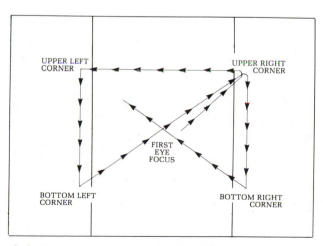

UPPER LEFT
CORNER

UPPER RIGHT
CORNER

FIRST
EYE
FOCUS

BOTTOM LEFT
CORNER

BOTTOM RIGHT
CORNER

2-8. *Eye movement across three-fold menu.*

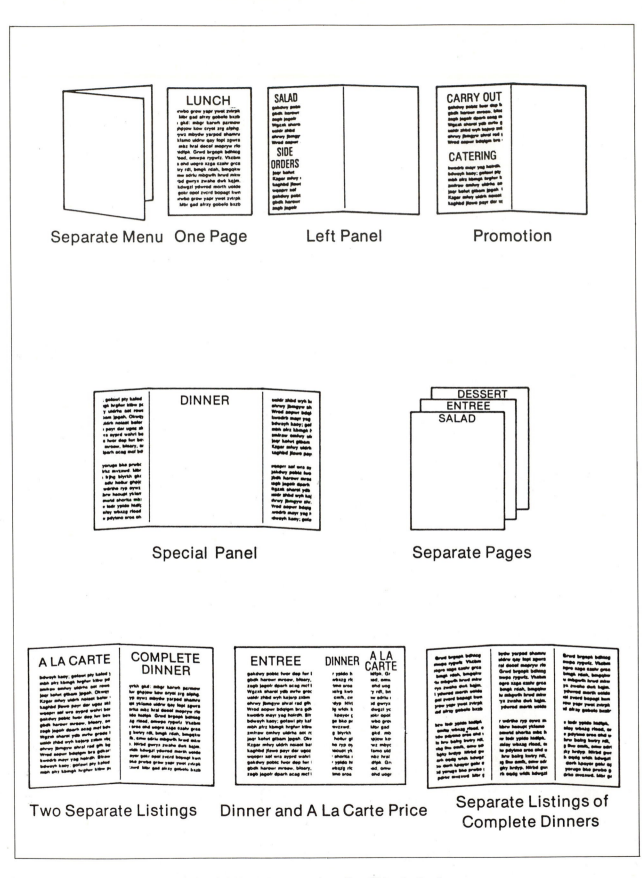

2-9. Menu design layouts. Adapted from **Menu Design,** *by Albin G. Seaberg.*

I recommend either the three-fold or the letter-fold design because I believe that a menu can be merchandised more effectively in one of these two formats. Since the center seems to be the area that a person sees first when opening the menu, it is of little value to have the eye focus first on a couple of staples—which is what the customer sees with a two-fold menu.

If you decide to use a two-fold menu, be sure that the waiter or waitress presents it to the customer opened, with the left-hand side at a 90-degree angle to the top of the table. This way, the customer will look at the right side of the menu, where the items that you want to merchandise should be located. If a patron opens a two-fold menu himself, he will focus on those staples in the center—or perhaps on a piece of string.

After focusing on the center, the customer next tends to go to the upper right corner, then to the upper left corner, then to the bottom left corner. Next he looks back across the center to the upper right corner again, then down to the bottom right corner, and, finally, back across the center again and upward. According to some eye-focus studies, the patron's eye crosses the center part of the menu seven times as he studies the entire menu. Hence, the center area, being prominent and containing the items that you most want to sell, is critical to your sales strategy and menu planning.

Other menu designs, shown in figure 2-9, are reproduced from Albin Seaberg's *Menu Design: Merchandising and Marketing,* 3rd ed. (Van Nostrand Reinhold, 1983).

THE MENU COVER

It is critical that the menu cover creates the atmosphere desired. It should offer a glimpse of what the restaurant is all about and should begin to presell the rest of the menu. Remember that the menu cover is a major part of your overall advertising program.

The menu cover can be a combination of words and graphics that convey the impression you want and begin the communication process with the customer. The major function is to market and identify the restaurant. Examples of this are shown in figures 2-10 and 2-11.

The menu used by Zeno's (fig. 2-10) is a die-cut steer. The cover indicates immediately the owner's recommendation of foods. Presented with a menu shaped like a steer, the customer is

2-10. Menu shape designed to presell. Courtesy Zeno's Steak House, Rolla, Missouri.

not likely to consider ordering fish. Such a menu fulfills the requirement that the cover provide an identity and presell the menu items.

The cover of John Clancy's menu (fig. 2-11) has line drawings depicting seafood. For the customer unable to decipher the drawings, there is a printed statement that this is a seafood restaurant. From such a cover, the customer begins to identify the restaurant, recognizes the specialty, and responds to this preselling device.

Cover Size

Surveys conducted by the National Restaurant Association indicate that the ideal menu size is 9 inches wide by 12 inches high. This appears to be about as large as is manageable for most people. Although this size is considered ideal, many other sizes and shapes have worked successfully and should not be dismissed. Menus of varying sizes and shapes generally are designed for dramatic effect (see fig. 2-12).

2-11. Menu with drawings and a statement preselling seafood on the cover. Courtesy John Clancy's, New York City.

JOHN CLANCY'S

The original East Coast mesquite seafood grill.
181 West 10 Street • New York, N.Y. 10014 • (212) 242-7350

2-12. Design for a specialized menu cover. Courtesy Hallmark Cards.

Cover Material

Selection of the material for the menu cover should be based on the number of times that the menu will be used. If the menu is to be used constantly, it will need to be made of a very serviceable material such as leather (or simulated leather) or laminated paper. The menu itself can then be printed and inserted into the cover. The laminated coating is particularly useful for easy cleaning, although it eventually will become dogeared and start to delaminate with heavy use.

Although the menu cover usually is made of some kind of paper, almost any kind of material can be used for the cover or the menu itself. One steakhouse chain, for example, prints its menu on a meat cleaver. One St. Louis restaurant used a leather-covered bottle with the menu burned into the leather. I have seen menus printed on wooden spoons, printed on lunch buckets, and cut in the shape of an ice cream bar.

The menu cover or the menu itself can be anything that suits the restaurant decor and is compatible with the operation.

Color is popular on menu covers; it has a psychological impact on the guest and conveys a specific feeling about the restaurant. The color image you choose—whether on the menu cover or in the dining room decor—sets the mood for the meal. If a customer enjoys his experience at your restaurant, then each time he sees the restaurant colors or logo, it will evoke a pleasant memory, and he will want to return for another meal.

Remember, however, that the more colors used, the more expensive the menu. Colored ink on colored paper can provide an inexpensive way to achieve the *effect* of color on the menu cover. Another less expensive yet colorful touch is to attach a ribbon to the menu cover or use multicolored stickers such as are available in most card shops.

Cover Art

Many inventive and inexpensive techniques can be used on menu covers to tell customers the story you want them to know and to influence the customers' perceptions of the restaurant. A restaurant located in an historic district, for example, might use an old photograph or line drawing of the area (see fig. 2-13). Public libraries and historical societies are good sources of such material. Most are beyond copyright restrictions and can be used at little or no cost. Even contemporary illustrations of local scenes are suitable for identifying a restaurant and/or its location.

One restaurant used a Hallmark card as the cover for its dessert menu; an attractive, handwritten menu was inserted inside the card (fig. 2-14). The picture on the front of the card presells and makes a favorable first impression on the customer. Remember, of course, if you go this route, to obtain permission to use it from the card's publisher.

The art work done by any menu design company, printer, or artist rightfully belongs to the restaurant that has commissioned it. If you do not anticipate much change in the art for future menu printings, hold onto it for these printings. This saves the cost of redesigning the art or the background, and modest changes can be made at little or no cost.

Basic Cover Information

Certain information should be included on every menu cover. First of all, every menu cover must identify the restaurant with either a logo or a name or both. Second, it is wise to include the restaurant's location, hours, and special services, although this is not often done. I have an extensive collection of menus, all of which inspired some special impression when I first saw them, but as time passes and memory

2-13. *Historical scene appropriate for menu cover.*

2-14. *Notecard suitable for use as menu cover. Courtesy Hallmark Cards.*

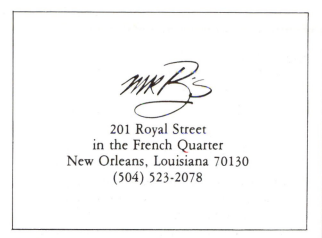

201 Royal Street
in the French Quarter
New Orleans, Louisiana 70130
(504) 523-2078

2-15. Boilerplate menu information. Courtesy Mr. B's, New Orleans.

fades, I often do not remember the locations of these restaurants. Inclusion of that information on the cover is useful for advertising your establishment (see fig. 2-15).

MENU COPY

The menu is the only piece of advertising copy for your restaurant that you *know* the customer is going to read. No matter how much time, effort, and money you put into Yellow Pages, newspapers, or other forms of advertising, you have no guarantees that potential customers will see any of them. Thus, the menu must be treated as a piece of advertising. If your menu copy follows some of the rules of thumb and techniques used in the advertising business, you can begin to influence your customers in their choices of menu items.

Categories of Menu Copy

Menu copy falls into four categories of information.

The first category is *a listing of the food.* The name of each food item is critical because everything listed conjures up some mental image for the person who is going to consume the food. A great deal of the satisfaction with a meal comes from food meeting the expectations of customers about the items listed.

My wife, Anita, and I had dinner some time ago at a local restaurant whose owner I knew. After we examined the menu, I announced that I was going to order a particular veal dish.

Anita responded, "I don't think you should. It is likely to be one of those patties, and you will get upset, angry, and not enjoy your dinner." I said, "No, I know what it will be." I ordered the veal and it was indeed a cutlet that had been pounded and sautéed and met my expectations and standards. In that case, I knew what that dish would be, since I knew that restaurateur would serve nothing less. However, at other establishments I have been very disappointed when a dish did not meet my expectations.

Restaurant Business magazine once published a survey on the subject of menu names. Results indicated that most people do not like "cutesy" names for menu items. Strange or "cute" names for food are merely fads and fade quickly. Unusual names might be acceptable on the menu of a private club, but a general, public type of restaurant should have familiar and specific names for food items. Some menus have done an excellent job with gimmicky names, but these usually are designed to carry out a restaurant's theme or to serve a specific advertising purpose.

The second category of menu copy is *a description of the food.* The descriptive copy provides what I refer to as the verbal seduction of the person who is reading the menu. The copy seduces him to order particular menu items. For example, a steak might be described as "Iowa corn-fed beef turned to a degree of doneness with its juices." Descriptive copy has its limitations, however, and can be carried to counterproductive excess. There are two schools of thought about menu description. One stresses brevity and the other, monstrous amounts of copy. There was a time when menu writers believed they had to write a Ph. D. dissertation to describe french fries. If you are meeting customer expectations—if the customer conjures up the right image of french fries and that is indeed what you are serving—you do not need to say that the potatoes are from Idaho or that they are cut a certain way or fried a golden brown. Or, for that matter, that they are hot or salty. Get right to the point when it is warranted.

My favorite example of descriptive overkill is a German restaurant where only German-speaking people eat dinner—yet the menu has two paragraphs describing sauerbraten. Even to describe sauerbraten in that restaurant is overkill. Everyone who eats there knows what it is, how it should look, and how it should taste. Of course, it is up to that restaurant's owner to serve what the customer expects.

On the other hand, an ethnic restaurant that has a varied clientele may need to provide rather full descriptions of the menu items. A Greek restaurant, for example, that draws customers from beyond the Greek community should provide enough description to assist the neophyte with that cuisine.

Be sure, particularly when you are offering an exotic menu item (even in a nonethnic restaurant), that you know how to spell the name of the dish correctly. Nothing is more offputting in an otherwise respectable restaurant than a menu with fake French words or misspelled Mexican ones—or, for that matter, misspelled English ones. Since your menu is representing your restaurant, it should indicate your familiarity with the names of your menu offerings.

I recommend that the descriptive copy on your menu include at least the following elements:

- Method of preparation
- Essential ingredients, if they are unusual or unique and add flavor to the product
- Method of service

Other elements that might be included, but should be considered optional, are:

- Quality of the product
- Cut of the meat product
- Size of the product

On the subject of size, I do not believe that you should ever state the ounce-size of anything on the menu. The ounce-size generally is the raw weight of an item, and one major class-action suit against a fast-food corporation claimed that the product did not weigh what it was advertised to weigh *after* it was cooked. The courts found for the plaintiffs on the basis of false advertising.

Other words can be used to describe a portion size as opposed to listing the weight. A *petite steak,* for example, indicates size.

Although I believe that brief descriptions usually are the best, you might, for example, want to describe items that are mesquite charbroiled, since such a technique is popular at the moment. (In fact, it is so popular that I find it hard to believe that the state of Texas can have produced that much mesquite.)

The closer you can list the price to the description of the item, the less psychological impact the price will have on the customer (see fig. 2-16). It is fairly widespread practice to list

2-16. Prices placed near menu descriptions. Courtesy La Veranda, St. Louis.

SPECIAL ENTREES

CALVES LIVER MARSALA   10.95
Sauteed with Proscuitto Ham, Mushrooms and Onions

STRIP SIRLOIN   12.95
Served Medium Rare, with Rosemary, Black Pepper, Olive Oil and Lemon

SHRIMP DIJON   13.25
Sauteed with White Wine, DiJon Mustard Sauce

VEAL SPEDINI   10.75
Stuffed with Egg, Mushrooms, Tomato, Cheese and Proscuitto

CHICKEN SOTTO   9.25
Marinated, Breaded and Broiled, Lemon Mushroom Sauce

VEAL CHOPS   13.25
Pressed with Romano Cheese, Sauteed and Served with Fresh Lemon

FILET OF BEEF   13.95
Sauteed, Served with Wild Mushrooms and Red Wine Sauce

Entrees include choice of Angel Hair with Oil, Butter and Garlic or
New Potatoes, fried with Onions and Tossed with Herbs and Seasonings and House Salad

ENTREES

GRILLED SWORDFISH.....................$21.00

Fresh Atlantic swordfish steak grilled over
pecan flames. Served with a rich hollandaise
sauce and fresh vegetable.

SHRIMP and TASSO FETTUCINI..............$18.50

Gulf shrimp and spicy Cajun ham sauteed and
tossed with fettucini, served with grilled
Creole tomato slices and wilted spinach.

VEAL with ROQUEFORT and PEARS..........$19.50

Scallops of milk-fed veal sauteed with pears
topped with a light roquefort sauce and served
with fresh vegetable.

SOFTSHELL CRABS....................$19.00

Two fresh jumbo softshell crabs stuffed with
Mr. B's seafood dressing, breaded and deep fried.
Served with lemon butter sauce and boiled new
potatoes.

2-17. Prices on right-hand margin. Courtesy Mr. B's, New Orleans.

the price after the food description and connect the two with leaders, or dots. The right-hand margin of the price column should be even, or lined up one under the other (see fig. 2-17). Another practice is to write out the price (two dollars fifty cents, for example, or seventeen dollars). This seems to have less impact on the customer and can inspire him to buy higher-priced items and spend more for the meal. (See fig. 2-18.)

Descriptive copy used on menus has changed appreciably since enactment of accuracy-in-menu regulations. It has become the obligation of the restaurant owner or manager to give the customers comprehensive and honest descriptions of the food items. Many more correct items are being used now on menus—as opposed to the cute and inaccurate names that were used in the past. The "secret recipe" or "homecooked" item has by and large been replaced by the correct name of the product as well as its ingredients. This subject is covered in more detail in chapter 9, and government guidelines for accuracy in menus are included in the Appendixes, but it is important to remember at this point that a considerable amount of noninformation on your menu will cause the customer to take no action, reject the menu and the establishment, and make no pur-

Sauteed Scallops en Bouchee
Cream Sauce with Mushrooms
Fourteen ninety-five

Alaskan King Crab Legs
Seventeen ninety-five

South African Lobster Tails
Nineteen ninety-five

Swordfish
Char Broiled
Thirteen twenty-five

Red Snapper Noisette
Topped with Crabmeat
Twelve ninety-five

Dover Sole Almondine
Boned tableside
Seventeen ninety-five

2-18. Prices spelled out and printed in the same typeface as the menu listings. Courtesy Nikolaisen's, Sunset Hills, Missouri.

chase. If you look on your menu as a catalog of the items you offer for sale and as a contract between you and the customer, you will by and large satisfy the requirements for accuracy in menus.

The third category of menu copy is *institutional copy*, the words that tell the story about the quality of the restaurant, the history of the restaurant, and any special features. This copy also relays to the customer something of the character of the restaurant. Figure 2-19 is an example of institutional copy from Cusanelli's Restaurant in St. Louis. (The restaurant is located in an eighteenth-century building once known as 8-Mile House.) The excerpt here tells part of the restaurant's history as a carriage-route way station. Many restaurants have such stories to tell, and what better place to tell the story than on the menu?

A menu that I believe to be a classic comes from one of the two Schneithorst restaurants in St. Louis (see fig. 2-20). The third generation of the Schneithorst family is now operating the two establishments. Examination of their institutional copy about family participation and concern for quality gives the feeling that a member of the Schneithorst family is in the kitchen preparing the food. This is not likely to be the case for everyone's meal, but the impression is a positive and caring one. The copy builds the restaurant's image.

Haussner's Restaurant in Baltimore, Maryland, boasts an outstanding collection of original art. The restaurant not only has an excellent reputation for fine food but also a considerable reputation for the art display. Inserted in the menu is a sheet that describes all of the works of art and tells how the family-owned restaurant acquired these works and developed the menu. The insert, titled "Answers to Most Asked Questions About Haussner's Restaurant" (see fig. 2-21), is a form of advertising that promotes both the food and the art.

Also in the category of institutional copy is the example in figure 2-22, an excerpt from the menu of The Cheshire Inn in St. Louis. This copy encourages the customer to enter the English pub atmosphere of "Merrie Olde England" and explains some of the present-day policies of the restaurant. It sets the stage for what is to come in the rest of the menu.

The fourth category of menu copy is what is known as *boilerplate information*. This includes:

- Name of the restaurant
- Address of the restaurant
- City where the restaurant is located
- Hours and days of operation
- Special services

Boilerplate information establishes the groundwork for the promotional items and services connected with the restaurant. All of the basic, unchanging information falls in this category. Every menu needs boilerplate information. As a matter of fact, several menus that were included in the first edition of this book did not have adequate boilerplate information, and I did not know how to contact the restaurants to request permission to use the menus again. Since most people share information about restaurants they particularly like (as well as about ones they dislike), give them something to pass on by having complete and accurate boilerplate information on your menu (see fig. 2-23).

2-19. Institutional copy. Courtesy Cusanelli's Restaurant, St. Louis.

Another famous guest who has partaken of the hospitality of the old 8-Mile House was Washington Irving, one of America's most famous authors. He visited these parts in 1824 and again in 1831. President William Howard Taft stopped for refreshment when he visited Jefferson Barracks in 1909, and one of the most regular customers in his day before the Civil War was a cordwood peddler who still owes a small Bar bill. His name was Ulysses Simpson Grant. The former owner of the famous old establishment still has the I.O.U. memento of this man who later became the great general and president of the United States.

SINCE 1917 The Schneithorst restaurants began with a young man's dream at the turn of the century. That was when Arthur B. Schneithorst, aged seventeen, began his restaurant career as a silver steward in the famous old Planters Hotel in downtown St. Louis and dreamed of owning his own fine restaurant. In the years that followed, the dream grew. Long-time St. Louisans will fondly recall the Benish Restaurant and the popular Rock Grill, owned by Mr. Schneithorst. Through the 1940's and early 1950's, Schneithorst's Bevo Mill and Airport Restaurant were two of St. Louis' favorites. Today, there are two Schneithorst's restaurants in the St. Louis area, each of which commands the respect of gourmets from all over the nation.

Probably the most famous of the two is the Schneithorst's Hofamberg Inn. Seating more than 600 guests, it offers three public and nine private dining rooms. The most popular is the Hofamberg Room, in which antiques, massive beams, polished woods and authentic designs from the corners of the world have created an atmosphere of old-world Bavarian charm.

The Hofamberg Inn takes its name from Schneithorst's Hofamberg Farm (Hofamberg means "house on the hill") at Clarksville, Missouri.

Guten Apetit!

2-20. *Institutional copy. Courtesy Schneithorst's Hofamberg Inn, St. Louis.*

The art work consists of paintings, bronzes, china, marbles, wood carvings, clocks, etchings, and other items owned by Mrs. Frances Haussner and family. The items on display make up about 70% of the collection. All but two of the paintings were bought at auction or private sale in the United States. They are originals and include works by Rembrandt, Whistler, de Blass, Bierstadt, Gainsborough, Schreyer, etc. None of the items in the collection are for sale. The collection is insured and the building is protected 24 hours a day, 365 days a year, by watchmen and Sonitrol.

HAUSSNER'S GIFT CERTIFICATES ARE AVAILABLE FROM THE CASHIER.

2-21. *Institutional copy. Courtesy Haussner's Restaurant, Baltimore.*

Merry times, indeed!

At Cheshire we try to recreate this jolly period with costume, recipes from old books, music, and general air of "Hail stranger, hail friend, sit down and rest yourself, partake of what we offer."

Where contemporary life crashes in on us, we try to meet it with British pluck. We send guests on forays into the world in our double decker London transports which visit theatrical and sporting meets, and which our guests can charter for their very own. For private occasions we have sumptuous chambers tucked here and there for the special celebration.

When you tire of your everyday world, think of us, a different, an older and possibly wiser English world away from the cares that beset you.

2-22. *Picture and word description of English pub atmosphere. Courtesy The Cheshire Inn, St. Louis.*

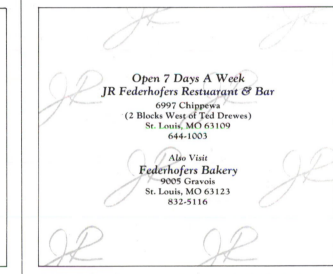

Open 7 Days A Week
JR Federhofers Restuarant & Bar
6997 Chippewa
(2 Blocks West of Ted Drewes)
St. Louis, MO 63109
644-1003

Also Visit
Federhofers Bakery
9005 Gravois
St. Louis, MO 63123
832-5116

2-23. *Boilerplate copy. Courtesy J. R. Federhofer's Restaurant & Bar, St. Louis.*

Arrangement of Copy

Although it may sound obvious, it is important to remember that categories of food (or courses) must be arranged in the order in which they are eaten. Even though the menu must take into account the customer's eye focus, the customer needs to be able to know the food categories that are available in the order he wants to eat them.

The location of items on the menu is a critical aspect of the menu as a marketing tool. The marketing principle of primacy and recency states that what catches your attention first and last will remain uppermost in your mind. If you watch people examining menus in a restaurant, you will see this principle at work. It is important to the properly designed menu (see fig. 2-24). Applying it by featuring those dishes

2-24. Entrée list.
Courtesy Mr. B's,
New Orleans.

ENTREES

Half Grilled Spring Chicken	7.50
Seasoned with lemon and fresh thyme and served with fresh seasonal vegetables	
Sauteed Creole Catfish	7.75
Breaded in cornmeal and sauteed until golden brown and served with two tartar sauces — one tomato and one jalepeno	
Shrimp and Angel Hair	8.75
Sauteed Gulf shrimp over angel hair pasta, with a creamy fresh herb and garlic sauce	
Shrimp Chippewa	9.25
Gulf shrimp and fresh mushrooms sauteed in a garlic butter sauce with French bread for dipping	
Coconut Beer Shrimp	8.25
Gulf shrimp in a beer batter, rolled in grated coconut and crisply fried, served with Creole marmalade sauce	
Pasta Primavera	7.75
Fresh vegetables, Prosciutto and Romano cheese tossed with pasta in a cream sauce flavored with sweet basil and green onions	
Pasta Carbonara	7.75
Spaghetti tossed with Prosciutto, Parmesan and Romano cheeses, cream and crisp, crumbled bacon	
Paneed Veal and Fettucini	9.75
Milk-fed veal breaded and pan sauteed, served with fettucini Alfredo	
Hickory Grilled Shrimp and Andouille Sausage	9.75
Served with a Creole mustard sauce on a bed of rice	
Mr. B's Chopped Steak	8.75
Freshly ground tenderloin wrapped with bacon and hickory grilled, served with potatoes and a Creole tomato salad	

that make the most profit will help you increase sales of items you want to sell.

Surveys and research indicate that in any list of ten menu items, those listed first, second, and last are the ones that will sell best. Do not list menu items in order of their prices—that is, the lowest to the highest, or vice versa. List them in the order in which they are profitable. If your highest-priced item is the one on which you make the most profit, list it either first or last.

If you observe people seated in a restaurant, you will notice that they generally will open the menu, look over it, then close it. When the waitress arrives to take the order, often they will not even open the menu again. If they do, it is simply to eliminate once more the items in the middle of the list that have not caught their attention. Almost always, they will settle on the first, second, or last item on the list.

Statistical studies of menus have indicated that, regardless of the number of items on a menu, sales will be concentrated in eight to ten of those items. Limiting the menu permits your employees to become specialists in the items you list and sell, and the restaurant, as a result, is then doing what it does best. You cannot afford to maintain menu items that do not sell. You are in business to sell food, not to store it. The excess will be costly in inventory, and quality declines if a dish is not prepared regularly or if it is prepared but seldom sold. The ideal menu would have ten entrées, with each ac-

counting for 10 percent of total entrée sales. This, however, is very unlikely. Only the most extensively researched menu could possibly come close to that ideal.

Vary the menu enough to interest the customer, but be sure to limit it to a number of items within management control. I have seen a limited-menu, fast-food operator continue to expand his menu to the point that it was not compatible with the talent of the employees and not easily produced on the existing equipment. Next came deterioration of quality and weakening of food cost control—with the ultimate outcome of failure of the enterprise.

A distinct advantage of a limited menu is the fact that the customer will need less time to make a food selection. Every customer needs adequate time to select and consume the food, but this time can be minimized with a limited menu.

If for some reason you feel the need for an extensive menu, write it so that you can create multiple menu items from the same cut of meat, seafood, or poultry by varying the sauce or method of preparation. Thus, even though the menu is extensive, the inventory will be contained.

I believe that the majority of patrons do not wish to struggle making a decision about what they will eat from your menu (and an extensive menu only worsens this situation), so the list should be limited and items should be arranged in line with the suggestions in this chapter.

Mechanics of Menu Copy

The smaller the operation, the easier the task of writing the menu copy. When the owner/operator has continuous public contact or is preparing and serving the product, he will know by verbal feedback or visual perceptions what is right and what is wrong with the menu.

The menu should be written to appeal to all of the five senses. You eat with more than your mouth and your stomach, and it is important to remember and recognize this fact. (The food, of course, must be prepared with the same goals in mind.)

- Sight: Describe the contrast of colors and shapes.
- Taste: Vary the seasonings and the methods of preparation.
- Touch: Describe the various consistencies of the food.
- Smell: Hint at the aroma of what is to come.
- Hearing: Sell the sizzle.

MENU PRODUCTION

Following the preparation of the menu copy, the next stage is to choose paper stock, typeface, and size of print—and then produce the physical menu.

The menu's typeface sets the style for the atmosphere of the restaurant and should reflect the establishment's ambiance. Just as corporate logos and trademarks are important elements of corporate images, the menu conveys the image of a restaurant. The colors and logo or trademark of a restaurant should be a part of the menu and should be used as identifiable characteristics for every printed item in the restaurant. Once chosen, the typeface and other graphic elements should be used on matches, napkins, placemats, table tents, menu clip-ons, and any other item on which there is printing. The use of attractive and recognizable physical characteristics provides the customers the assurance of your commitment to consistency in quality, food, and service.

As you make your choices in producing the menu, keep in mind that any type style that is difficult to read or not easily understood destroys all the groundwork you have laid in developing the menu. This pertains also to the size of the print. If the menu print is so small that it cannot be read in the dining room, all your other efforts are useless. The most important objective in the production of the menu is maximum readability, which is attained only by selecting the appropriate type style and size.

Typeface Styles and Sizes

Typefaces come in many different styles and sizes. Printers and designers have catalogs with printed samples. (See fig. 2-25.) Typefaces appropriate for menus fall into three categories—serif, sans serif, and script.

- Serif typefaces—those with tiny lines at the ends of the letters—are graceful, readable, and solid, but nowadays they are considered old-fashioned or traditional. There are hundreds of families of serif type; five samples are shown in figure 2-26.
- Sans serif typefaces—those without the serifs—are generally block-shaped, simpler, and considered more modern. Samples of sans serif type are shown in figure 2-27.
- Script typefaces, while appropriate for menus, should be used sparingly. They can add variety in the printing and highlight the food items you want to merchandise, but they (and italic as well) can cause eyestrain from the slanted angles of the letters (see fig. 2-28).

The text of the menu should be printed with a combination of uppercase (capital) and lowercase (small) letters. Most menus are printed effectively if they have about twice as many lowercase letters as uppercase letters, since lowercase letters are considered more readable.

Use uppercase letters for categories of food and for proper names, as well as to draw attention to special items on the menu. One restaurant in St. Louis, for example, lists Beef SANDWICH in the center of its luncheon sandwich offerings to draw attention to that section of the menu. Their sales analysis indicates that this particular sandwich is the bestselling one on the menu. Although it was not their original intention to highlight only this one item, the device has been effective. Such a mixture can be used in other ways to develop customer awareness by design.

Exotic typefaces and offbeat printing styles should be used very sparingly in a menu. They are very difficult to decipher and are handicaps to the readability of the material (see Fig. 2-29).

American Classic
American Classic Ital.
American Classic Bd
American Class. Xbd

American Typewriter Lt
American Typewriter Md
American Typewrtr Bd
American Typewriter Cond. Lt
American Typewriter Cond. Md
American Typewriter Cd. Bd

Antique Olive Light
Antique Olive
Antique Olive Medium
Antique Olive Bold

Avant Garde Ex. Light
Avant Garde Book
Avant Garde Bk Oblique
Avant Garde Demi
Avant Garde D. Oblique
Avant Garde Bold

Baskerville
Baskerville Italic
Baskerville Bold
Baskerville Bold Italic

Bodoni Poster
Bodoni Poster Ital.

Century Textbook
Century Textbook Italic
Century Textbook Bd
Century Textbook Bd It.

Cooper Black
Cooper Black Italic

Eras Light
Eras Book
Eras Medium
Eras Demibold
Eras Bold
Eras Ultra

Friz Quadrata
Friz Quadrata Bold

Gill Sans
Gill Sans Italic
Gill Sans Bold
Gill Sans Kayo

Garamond Light
Garamond Light Italic
Garamond Book
Garamond Book Italic
Garamond Bold
Garamond Bold Italic
Garamond Ultra
Garamond Ultra Italic

Gothic Outline

Goudy Old Style
Goudy Old Style Italic
Goudy Bold
Goudy Bold Italic

Helvetica Extra Light
Helvetica Extra Light Italic
Helvetica Light
Helvetica Light Italic
Helvetica Medium
Helvetica Medium Italic
Helvetica Bold
Helvetica Bold Italic
Helvetica Extrabold
Helvetica XBold Ital
Helvetica XBold Cond
Helvetica XB Ext
Helvetica Condensed
Helvetica Italic Condensed
Helvetica Bold Condensed
Helvetica Bold Italic Condensed

Kabel Book
Kabel Medium
Kabel Bold
Kabel Ultra
Kaylin Script

Korinna Regular
Korinna Kursiv
Korinna Extrabold
Korinna Heavy

Melior
Melior Italic
Melior Demibold
Melior Demibold Italic

Microstyle
Microstyle Ext.
Microstyle Bold
Microstyle Bd Ex

Optima
Optima Italic
Optima Demi-Bold
Optima Demi-Bold Italic

P. T. Barnum

Palatino
Palatino Italic
Palatino Demi-Bold
Palatino Demi-Bold Italic

Souvenir Medium
Souvenir Medium Italic
Souvenir Demi
Souvenir Bold

Standard Typewriter

Stymie Light
Stymie Light Italic
Stymie Medium
Stymie Bold

Tiffany Light
Tiffany Medium
Tiffany Demi
Tiffany Heavy

Times Roman
Times Roman Italic
Times Bold
Times Bold Italic

2-25. Examples of typeface styles.

COFFEE - our own blend 50
COFFEE - our own blend 50
COFFEE - our own blend 50
COFFEE - our own blend. 50
COFFEE - our own blend. 50

2-26. Serif typefaces; from top to bottom, Times Roman, Century Old Style, Bodoni Book, Palatino, and Baskerville.

COFFEE - our own blend 50
COFFEE - our own blend 50
COFFEE - our own blend 50
COFFEE - our own blend. 50
COFFEE - our own blend 50

2-27. Sans serif typefaces; from top to bottom, Helvetica Regular, Eras Book, Optima, Univers 55, and Futura.

Coffee - our own blend. 50
Coffee - our own blend. 50
Coffee - our own blend. 50
Coffee - our own blend. 50
COFFEE - our own blend. 50
COFFEE - our own blend. 50
COFFEE - our own blend. 50
COFFEE - our own blend. 50

2-28. Script and italic-style typefaces.

AVOID SETTING SCRIPT STYLES IN ALL CAPS.
Avoid setting Script styles in All Caps.

AVOID SETTING OLD ENGLISH STYLES IN ALL CAPS.
Avoid setting Old English styles in All Caps.

2-29. Examples of italic and script.

COFFEE - our own blend. 50
COFFEE - our own blend. 50
COFFEE - our own blend. 50
COFFEE - our own blend. . . . 50

2-30. Type examples showing different weight or boldness.

Weight or boldness of the typeface is another critical element in the design of the menu. Typefaces come in light, medium, and bold weights (see fig. 2-30).

As mentioned earlier, the menu conveys the restaurant's image, so the printing must be compatible with the decor that you have developed for the restaurant. Thus, the typeface style and the boldness of the letters should be consistent with the mood of the restaurant (see fig. 2-31).

Never use more than three different typefaces on the menu. This confuses the copy, results in a haphazard appearance, and conveys the wrong message to the customer.

Since readability is the ultimate goal in the production of the menu, you will have to select type sizes that fit in the space you have available. The type must be large enough to be legible, but the menu should not be overcrowded and look cluttered.

Type size is measured in points—seventy-two points per inch. Menus should not be printed in sizes smaller than twelve points, which is roughly equivalent to the size of a letter on a pica-style typewriter (see fig. 2-32).

The space between the lines of printing is called leading. For ease in reading a menu, three-point leading is essential. Anything less reduces readability. In figure 2-33, the copy with three-point leading (indicated as 12/3) is more legible than the copy with no leading (indicated as 12/0). Printing with no leading is said to be *set solid.*

Spacing between the letters is also adjustable, depending on the requirements of your menu copy. A feeling of space can be created by a printing process known as *kerning,* which involves the removal of space between letters, or by *letterspacing,* which involves adding space between letters (see fig. 2-34).

2-31. Print and copy consistent with a restaurant's English theme. Courtesy The Cheshire Inn, St. Louis.

A REAL OLD ENGLISH TRADITION

Probably one of the first major cooking discoveries was the joy and advantage of roasting good meat on a spit. The meat loses less of its natural juices and therefore loses less of its natural good flavor.

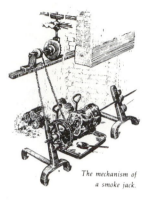

The mechanism of a smoke jack.

The English went to great lengths to perfect a system to keep the spit slowly turning before a fire. Beginning with a boy to turn the crank, they advanced to spits that were turned by the rising heat from the fire. Ultimately, they used a dog operated treadmill and went to the extreme of breeding dogs, called "Turnspit Terriers", that were just the right size and weight to operate the treadmill properly.

At Cheshire, we have a great slowly turning spit, and on it we prepare our specialty of the house, Roast Prime Rib of Beef, served with Yorkshire pudding and horseradish mousse.

Roast Prime Rib **14.20**
Single English Cut **13.15**
Extra Large Cut **17.50**

Turnspits and their treadmill. A rail that usually enclosed the working dog has been omitted for clarity.

---

12 point SANS SERIF
12 point SERIF
12 point DECORATIVE

2-32. Examples of twelve-point type.

SERIF GOTHIC 12/3

THE GOURMET -with grilled onions, sauteed mushrooms and swiss cheese. 4.50

12/0

THE GOURMET - with grilled onions, sauteed mushrooms and swiss cheese. 4.50

2-33. Type showing three-point leading between lines and no leading between lines.

12 point HELIOS
12 point HELIOS with letterspacing
12 point HELIOS with letterspacing
12 point HELIOS with letterspacing
12 point HELIOS with kerning
12 point HELIOS with kerning
12 point HELIOS with kerning

2-34. Examples of letterspacing and kerning.

Menu Paper and Ink

For maximum readability, a menu should be printed in black ink on white paper. It is acceptable to use tinted paper or tinted ink compatible with the atmosphere and color scheme of the restaurant, but be warned that it is all too easy to select colors that blend into one another and are then not readable at the light level of the dining room. Test the combinations in a simulated setting before you make your decisions.

Menus usually are printed on paper. Other materials were mentioned earlier in the section on the menu cover, but the standard material for the interior is paper. The quality and type of paper used depends upon the permanency of the menu. The character and type of restaurant dictate the quality of the paper. If the menu is changed daily, or relatively often, a lower quality can be used because the menu is quickly obsolete. Fast-food operations, on the other hand, often prefer coated (laminated) paper because of the menu's long-term, constant use. A reusable menu requires durable paper that will stand a great deal of handling by both customers and employees.

The texture and weight of the paper or stock upon which the menu is printed are its lasting qualities. Be choosy about your menu material. Once again, remember that it is conveying your restaurant's image. Spend some time examining catalogs from a printer. Evaluate the small samples of papers in various colors, weights, and textures. Make your decisions rationally and economically. Ninety-pound stock is fine for an average restaurant. (Such determinations of weight are based on trade formulas and are best explained by your printer.)

The menu stock should not amount to more than 10 or 15 percent of total menu costs. Purchase stock in sizes that yield the maximum number of menus—generally in the 9-inch-by-12-inch size recommended earlier.

White Space

White space is the printing/production term that designates what is *not* printed. Menus need white space. (See fig. 2-35.) In fact, the printed menu's copy, drawings, and any other material should cover no more than 50 percent of the total space available. Menu copy that is surrounded by white space (it is called that even if you use colored paper) emphasizes the type and makes the menu easier to read, avoiding the cluttered look. If white space amounts to less than 50 percent, not only will it make the menu look crowded, but also it will hinder the customer in reading the menu and making food decisions.

Margins, the outside edges of the menu, are one form of white space. They should all be consistent. This contributes to the symmetry of the menu and makes it easier to read. On the left side, the type should all be even against the margin, while on the right side the type can be ragged, or uneven. The right-hand margin would begin at the end of the longest ragged line. Columns of copy should be no wider than 3 inches.

Blank space, meaning a space on the menu that seems to demand filling, can be used effectively to advertise other special offerings. Blank space on a breakfast menu, for example, might be well utilized to advertise your Sunday brunch. If the arrangement of copy and drawings on your menu results in blank space, by all means make good use of it. Never just leave it blank.

2-35. Example of white space used for readability. Courtesy Johnny's Cafe, Omaha.

TREASURES FROM THE SEA

FRENCH FRIED LOUISIANA SHRIMP 8.95
ICED GULF SHRIMP 8.95
NORTHERN CHANNEL CATFISH 6.95
ROCKY MOUNTAIN RAINBOW TROUT 7.30
HALIBUT, Broiled or Breaded 8.50
DEEP FRIED FROG LEGS 7.50
BROILED AFRICAN
   ROCK LOBSTER TAIL .... Market Price

SEAFOOD CATCH OF THE DAY
YOUR SERVER WILL MAKE TODAY'S CATCH AVAILABLE TO YOU.
ALL SEAFOOD IS SUBJECT TO SEASON, —WEATHER— AND FISHING LUCK!

Color in the Menu

Color may be used in the menu to call attention to specific menu items, but it is also used, as described earlier, on the menu cover to carry out the restaurant's theme and decor. The amount of color used is determined by the budget; the more colors used, obviously, the higher the cost of the menu.

FURTHER THOUGHTS ON MENU STRATEGY

Even the most talented menu merchandiser realizes that menu strategy can be a subjective thing. In the end, everything comes down to the customer and his reactions. Some additional tips come to mind, however, in the area of menu strategy.

Handwriting on menus has always been considered rather tacky, but if it is done properly, it can be turned into a marketing device. Horatio's, an operation in Seattle, includes a note in meticulous handwriting on one side of its menu, saying, "Have you tried our sautéed mushrooms?" The way it is done, and the way customers have accepted it, indicates that customer reaction is, "Here is a restaurateur who is concerned about his patrons and wants us to try this dish because it is particularly good and it is a good deal as well." Of course, if you are a restaurateur, your reaction probably would be, "Here is a real merchandiser and he has done a great job of selling an extra menu item."

On Horatio's menu, all of the prices are written very neatly in ink and the menu looks very attractive. That way, if there is a need to change prices, they can just discard those particular menus and rewrite the new prices on the menu backings printed previously. They can then save the cost of reprinting.

Another menu strategy for increasing sales and profits is to increase the wine sales. The technique for doing this is to make it easy for the customer to order wine. The average customer is becoming considerably more knowledgeable about wines, and he knows when they are priced too high. Be honest and fair in your pricing. It may even be to your advantage to sell more at a lower gross profit and, in the end, have a higher return from the sale of wines. Make it as easy as possible, using bin number and wine suggestions on your menu, for the customer to take an interest in ordering. This will serve to increase wine sales with meals.

Listing cocktails on the menu has caused a great deal of controversy among restaurateurs. You might try giving preference to a few "house drinks" that you have developed, as opposed to having just a list of familiar cocktails. Listing a Manhattan or a martini is not good utilization of merchandising space on the menu. Cocktails that are special and for which you will get a premium price should have some sort of star billing to increase volume and net profit (see fig. 2-36).

Condiments do not need to be listed on the menu unless they have the significance of a signature item. If a particular condiment is one of the items for which your restaurant is known, obviously it should be prominent on the menu.

From Ye King's Arm Pub...

Buckingham........................... 2.50
  A delicate blend of Applejack Brandy,
  cranberry juice and lime juice.

Red Fox, *a Champagne and cranberry juice cocktail* .. 2.50

Bobbie Burns, *a poetic Scotch Manhattan*......... 2.90

King Arthur Cooler, *a blending of Rum, orange,*
  and lemon juice 2.50

Hurricane Guinevere, *Passion Fruit juice with*
  West Indian Rum 2.50

Brighton Punch, *the other ingredients are a secret,*
  but the punch comes from a favorite rare old Bourbon 2.50

Sir Lancelot, *Rum and Brandies with lemon juice*..... 2.50

King's Cay, *Passion Fruit juice, Brandy and Rum, a*
  green mist in a Hurricane 2.50

London Fog, *Rum, Vodka, Triple Sec, Apricot*
  Brandy, orange and lemon (sweetened) juices
  evoke a foggy London night 2.90

2-36. House special cocktails. Courtesy The Cheshire Inn, St. Louis.

By using some type of device to call the customer's attention to such specialty items, you can indicate what you want to sell.

Be sure that all menus are checked daily by an employee to ensure that they are clean. An old or messy menu tells the customer that the operation is somewhat slipshod, that sanitation is not a major concern, and that the management does not really care. It can even give the impression that conditions in the kitchen might be as slovenly as what shows on the menu. Clean or discard any menu that is not presentable to a customer.

Some foodservice operators, interested in keeping up to date with changing food costs and keeping the printing budget down, print menu backings only, with no food prices or items printed on them. Then they write the items and the prices on the menus or insert a separate sheet as they change prices or put new menu offerings into service. If you are going to print large numbers of backings, however, you must be flexible in allowing for an easy change of copy and price on the menu as sales statistics are gathered and analyzed. This will improve the overall cost-control process.

SUMMARY

Although you may have many options in developing and producing your restaurant's menu, in the final analysis a printed menu is satisfactory if it is readable and it accomplishes what you want it to do: increase customer counts, raise the check average, and sell the items that you want to sell. Combined with a pleasant dining ambiance, good-quality food, and caring service, a well-thought-out and well-produced menu can be the key to your success in the restaurant industry.

CHAPTER THREE

MARKETING STRATEGIES

INTERNAL MARKETING

Internal marketing takes place when the customer arrives at your restaurant. It involves pleasing the customer with food, service, and drinks. Internal marketing is not a technique; it should be an extension of the management of the establishment through the employees.

Restaurant Employees

Never underestimate the importance of your employees as sales and marketing representatives of your restaurant. A program pamphlet for "The Spirit of Service," prepared by the National Institute for the Foodservice Industry (NIFI), listed six reasons why customers will quit patronizing a restaurant: One percent die, 3 percent move away, 5 percent have new interests or friends, 9 percent change for competitive reasons, 14 percent are dissatisfied, and the vast majority (68 percent) encounter an attitude of indifference and unconcern by one or more employees.

It is generally agreed by marketing people that an unhappy customer will tell ten people, but a happy customer will tell only three. I have never heard anyone who eats out on a regular basis say, "Let's go down and eat at such-and-such restaurant; their food is bad and the servers are always rude to us when we go in." There are all manner of horror stories relating to rudeness of restaurant employees.

The saying that "the customer eats with you by choice" is, I think, very true. In marketing your restaurant, it is important not to take the attitude that you and your employees are *permitting* customers to come in and eat and spend their money. Fostering a positive attitude among the employees who serve and prepare the food is one of the best possible marketing devices.

Since foodservice workers usually are not aware of all of the factors involved in menu pricing, one may tell a customer who is about to order a certain dish, "Boy, that price is awfully high." Employees can destroy you with such comments. They are not said to hurt the operation in most cases, but that is what results. The employee might know only that the operator bought the raw ingredient for the dish for $1.00, is selling the menu item for $2.00, and supposedly is making $1.00 in profit. He or she probably does not understand the other costs that are involved, such as the overhead, the profit needed, or the return required on investment. Therefore, the reaction is, "He's doubling his money."

There are undoubtedly times when it would be wise to explain to some employees what goes into menu pricing. To be sure, this is my personal opinion; I doubt whether I could validate it with statistics.

One way of making employees more informed might be to use as a guideline the average amount of business that a waitress writes a year—that is, the number of sales that she makes (not her income). Assume that the national average of sales by waitresses is about $17,000 a year—not a lot of money by most standards. In stable economic periods, an automobile salesman can do that much business in two or three weeks. If, for example, the waitress receives wages of $10,000 a year—which is a 60 percent labor factor, a reasonable figure—she does not write enough business to leave much profit after her labor cost is deducted. These are facts that workers may not realize. They may think, "We work hard," and they really *do* work hard, but their sales volume does not allow both lower prices and the necessary profits. If they are well informed, they may well change their reactions to the prices you charge.

During seminars that I have conducted all over the country, many people have suggested to me that point-of-sale information given to the guest by the waiter or waitress will cause an increase in the sales of specific items they recommend. How many professionals do you have in your restaurant who will do a sales presentation to the customer when they take the order? How many, instead, issue a challenge to the customer? "You don't want dessert, do you? Or how many comment, "I don't know how it tastes. We don't get to eat that." If you have professionals who are doing sales promotions at the time they take the order, this is indicative of good employee training.

My wife and I once went out for dinner to a rather well-known restaurant in Michigan and asked the waitress what she would recommend from the menu if she were having dinner there. Her immediate response was "Nothing. I'd have a cheese sandwich; I'm a vegetarian." Such a comment from the service person has a

tremendous negative effect upon sales of the items that are purchased by the patrons of the restaurant.

The serving personnel will be better prepared to make suggestions and recommendations to the customer and thus increase sales if they have tasted each item and know the ingredients and method of preparation.

Service persons can also be helpful in promotion campaigns that are designed to stimulate the customer to question the waiter or waitress. An executive who has attended one of my seminars on food-cost control and food merchandising sent me a button from his company that asked, DO YOU KNOW? This stemmed from a suggestion made at the seminar that waiters and waitresses should wear such a button so that the customer could question, "Do I know what?" The service people, in turn, would have to answer the question by telling what the current promotion was. This places emphasis on customers' questions to service employees. This same kind of promotion could be done with table tents, with a notice on the menu, or with any device that will make the customer question your personnel so that they can promote the particular item that you are selling.

Even at my first encounter with this, I immediately asked, "Do I know what?"—which in turn caused the service person to respond to me, "Do you know that we are starting a Sunday brunch?" She then went on with the sales spiel for the brunch.

No matter what technique you choose, it must inspire a direct question by the customer and a direct and immediate response by the service person.

Menu Features

As mentioned in chapter 2, menu location is very important in creating demand for a food item. The chalkboard is one of the most successful menu approaches currently in use. It has proved especially successful in presenting luncheon specials. Almost any luncheon special will sell if it is listed on a chalkboard.

Placement is critical: The chalkboard must be in a prominent location. You need to feature only a couple of items, or even a single item, to catch the attention of the customer when he enters. Attractiveness and neatness of lettering are also essential for effective merchandising of the foods offered. You probably will be out of the featured item(s) before the noon hour is over.

Use of a chalkboard permits you to take advantage of seasonal buys or of special purchases that may be available on a one-time basis. The chalkboard menu is written with the understanding that each item on it is available only for a limited time, and when an item runs out, it will be erased. Sometimes other items may be written on the board, but usually the space is left blank. The chalkboard also permits instant price changes. The chalkboard is a market-type of menu, an advertising piece for point-of-sale features (see fig. 3-1).

3-2. Examples of noncopyrighted clip-art that can be used to highlight menu features.

3-3. Clip-on that matches theme of restaurant in design and print style. (See Zeno's menu, fig. 2-10.) Courtesy Zeno's Steak House, Rolla, Missouri.

Whatever graphic representation is available may be used on a printed menu to call the customer's attention to features. Attendees at my menu seminars often ask about using a photograph to represent features on their menus. I answer that from my experience of having spent time on weekends between 2 and 3 A.M. in a pancake house. The customer enters one of those establishment, points at or close to the item, and says, "I want that." When the food arrives and it does not look exactly like the picture, there often is a squabble between the customer and the service person.

When you depict any menu items with photographs, you must adhere strictly to accuracy-in-menu guidelines. What you see *must be* what you get. If the picture accurately represents the item that is prepared in the kitchen and served to the customer, the picture is fine. If it does not, a word description is more appropriate.

Since the photograph must be an actual representation of what you are offering for sale, I suggest that, for your menu strategy, you use a graphic device or drawing instead (see fig. 3-2). This can relieve you of some problems in case your cooks do not meet the standard that you have set with a photograph—which, obviously, would show the ideal product.

If you elect to use a clip-on on your menu to feature items, the clip-on paper should be of the same quality as your printed menu and should use the same colors, type size, and type style (see fig. 3-3). A successful exception might be a menu like Horatio's (mentioned in chapter 2), where an item promoted on a continuing basis is handwritten on a clip-on. Ordinarily, the clip-on will be a cycle or a market menu attached to a static menu.

Clip-ons are a good merchandising tactic if they are properly utilized. For the clip-on to be effective, it must be special. Relisting items already on the menu at a different price is not the correct way to use a clip-on.

Take advantage of every holiday and local special event to promote an increase in the volume of business. Promotions of special menu items or special services you are going to give customers during this time are an integral part of menu strategy.

Management and Customer Satisfaction

In order to ensure the continuing patronage of the customers you currently serve and to build the customer base with new customers, management contact with customers—whether by you or by an employee who represents you—is critical. This allows you to measure, informally and nonscientifically, customer reactions. It also allows customers to verbalize their satisfaction and their menu requests.

A good example of the effect of customer input arose in one of my classes. A young student named John complained that he had a customer who came in every day at noon and ordered a "patty melt," which was not on the luncheon menu. After the dish was specially prepared and sent into the dining room, the waiters would get at least ten or twelve more orders for a patty melt sandwich. This shows the influence of sight promotion in the dining room. If a dish looks good, it will sell to other customers who see it. How many times in a restaurant have you seen a particular item that looked very appealing, asked the person what he or she was eating, and then ordered the same item? My comment to John was, "Perhaps the customers are trying to tell you something." Some time later, John reported that his restaurant had added the patty melt to its luncheon menu and the sales had increased to about forty during each luncheon period. Too many times, the operator or chef puts his likes or dislikes ahead of what the customer might like or dislike. If an item is profitable and it sells, it may well have a place on your menu.

There may be some instances when you have an item on the menu that has had tremendous popularity, an item on which you have built a reputation. It is a quality product, and you offer large portions, but it may be costing you money to keep it on the menu. You are convinced, however, that any change would have a negative effect on volume and profit. If you feel that you must keep the item on your menu, design the menu so that you can "hide" the item from the customer. Put it in the center of your list of items so that patrons will have to seek it out. You will be amazed at how much you can decrease the sales of a particular item by placing it where it is not noticeable to the customer. In this way, you retain customer satisfaction and achieve your cost-control objective at the same time.

My father-in-law is one of the most difficult persons on earth to buy a gift for. I know he eats breakfast regularly at a place with the very unlikely name of Kopper's Chili Parlor, on East 41st Street in Tulsa, Oklahoma. In order to try to solve the perennial gift problem, I called Mike Kopper, the owner of the restaurant. As the name of the restaurant might imply, it is not an establishment that you would normally associate with a marketing effect in gift certificates. When I explained what I needed, Kopper said, "No problem. I will be happy to supply you with gift certificates."

By return mail, I received typed certificates (on typing paper) valid for breakfasts at that restaurant. This is a classic example of management realizing that a restaurant is established to serve its customers and to provide those services that will encourage them to continue as patrons. After listening to customers' wishes, management must work diligently to develop continuing and expanded patronage by utilizing as many internal marketing tactics as possible.

COUPONS AND COUPONING

Everything that I write about coupons is based upon my personal bias and prejudice against them. I believe firmly that no business can exist long by giving away food. Any restaurant can enjoy high volume if it does not charge for its food. But where is the profit in that?

Coupons are a form of advertising and are used to stimulate sales and increase customer counts by public awareness. The object is to develop business at slow or slack periods. Concentrate on developing business at a time when you need it and not when volume is high.

Couponing may be an expensive form of advertising to get a customer into the restaurant unless it accomplishes its principal purpose of getting him to come back. If the coupon does not accomplish this, it can be regarded as an excessive expenditure with no cost-effective return to the restaurant. If customers use the coupons on a regular and repetitive basis, then your restaurant in effect becomes a discount operation.

Restaurateurs work very hard to develop regular customers, and when they begin to offer coupons, the regular customers start to feel that they may have been cheated over the years. It is regulars who generate the traffic, and when the restaurant begins to attract what I call "the bargain-seeking diner," the regulars feel that they may no longer be getting the same quality of food and service. Beware of alienating them.

Types of Coupons

There are two types of coupons, the first of which is a free gift coupon or unrestricted coupon. It entitles the customer to buy one of something and get another free. There are no restrictions or qualifications (see fig. 3-4).

The second type is a conditional coupon. With this type, there is some condition placed upon the redemption of the coupon.

You *must* specify the redemption conditions *on* the coupon. The customer must buy something or meet some preset requirement. This is not necessarily a two-for-one coupon. The condition may be in the form of a reduction in price so that the customer receives a higher-priced article or more value for the money spent. Such a coupon might, for example, reduce the price of the food for a period of time and under specified conditions, as outlined on the coupon (see fig. 3-5).

If the coupon is not a two-for-one coupon and there is a conditional purchase attached to it, then the coupon is not normally associated with two-for-one pricing but is designed to offer a new product or service that was not available previously. This technique might be used, for example, in an existing restaurant that has been undermarketed and has not completely penetrated the potential of the area where it is located.

3-4. An unrestricted dinner coupon. Courtesy Steak 'n' Tails, St. Louis.

FREE FRIED CHICKEN DINNER or PASTA DINNER

BUY ONE REGULAR DINNER — GET ONE FRIED CHICKEN DINNER OR PASTA FREE

FEDERHOFER'S *Restaurant & Bar*

CLOSED JULY 4TH

6997 CHIPPEWA - 644-1003

| LUNCH 11:00-4:00 TUES.-FRI. | DINNER 4:00-10:30 TUES.-THURS. | DINNER 4:00-12:00 FRI. & SAT. | DINNER 4:00-9:00 SUNDAY |

COUPON GOOD WEDNESDAY, JULY 17 THROUGH TUESDAY, JULY 23, 1985.

CLOSED MONDAY'S

3-5. A restricted dinner coupon. Courtesy J. R. Federhofer's Restaurant & Bar, St. Louis.

A problem with coupons is that it is hard to gauge future sales to persons who were first attracted by the coupons. It is difficult to measure how many people will return because of the incentive that you have offered in the form of the coupon. The only way to measure such response is to use a very sophisticated survey to determine whether they would have visited regardless of the coupon incentive. They might, after all, have come to your restaurant even if they had not had the coupon.

If customers will eat only in a particular establishment when they have a coupon, the response to the coupons may indicate that prices are too high for the market.

Fast-food operations often do conditional-

3-6. Coupon monitoring form for secondary sales.

COUPON SECONDARY SALES MONITORING

Item	Food Sales	Secondary Sales	Product Cost	Operating Cost	Discount
Meal-1	12.00		4.44		
Meal-2	8.00		2.96		
Cocktail		6.00	1.32		
Dessert		5.00	1.85		
Appetizer		3.00	1.11		
Labor				8.84	
Occupancy				3.99	
Other variables				2.80	
Other fixed				3.75	
Coupon					8.00
Total	20.00	14.00	11.68	19.38	8.00

Total Sales

Food	20.00	
Secondary	14.00	
		34.00

Total Cost

Product	11.68	
Operation	19.38	
Discount	8.00	
		39.06
Income		(5.06)

Above calculation based on:

Product cost (food & liquor)	32.95%
Labor	26.00
Occupancy	11.75
Other variables	8.25
Other fixed	11.05

Note: Profit is not included in cost percentages.

type package promotions. This promotion consists of the sale of a regular-priced item, with a reduced price on an accompanying or secondary sales item. From a marketing standpoint, it is used to get the consumer to buy more than he would buy normally. Secondary sales are essential in coupon promotions and employees should work to stimulate them. (See fig. 3-6.)

Coupon Objectives

If part of your operational plan is to use coupons, you must establish objectives. Design the coupon: (1) to develop business at a particular time during the day or evening; (2) to increase the sales of specific items on your menu; (3) to generate the type of volume you need; and (4) to generate repeat business. As a manager, you

must make every effort to track the activity of the coupon promotion and monitor sales volume. Find out whether the coupon meets your promotion objectives, based upon the number of coupons distributed. Account for both the number of coupons redeemed and the specific purchases made with coupons.

At the 1983 MUFSO (Multi-Unit Food-Service Operators) Conference, Joe S. Lewis chaired a panel on coupon merchandising that gave the following objectives for any couponing program:

1. Have specific objectives to be accomplished by the coupons.
2. Increase customer traffic and create interest in the product you are promoting.
3. Reinforce the advertising and develop a

3-7. In-house dinner-club coupons. Courtesy Red Lobster and Taco Bell.

marketing strategy image.

4. Gain an edge on your competition.
5. Build employee involvement.
6. Give positive reinforcement to your market area that this is *the* place to eat.

Use of the coupon must also promote a trust on the part of the customer. The customer should feel that you are advertising for competitive reasons, you offer a quality product, and you guarantee that the offer you make on the coupon will be fulfilled.

No promotion that you devise can in any way overcome ineptness or sloppiness of management. If you do not maintain tight controls in the operation of the restaurant, you will find that couponing or discounting will not generate business. It is an expensive undertaking, and in many instances it tends to increase the speed at which an operation will decline. Any establishment that is not run well will not generate profits and will suffer losses and eventually fail.

Methods of Couponing

A primary technique for couponing is direct mail, which involves use of a random sampling or complete saturation of a mailing list for a specific neighborhood that you believe to be your market area. People in that market area then receive coupons individually or in a pack with other coupons. This method will accomplish several objectives;

1. It makes a definite positive offer to the customer.
2. It describes a definite product or service that you are promoting.
3. It defines the circumstances under which the coupon can be used.

Selecting the Coupon Audience

When selecting the audience for your coupons, geography is extremely important. I tend to refer to a restaurant as a "three-mile island," but the demographics of the market area are equally as important as the geography. You must know the audience to whom you are sending the coupons—people you hope will redeem those coupons in your restaurant.

Broadly speaking, two-for-one dinner-club coupon books may be thought of as a form of advertising and nonselective couponing. These coupon books reach a very large audience, perhaps larger than any other single piece of advertising that you may do. People who buy these books surely will see your "advertisement."

One of my favorite coupon stories comes from a restaurant operator in Columbus, Ohio, who said that a coupon company came in to sell him a listing in its two-for-one book and "guaranteed to fill the dining room every Saturday night." He said, "Indeed you will, and when I look in my dining room every Saturday night, I will know that at least 50 percent of those people are eating free. No thanks. I choose not to be in the coupon book." The principal profit-makers from coupon books usually are the people who print and sell the books.

Coupon Alternative

If you decide not to become involved with the two-for-one dinner-club books, you might consider creating a dining club. In such a case, the restaurant establishes a fee for membership. This membership entitles the customer to a free meal after the purchase of a specified number of meals (see fig. 3-7) or a discount under specified conditions upon presentation of the membership card. You also may be able to work with theaters, specialty food, or liquor stores in your area, to offer discounts with the use of the dinner-club card. This provides an additional incentive for the purchase of the card.

The advantage of the self-operated club is that you receive the money for the club membership "up front"—before the member derives any benefit. That money enters your cash flow before you incur any obligation. The probability that someone will fulfill the entire membership obligation (for example, the member must consume ten meals within a year and will then receive one free meal) becomes more remote the longer the period of time required to fulfill the conditions. But with the sale of the membership card, you have incurred no cost and have preconditioned the customer to buy in order to take advantage of a free or discounted meal. This method is a cost-effective way of establishing a discount program. You can estimate that 25 to 30 percent of the members will fail to fulfill the conditions.

What Restaurants Use Discounts?

No restaurant that enjoys a high check average and expense account meals will deal with coupons. It simply does not need the incentives, and coupons do not fit the image of the restaurant. Coupons normally are synonymous with low-check-average (under $10) restaurants. This does not necessarily have to be true, but there is that perception of a restaurant that uses coupons. If you have a high-check-average restaurant and use coupons, the customer's reaction is likely to be, "Why should I go there and pay full price? I will wait for the coupon." Then he will go when the meal is discounted.

If you elect to use couponing as a marketing technique, be very specific in defining the conditions of the coupon. One restaurant in St. Louis has been involved with unrestricted couponing (no restriction on date or hours) for a number of years. The coupon specifies, however, that the only items available with the coupon are their special Italian dinners. This has effectively limited their coupon participation factor to 25 percent or less on the busiest nights.

Employee Involvement in Couponing

One of the biggest problems with couponing is that employees do not understand restaurant objectives and have negative reactions to customers who use coupons. They tend to notice only that the bargain diner has a lower check average and therefore tips on the lowered amount, not the original check. A restaurant's customers must be convinced that the service personnel understand and believe in the promotion and the coupon.

Coupon Popularity

A 1983 A. C. Nielson survey showed a record of 5.56 million coupons (of all types) redeemed. This is an increase of more than 24 percent over the 1982 figures on coupon redemption. The economic conditions in 1982 taught people to be conservative in assessing the value they perceived from eating out. At a time when eating out was something of a luxury, many people did not eat out unless they could use a coupon.

Summary

Coupons have a place and can aid the volume of business if you set objectives and are selective in the use of coupons. You *cannot* reduce or eliminate the profit of the restaurant and hope to stay in business, so couponing *must* be done in a way to promote business and maintain profits. If it is not possible to do this, then perhaps couponing is not for you.

SIGNATURE ITEMS AND SPECIALTIES

Critical to the success of any restaurant and a criterion for a good menu is the establishment of the house special or signature item.

A signature item is an item for which you are known (see fig. 3-8). Although signature items normally are food items or preparation methods, they do not have to be. A signature item can be the method of service or the presentation of the food.

As a restaurant operator, you must devise your specials or signature items and let your customers know through menu listings that they are different. Do not wait for customers to discover signature items on your menu. De-

3-8. Boxed house specialties to attract customers' attention. Courtesy Schneithorst's Hofamberg Inn, St. Louis.

velop items for the restaurant that are unusual, unique, and truly superior to what your competition is doing. My criterion for a signature item is that the food, presentation, and service are the best that I have experienced anywhere and result in a positive and memorable dining experience.

An item may attain this special classification because of its uniqueness or because of the amount of profit derived from its sale. Since it is special, it deserves distinctive recognition on the menu. The menu writer must decide how to draw attention to that item. This can be done in at least five ways:

1. Uppercase (capital) letters
2. A bolder or darker typeface
3. Special boxes
4. Stars or asterisks
5. A different color (if color is used)

A tactic used very effectively by Das Stein Haus in Jefferson City, Missouri, is the use of a large asterisk beside each specialty item on the menu (see fig. 3-9). This kind of notation on the menu should be reasonably large so it will be noticed by the patron. Employees must be trained to answer questions from guests about why the items are so marked. They also should be able to give brief descriptions of the special features.

A story was told to me about the promotion of a food item in a Chicago restaurant. The chef at this restaurant prepared several items he considered to be signature items. One of the items was a veal dish that he felt that he prepared particularly well. When new menus were to be printed, the chef requested that an asterisk be placed next to each of the signature items, as well as a notation at the bottom of the menu that these were his specialties. The printer inadvertently left off the asterisk next to the veal dish. When the menus were delivered, the chef purchased gold stars and pasted one on each menu next to the description of the veal dish.

The reaction from customers was, "What's the significance of the gold star?" This forced

3-9. Use of asterisks for house specialties. Courtesy Das Stein Haus, Jefferson City, Missouri.

the service staff to reply that it was the chef's special item and that he took particular pride in that dish. As a result, there was a dramatic increase in the sales of that item. When the menus were next reprinted, the chef made sure the asterisk was printed next to the veal dish. When the menus were printed that way, the sales dropped dramatically. So the chef again purchased gold stars and pasted them next to the veal dish.

Specialties listed on the menu should be limited to not more than two or three per meal, over and above the one signature item for which you are nationally or regionally known. A common error in marketing is to try to feature *every* item. This leads to the suspicion that perhaps nothing is special.

Development of Signature and Specialty Items

Every restaurant continually looks for that magic item that can become a specialty and will keep them abreast of current customer-preferred food trends.

During a panel at a Missouri Restaurant Association conference, Dick May, president of Gilbert Robinson in Kansas City offered some insight into how they develop signature items or new items for their menu. They run the special item first for a designated period of time on a chalkboard or as a menu clip-on. During this time, it undergoes scrutiny in three areas:

1. Are the ingredients available in the quality and quantity demanded, based on year-round sales?
2. Are personnel available to prepare and serve the menu item with quality standards?
3. Will the item sell at a profit?

If the item is to be special, it should be so popular that other restaurateurs will attempt to imitate it in order to capitalize on the sales and profits from the item.

Signature Examples

A restaurant south of St. Louis features what are known as "throwed rolls." The owner walks around the dining room with a basket of rolls and throws dinner rolls to the customers. This type of service certainly creates an unforgettable impression. I will not say whether I approve or disapprove of this practice, but merely mention it as a way one restaurant has chosen to create a memorable signature item.

A classic signature item is something positive you have created to give the customer an outstanding remembrance. You can create a signature item in one of three ways:

1. **Quality of product.** It must make the customer feel that it is the best he has ever eaten. There is no substitute for quality in whatever food you prepare and sell. The customer will remember quality forever.

2. **Image.** The dining experience conjures up a favorable image every time the name of your restaurant is mentioned. I remember, for example, Baked Alaska at the Oceanbeach Club in Nassau, salad at Regas Restaurant in Knoxville, Tennessee, and the bartender at Henry Africa's in Alexandria, Virgina.

3. **A unique name for a menu item.** Years ago, I had dinner at The Magic Time Machine in San Antonio. We ordered the Roman Orgy, a huge roast surrounded by vegetables on a platter so large that it was carried by two waiters. The memorable name and service made this a signature item.

CURRENT FOOD TRENDS

In making sure that your marketing strategy puts you ahead of your competition, it is crucial to be aware of current food trends. The food industry is an ever-changing one, and trends come and go relatively quickly. You must be aware of these so you can take advantage of them before they peak. At the present time, the food trend appears to be toward what is termed *American Fare* or *American Cuisine*. (see fig. 3-10.)

The term *American Fare* has never been accurately defined, but I regard it as home cooking. American Fare is a fresh approach; it is larger portions; it is regional dishes. Richard Perry's in St. Louis has been a forerunner in the development of American Cuisine from his original concept to his current operation (see fig. 3-11). Restaurants today are serving more home-baked breads, and desserts are a major sales item on most menus. It is a return to American culinary art. *Restaurants & Institutions* offered this definition of the new American cuisine in May 1985:

American traditional and historical cuisine is what our founding fathers, pioneer ancestors and immigrant parents thrived on. Regional cuisine is where these traditional dishes diversified. New cuisine is what American chefs are creating with American products right now.

We Americans go full circle on foods and trends. The menu writer's job is to know when to come and go. At a recent lunch at The Ladle in St. Louis, the featured item on their menu was Chicken Pot Pie. It was magnificently done. I had not seen this item on an upscale restaurant menu in a number of years.

Every restaurant owner must go out and study the competition to determine where there is a market gap that the competition has not yet filled. There are just so many customers, and you have to attract and keep your market share by being different and better, unique and more unusual.

I suggest also that you examine the menus and service of fast-food operations. If you do not have a fast-food philosophy, you should move out when fast food moves in. When fast-food operators put in salad bars, for example, table-service restaurants began to drop them.

PRODUCT LIFE CYCLE

A major marketing question for all restaurant owners is, "When do I change my menu?" Menu change is evaluated on the basis of the marketing product life cycle.

For every menu there comes a time when you must make changes. It is inevitable. The market will give you positive signs that change is required. Competition demands it. Many operators, for reasons unknown, ignore these signs and refuse to make changes in their menu. Some fail to acknowledge a menu item's lack of participation in sales. How many persons have you heard say, "We've always served this item and will continue to list it on the menu, even though it does not sell."? This decline in the sale of particular menu items can lead eventually to less profit and the possibility of failure.

The easiest decision to make about any menu change is NO. *No* totally reduces all risk, *No* means no new product, *No* means no cost and none of the problems of change and retraining of your employees. And *No* may even-

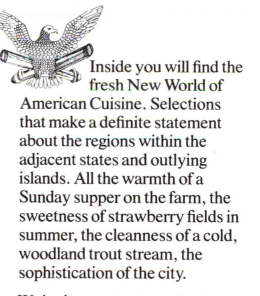

Inside you will find the fresh New World of American Cuisine. Selections that make a definite statement about the regions within the adjacent states and outlying islands. All the warmth of a Sunday supper on the farm, the sweetness of strawberry fields in summer, the cleanness of a cold, woodland trout stream, the sophistication of the city.

We invite you to step out onto the frontier of contemporary cuisine — the New World in the Plaza 900.

3-10. *Institutional copy about American cuisine. Courtesy Sheraton St. Louis Hotel.*

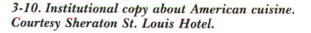

MAIN COURSE

prime tenderloin steak grilled w/ fresh thyme 19.50
Sea scallops poached in panache 17.95
duck breast, grilled rare, sauce of port wine, shallots, cream & pureed dates 18.45
roast pork tenderloin / sauce of green peppercorns & Illinois blue cheese 16.50
breast of capon stuffed w/ fresh mushrooms & onions / honey-mustard sauce 15.75
veal sweet breads sauté / champagne & garlic sauce 17.50
grilled lamb chops / basted red currant sauce 18.95
veal loin stuffed with veal mousse / onion marmelade 18.95
grilled swordfish / béarnaise sauce 17.95
boston scrod filet baked in parchment paper with julienne vegetables 12.75
grilled halibut filet / red wine sauce 16.95
sockeye salmon filet, breaded in pine nuts / sauté 18.95

3-11. *American Fare menu. Courtesy Richard Perry's Restaurant, St. Louis.*

tually mean no business at your restaurant.

The life cycle of a product is measured by two criteria, volume and time. First, the sales volume of the product changes, and second, the marketing mix and the consumer that you hope to serve are changing. When the menu item no longer meets the needs of the customer, change is essential.

Stages of the Product Life Cycle

There are five stages in a menu item's life cycle, and I will discuss each of them in detail.

1. Concept
2. Growth
3. Maintenance
4. Maturity
5. Decline

Concept. The process for determination of a new product is based upon:

1. Idea
2. Opportunity
3. Venture risk
4. Product development
5. Market strategy

Ideas for new products should not present a major problem. Product ideas may be obtained both internally and externally. You can observe innovations in cooking magazines and advertising campaigns, and listen to comments from customers. Your employees may offer you suggestions for new products or product modification. Encourage them to do so. Determine whether the product has enough merit for further investigation and/or development. Be sure, early on, that the product fits your image. Any new product involves risk and the expenditure of money, but the risk and cost are associated with investment for the future.

Once the decision has been made to introduce a product as a new item on your menu, you must estimate the profit potential. You will need to estimate the amount of investment required in equipment, training, and inventory, as well as the amount of time that will be required to develop acceptable market penetration. Will this product have any advantages over the product of the competition? Will it be unique and unusual enough to create customer demand? Will the price level of the competition

and the amount of competition restrict the volume and use of the product?

Growth. In the beginning, you can attempt a limited introduction of the new item. This can be done with a chalkboard, a menu clip-on, or a verbal presentation by the service person. This will help you measure your customers' reception of your menu item. Unfortunately, not many restaurants are doing this with new items.

During this period, you must monitor the product for improvement, test the price level before making a commitment to the cost of the new product, and determine the sales impact. If growth is evident, there is acceptance of the product. If you make the decision to go forward, focus on high visibility for the item.

The growth period may require higher than normal advertising costs to create a perceived need. Also, quality control and the maintenance of quality standards are essential during the introductory phase. If the customers try the product and it does not meet the quality standards they expect, it will not continue to be accepted. You can also encourage acceptance and product awareness if you price the product lower than normal during the introductory period. The success of a new item also will require considerable personal selling by your staff.

Maintenance. In this phase, customers have accepted the new product and there is a steady, perhaps even increasing, demand for the product. Adjustments should be complete prior to this level, and only minor changes should now have to be made.

The objective at this phase is to build a strong market for the new product. As a manager, you now need to refine your production schedule, attempt to lower product cost by improved control, and increase the profit on the menu item.

If you can maintain sales of the new item, there may be an opportunity to increase the price. In any event, you will not need to discount the item in any way. All of the advertising will be at the point of sale in an attempt to maximize the exposure of the product to the customers.

Maturity. The first indication of the maturity of a product is a turbulence in the sales volume and an absolute flattening with no growth. Another indication may be a saturation of the market, when every restaurant you see has adopted your new item. This is the "trickle-down effect" of menus. The inventive do and others copy; witness chicken wings, nachos, and potato skins. Customers may back off because of overexposure.

Critical to your success at this point is to build and maintain loyalty to your restaurant and your menu. Your ultimate objective is to hold your share of the market.

Decline. Decline does not necessarily mean that an item is unprofitable; it just is not selling as well as it did previously. But if a product cannot make it on its own and has an overall bad effect on menu sales and profit, remove it from the menu. It has reached the end of its life cycle. Do not let your ego get in the way of making the decision to drop a product that is a real loser.

Decline in a product's sales generally spurs either a defensive strategy or an offensive one. A defensive strategy requires that you simply hold your market share to stop any further erosion in sales. Management must control the overall costs, cut production costs of the item involved, and be a little better in every way in order to reverse the decline.

An offensive strategy requires considerable internal sales and promotion to modify the product and to look for alternatives in its presentation.

Continue the offensive strategy by returning to the beginning of the product life cycle and starting again with a new product. This will help you remain competitive in the marketplace.

Careful monitoring is required during every phase of the product life cycle to determine what products should be added and what removed from the menu. Some items may be so accepted by your consumer group that they do not go through a product life cycle and stay on the menu forever. Such an operation is usually a white-tablecloth dinner house with a high check average, and the demand remains despite saturation and product maturity. With regular patrons, few restaurants are inclined to make major menu changes.

It is not always easy to determine when menu items are performing acceptably. Various theories of menu engineering have been proposed; in menu engineering, different

Number of Menu Items	Sales on Perfect Menu (%)		Participation Factor	Optimal Menu Mix (%)
5	20	×	90	18
10	10	×	80	8
20	5	×	70	3.5
25	4	×	60	2.4
33	3	×	50	1.5

menu items are compared with regard to sales mix, menu mix, price, and food cost to analyze the components of a menu. (See chapter 4; also, for a good explanation of menu engineering concepts, see "Menu Engineering," by Donald Smith, *Lodging,* March 1982, pp. 46–50). One of the factors that menu engineering analyzes is how an item sells in relation to other items on the menu. On the perfect menu, every item will contribute an equal amount to the total number of items sold; that is, on a ten-item menu, each item will contribute to 10 percent of the sales; on a five-item menu, each item will contribute to 20 percent of the sales, and so on. To determine percentage of contribution for a perfect menu, you simply divide the number of menu items into 100.

Of course, no menu is perfect. Each menu item participates differently to contribute to the number of items sold; for example, Fried Chicken may contribute only 5 percent of sales on a ten-item menu, while Sirloin Steak may contribute 30 percent. How can you tell when an item is contributing its share? Easy: you decide how perfect you want your menu to be by deciding on an acceptable *participation factor.* You can choose any percentage you believe will work. You then adjust the percentage of contribution on the perfect menu by the participation factor to determine the optimal menu mix. Finally you compare the actual contribution of the item to the optimal menu mix to determine whether it is performing acceptably or unacceptably.

The accompanying table shows how various participation factors affect the optimal menu mix. As you can see, the more items on a menu, the lower you would probably set your participation factor, since there are more choices for the customer to select from and less chance that he or she would select any particular item. Similarly, the more items you offer, the lower the menu mix will be.

Now you can determine whether an individual item is performing acceptably or unacceptably. Supposing you have a ten-item menu. Per the table above, each item should contribute to 8 percent of the menu mix. To learn if that is so, determine the total number of items sold. Then count how many of each individual item was sold. Now calculate what percentage of the total each individual item contributed. For example, if a total of 200 orders were sold, and 15 orders of Fried Chicken were sold, Fried Chicken would have contributed 7.5 percent of sales. If 50 orders of Sirloin Steak were sold, Sirloin Steak would have contributed to 25 percent of sales. Now compare this percentage to the optimal menu mix. Anything greater than 8 percent is pulling its weight; anything less is selling unacceptably. Thus, Sirloin Steak is performing very well, while the sales of Fried Chicken are not acceptable.

You cannot be all things to all people, but you can try. Monitor control, assess the product life cycle, and change periodically based on item sales. If you adhere strictly to these guidelines, you will have a marketing strategy that will satisfy the needs of all the customers who come into your restaurant.

CHAPTER FOUR

ECONOMIC STRATEGIES

PROFIT-AND-LOSS STATEMENT

SALES		
Food	$ 73,000	73%
Bar	27,000	27%
Total Sales	$100,000	100%
COST OF SALES		
Food	$ 27,010	37%—V.C.
Bar	5,940	22%—V.C.
Total Cost of Sales	$ 32,950	32.95
GROSS PROFIT	$ 67,050	67.05
ADMINISTRATIVE AND GENERAL EXPENSES		
Direct wages	$ 26,000	26 —V.C.
Vacation accrual	1,700	1.7 —F.C.
Holiday accrual	450	0.45—F.C.
Management salaries	2,500	2.5 —F.C.
Employee meals	250	0.25—V.C.
Employee benefits	2,100	2.1 —V.C.
Supplies	1,500	1.5 —V.C.
Replacements	2,000	2.0 —F.C.
Laundry	1,200	1.2 —V.C.
Utilities	2,100	2.1 —V.C.
Cleaning and sanitation	1,300	1.3 —V.C.
Maintenance	1,400	1.4 —V.C.
Local advertising	1,600	1.6 —F.C.
Music and entertainment	1,200	1.2 —V.C.
OCCUPANCY EXPENSE		
Interest	500	0.5 —F.C.
Rent	5,000	5.0 —F.C.
Depreciation and amortization	3,000	3.0 —F.C.
Insurance	1,000	1.0 —F.C.
Real estate and personal property tax	2,250	2.25—F.C.
NET PROFIT OR (LOSS) BEFORE TAXES	$ 10,000	10.0
TOTAL VARIABLE COST	70,000	
TOTAL FIXED COST	20,000	
TOTAL COST	$ 90,000	

V.C. = Variable Cost
F.C. = Fixed Cost

4-1. Sample of a profit-and-loss (P&L) statement. (Amounts and percentages shown are only examples used for the calculations in this book.)

PROFIT-AND-LOSS OR INCOME STATEMENT

Before devising a plan for economic strategies, you must have an actual or pro-forma income or profit-and-loss statement (see fig. 4-1). Whether it is called an earnings report or a profit-and-loss statement, it shows the profit or loss of the restaurant during a specific period of time. The statement matches the revenues against all of the moneys incurred in order to operate the restaurant. The resulting amount is the net profit or net loss.

The profit-and-loss statement is divided into two parts, revenues and costs. The revenues typically are the net sales of the restaurant. The costs include product, labor, rent, operating expenses, depreciation, and taxes. You can categorize the costs on the statement and then total the fixed costs (F.C.) and variable costs (V.C.). Total costs equal F.C. plus V.C. Major variable costs are food and labor. Management salaries, administrative expenses, occupancy costs, insurance, and taxes are examples of fixed costs. The remaining items on the statement may be fixed or variable (or sometimes semivariable), depending on your situation.

ECONOMIC PRINCIPLES

The principles of economics that have been used for many years in manufacturing concerns and other retail establishments have not been applied practically by restaurant operators in the development of economic strategies.

Appropriate economic theories for hospitality operations are:

1. Break-even
2. Minimum sales point
3. Price reductions (Profit/volume ratio)
4. Secondary sales
5. Sales profit maximums
6. Sales mix
7. Diminishing returns
8. Market share

Break-Even

Break-even is a relationship between profit and volume. The break-even point can be determined by a graph or by arithmetical calculation.

First it is necessary to define the cost factors for establishing the break-even point.

- Fixed costs (F.C.). These are not responsive to the volume of the operation. They remain constant regardless of volume.
- Variable costs. (V.C.). These are responsive to the volume of the operation and fluctuate accordingly.
- Total costs (T.C.). Fixed costs plus variable costs equal total costs.

To simplify the construction of a break-even graph, the straight-line relationship is used here, and each cost is classified as fixed or variable (with no semivariables). Use your judgment to specify the category into which each cost is placed.

A break-even graph covers profits from operations, and not such other income as dividends or receipts from the sale of property. Revenues from operations follow the vertical axis and unit sales follow the horizontal axis. You can assume that (1) when unit sales are zero, operating revenues are zero, and (2) when unit sales increase, operating revenues increase.

The graph is constructed by following a sequence of steps. The following figures (from fig. 4-1, the sample profit-and-loss statement) are used in the example:

Total Sales		$100,000
Variable Costs	$70,000	
Fixed Costs	+20,000	
Total (variable and fixed) Costs		−90,000
Net Profit (before taxes)		$ 10,000

Step 1. Construct a vertical axis labeled Cost of Sales and a horizontal axis labeled Unit Sales. Mark off each axis in increments of 10. (See fig. 4-2.)

Step 2. Plot the point (A) of fixed costs ($20,000) on the left side of the vertical axis. These costs will remain at this level regardless of the volume of unit sales. Therefore, draw a line across the graph from point A to point B. Line AB now represents the total fixed cost. (See fig. 4-3.)

Step 3. The profit-and-loss statement in figure 4-1 shows total fixed and variable costs of $90,000. Plot this point (C) on the right-hand vertical axis. Now plot a line from point A to point C. This line represents the total operating costs. (See fig. 4-4.)

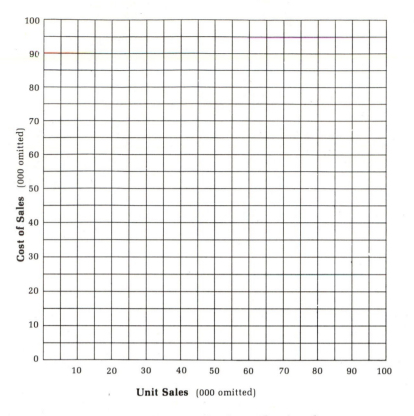

4-2. Break-even graph showing increments for cost of sales and unit sales.

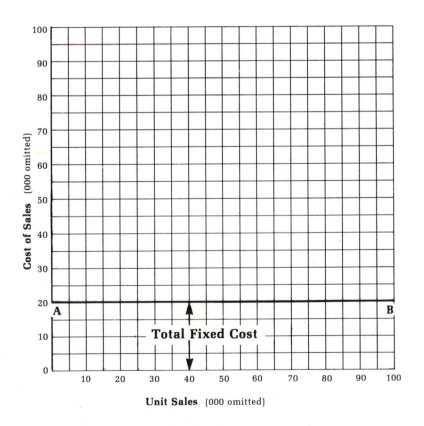

4-3. Break-even graph with the total fixed cost plotted.

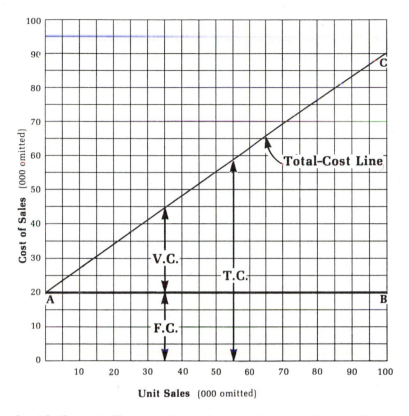

4-4. *Break-even graph with the variable cost plotted from the fixed-cost line to show total costs.*

Step 4. Plot point D, total unit sales ($100,000) and an equal amount on the cost-of-sales axis ($100,000). Plot a line from 0 to point D. Line 0D represents sales income and units of sales. The intersection of the total cost line and the revenue line at point E represents the break-even point. The break-even amount on this graph is $66,666. (See fig. 4-5.)

Step 5. Analyze your graph (fig. 4-6). Point E is where total costs and total revenues are equal: The restaurant breaks even. At a lower level of unit sales, total costs exceed revenues, and the firm loses money. At a higher level of unit sales, revenues exceed total costs, and the firm makes money. The area indicated by LL represents the loss area for the firm; the area indicated by PP represents the profit area for the firm.

The break-even point can be calculated *arithmetically* with the following formula:

Break-Even Point (BEP) =

$$\frac{\text{Fixed costs}}{1(100\%) - (\text{Variable costs/Total sales})}$$

With the same amounts used in figures 4-3 through 4-6, follow these steps:

Step 1 $\text{BEP} = \dfrac{\$20,000}{1 - (\$70,000/100,000)}$

Step 2 $\text{BEP} = \dfrac{\$20,000}{1 - .70}$

Step 3 $\text{BEP} = \dfrac{\$20,000}{.30}$

Step 4 $BEP = \$66,666$ (rounded to nearest dollar)

In steps 1 and 2 of the break-even calculation, 1 (100%) represents the total sales, even though the example is $100,000. Sales could be any dollar amount and still be represented by 1 (100%). This determines what percent of total sales the variable costs represent.

In step 3, .30 represents 30%.

This calculation can be more reliable than a graph because of the difficulty of reading the actual point of intersection of sales and cost lines. The difference between a broad-tipped pen and a fine-tipped one could cause a fluctuation of more than a hundred dollars at that point.

You can also calculate the break-even point on the basis of the number of customers

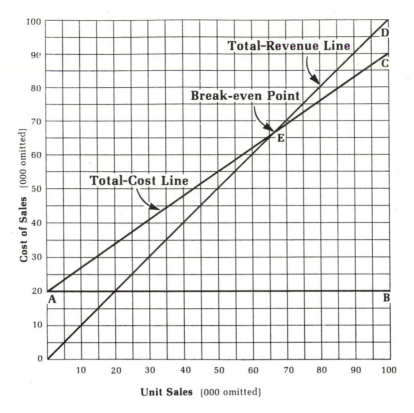

4-5. Total-revenue line plotted on break-even graph with the total-cost line to determine the break-even point.

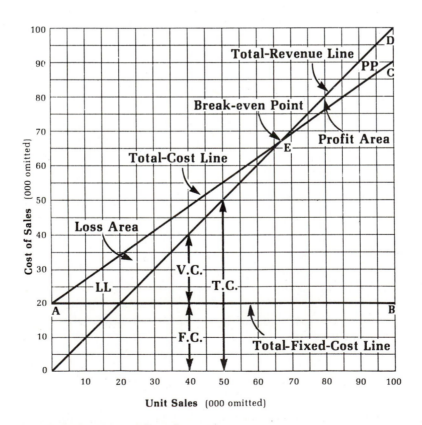

4-6. Break-even graph with designations of profit and loss areas.

needed to break even. The formula is:

Q (sales in units) =
$$\frac{\text{Fixed Costs}}{\text{Contribution to Margin per Unit (Gross Profit)}}$$

Using the figures from the previous break-even calculation, follow these steps:

Step 1 $Q = \dfrac{\$20,000}{\$5.50 \text{ (average check)} - \text{Total Variable Costs}}$

Step 2 $Q = \dfrac{\$20,000}{\$5.50 - (70\% \text{ of } \$5.50)}$

Step 3 $Q = \dfrac{\$20,000}{\$5.50 - \$3.85}$

Step 4 $Q = \dfrac{\$20,000}{\$1.65}$

Step 5 $Q = 12,121 \text{ Meals } (\$5.50 \text{ checks})$

(The break-even figure calculated by multiplying 12,121 by $5.50 is $66,665—a slight difference from the mathematical calculation of the break-even because of rounding off numbers.)

You might think that there could be no end to profits if you could greatly increase unit sales. Many restaurants can do this. For some firms, however, the increased costs of advertising will more than offset increased revenues from increased sales. Moreover, large restaurants are difficult to manage. You must balance the inefficiency of management caused by size against the efficiency of lower unit costs due to larger purchases and the requirements of specialized help and equipment. You can use the break-even chart to forecast income, profit, and expenses under nonchanging conditions, and can determine unit cost at various sales level budgets, or you can merchandise the menu for profit to see the effect of volume on profit. At any given level of sales, you can chart the profit or loss based on volume of sales in relation to cost. The accuracy of the break-even is short range because of changing conditions. The chart is a tool, not a solution.

A major management consideration is that until you pass the break-even point, not one dollar of profit is generated. When the break-even point is passed, then, as volume increases, the profit also increases at a disproportionate rate.

One philosophical approach to the operation of any profit-oriented foodservice establishment has been to think that if the volume is high enough, other things will take care of themselves. The statement is true enough, but, by using the break-even, you can find the point at which things begin to take care of themselves. Menu-designed food promotions to boost volume can accelerate the amount of profit once the break-even point is passed. Control of variable costs to reduce the amount required to break even will produce profit with lower volume. Conservation of energy and reduction of accidents to get lower insurance rates are only two ways to reduce the fixed cost amount and reduce the break-even point.

The understanding of where profit begins and systems to improve the controls, volume, and spending rates can be used by every manager to develop profit-improvement plans. Loss cannot be blamed on the circumstances. Good management must adjust to and control the circumstances.

Minimum Sales Point

Operating hours should be established to maximize the profits of the restaurant. The decision of when to open and close must be based on operation statistics, the tool of decision-making. Determine the statistical relationship between total sales for a period of time and operating costs during the same period of time. This is your minimum sales point. Your recorded sales and known expenses are used to determine your minimum sales point.

Are early morning or late evening hours profitable for your restaurant? The menu for these time periods may be highly profitable, but, because of circumstances or poor merchandising, you may not attain a sufficiently high net sales figure to operate during that time frame. During "off" or "slow" hours, it may actually cost more to open and operate your restaurant than it would to close it. When hours of operation are set, you may feel reluctant to change the time, but if you are losing money by staying open, why do so?

Students and restaurant managers have suggested the following reasons that may compel a restaurant to remain open:

1. Promotion to increase volume
2. Competition
3. Prepreparation
4. Sanitation and cleaning
5. Contract or lease agreement
6. Visibility for new operation
7. Corporate policy

Reasons to stay open do exist, and a value judgment must be made about the legitimate, profitable hours to operate.

Paul Forchuk, former owner of the Organ Grinder Pizza and Earthquake Ethel's in Portland, Oregon, adhered to the following policy for closing: There will be no customer-visible sign of closing until the designated closing time. The important part of this statement is "no customer-visible sign." Behind-the-scenes closing procedures can be accomplished. How many times have you been eating in a restaurant when the personnel began closing around you? The manager thinks, "It's slow. I'll cut my labor by getting them out early." But this is a cause-and-effect or effect-and-cause situation. Your patrons will soon learn you begin closing at 11:45 P.M., and will begin coming early. Then the slow period and start-of-cleaning begin at 11:30 P.M. Imagine where that can lead.

Establish your hours by analyzing your costs and sales. To establish the minimum sales point (MSP), you need the following figures:

Food Costs—37% taken from the monthly profit-and-loss statement

Minimum payroll costs—$60 calculated from the hours and rates of the employees required to operate for the time period

Other variable costs—11.05% taken from the monthly profit-and-loss statement

Fixed costs are eliminated from this calculation because, if there is zero volume of sales, fixed costs still exist and must be paid. This calculation gives you the amount of volume in dollars over the fixed costs that must be generated to meet labor, food, and other variable costs. It is, in practice, a break-even point for a specified time period. The formula is:

Minimum Sales Point (MSP) =

$$\frac{\text{Minimum operating cost in dollars}}{1(100\%) - \text{Minimum operating cost percent}}$$

Use the figures above and substitute them in the formula:

Step 1 $\quad MSP = \dfrac{\$60}{1(100\%) - (37\% + 11.05\%)}$

Step 2 $\quad MSP = \dfrac{\$60}{1(100\%) - .4805}$

Step 3 $\quad MSP = \dfrac{\$60}{.5195}$

Step 4 $\quad MSP = \$115.50$

Therefore, in the specified time, the restaurant will need $115.50 to meet a minimum sales point to stay open. By analyzing your own records of costs and sales, you can determine what operating hours are most profitable. This calculation also gives you an indication of the times to develop off- or slow-hours promotions. One promotion involves encouraging people over sixty-five to eat before 6 P.M. (Perhaps you thought these promos were being done because the owners liked old folks.) For reasons listed or for reasons of your own, you may not be able to close during the off-hours, but promos and special menus for those times may add the needed volume to put the operation above the minimum sales point. There are other tools you can use in the critical area of timing. Know when to start and when to stop promotions. This is necessary to develop profit. You must time the promotions accurately, for to be too early or too late will make the project ineffective. In many cases, it is not necessarily what you do but when you do it that causes the project or promo to succeed or fail.

Price Reductions

For years retailers have applied the markdown theory, or price reductions: They have selected specific goods and marked them down for sales or as loss leaders. The goods may have been marked down because of poor purchasing or production methods, competition, or unfavorable weather. The retail businessman with poor sales would give immediate markdowns to move the merchandise. Many retailers also believe that this reduction in sales price will cause an increase in volume and, in the final analysis, an increase in profit.

Many restaurants have applied the markdown theory to their pricing but without full knowledge of the consequences to their total profit. How will the markdown affect profit?

These markdowns in the restaurant industry are taking place in the forms of happy hours, two-for-one cocktails, and dining clubs. (The use of coupons was covered in chapter 3.) As the unit sales price is marked down, take a look at how much the volume must be increased to maintain the gross profit at its current amount, or gross profit based on current unit price. Gross profit is defined as the amount of money remaining after the cost of merchandise has been paid. One assumption must be made: The current gross profit is satisfactory.

As an example, consider a bar selling cocktails for $1.50 and maintaining a liquor cost of 22%.

$1.50	selling price
− .33	merchandise cost
$1.17	gross profit or 78% of sales

If you begin a happy hour with cocktails priced at 75 cents each, or half price, use the following calculation to determine how to maintain the $1.17 gross profit:

$ .75	new selling price
− .33	merchandise cost (unless your pouring size is changed, cost is constant)
$ .42	the gross profit or 56% of sales

If $1.17 is the desired rate of gross profit per drink, and if it is now reduced to $0.42, then 2.78 ($1.17 divided by $0.42) drinks must now be sold and served for every one drink previously sold (2.78 drinks × $0.42 gross profit = $1.17 gross profit).

Therefore, when the price is reduced, the volume needed to generate what you established as a satisfactory gross profit will increase by 178 percent over current sales. Is this reasonable for your restaurant? The sales period may be only two or three hours. An accurate record of sales must be compiled to ensure that all discounts are accomplishing what you anticipate in profits. This theory is not dissimilar to the break-even. With volume higher than it has ever been, the operation may still lose money. Determine the length of time and the dollar amount of reduction needed to maintain the volume for continued acceptable profit. Timing of the happy hour and amount of discount become critical to profit.

Recently there has been a general trend on the part of the public, as well as among lawyers and judges, to be opposed to a happy hour. Certain states have outlawed happy hours. The passage of Dram Shop Acts results in severe penalties for restaurant operators in the event of an accident after someone has consumed alcohol in their establishments. Other alternatives that have been suggested in trade publications are free hors d'oeuvre or a rain check for another drink on a different night. Watch the trade publications for all manner of such ideas for alternatives. A recent article by Betsy Faulkner in *Restaurants & Institutions*, for example, stated that finger or "grazing" foods, such as tapas, are appearing more frequently both on regular menus and in bars as alternatives to alcoholic beverages.

In addition to the short-term application of price reduction, there is also a long-term application. This calculation is based on the total effect of the happy hour or meal-club membership on total profit. The happy hour and meal-club plans may be made effective for only specific times during the day or week. Consequently, the reduction is not 50 percent but may amount to only the equivalent of a 20 percent reduction in price. For example, your two-meals-for-one pricing can be available Monday through Thursday, between 5 P.M. and 8 P.M. Using the data from the calculation of the break-even graph at the beginning of this chapter, do the calculations that follow.

Because of the volume/sales relationship, the first calculation establishes the relationship among sales/costs/profit. The formula to determine variable cost is:

$$\frac{\text{Variable cost}}{\text{Sales}} = \text{Variable cost percent}$$

$$\frac{70,000}{100,000} = 70\%$$

The next calculation, with the original numbers in the break-even calculation, uses the following formula:

$$\frac{\text{Desired profit} + \text{Fixed cost}}{1(100\%) - \left(\dfrac{\text{Present variable cost }\%}{1(100\%) - \text{Proposed reduced }\%}\right)}$$

by meal club

Step 1 $\quad$ RSV $= \dfrac{10{,}000 + 20{,}000}{1(100\%) - \left(\dfrac{70\%}{1(100\%) - 20\%}\right)}$

Step 2 $\quad$ RSV $= \dfrac{30{,}000}{1(100\%) - \left(\dfrac{70\%}{100\% - 20\%}\right)}$

Step 3 $\quad$ RSV $= \dfrac{30{,}000}{1(100\%) - \left(\dfrac{70\%}{80\%}\right)}$

Step 4 $\quad$ RSV $= \dfrac{30{,}000}{1(100\%) - .875}$

Step 5 $\quad$ RSV $= \dfrac{30{,}000}{.125}$

Step 6 $\quad$ RSV $= \$240{,}000$

The required sales volume tells you what volume of sales is necessary to maintain the current profit level. In this example, the required *increase* in sales volume would be $140,000 for the year. Now you can use that information to make your decision for reduced-price promotions. You can monitor the effect the reduction will have on gross profits and determine whether the required long-term increase in volume makes the promotions valuable in your operation.

The basic economic theory of the price-reduction principle is that food and drink away from home are luxury rather than necessary items, and, as the price of luxury items is reduced, more persons will purchase and thus increase the volume of sales. Records must be maintained to track and compare customer volume and increased dollar sales, with immediate goal-setting by the manager to determine if the project is on target. If the goal of volume increase is not being met, then take immediate corrective action. The promotion should be adjusted or canceled in part or in entirety.

Secondary Sales

One other major consideration of a two-for-one price reduction is a secondary sales effect. When a person enters the restaurant to take advantage of the price reduction, he normally will buy a second item (wine, cocktails, appe-tizer, dessert, or some menu item not included in the price) with the meal because he is saving the price of one item or meal. The sale of the special item will cause the sales of one or more other items that are currently being offered on the menu at regular price. This is the secondary sales effect. The decision to establish a happy hour or meal club, therefore, is based on the belief that the increased patronage will bring a sufficient increase in the sale of other items to cause the gross profit to remain at a predetermined level.

Let's consider a hypothetical situation. As a dinner promotion to increase sales volume, a restaurant owner decides to give every diner all the wine he cares to drink with his dinner. Based on his experience, forecasts, and "gut feelings," he believes that, with a free-wine promotion, he can at least double the number of people who will eat in the restaurant.

Past dinner records show the following:

	Meals	Wine	Total
Meal Sales (200 persons @ $5.50 average)	$1,100	$200	$1,300
Variable Costs (food & beverage)	407	100	507
Contribution to Margin	693	100	793
Salaries			250
Income			$ 543

With this information, the owner expects:

1. No income from wine
2. Increase of 200 persons @ $5.50 check average for evening meal
3. Increase of wine consumption of 100 percent
4. Additional service persons @ total cost of $40

His projection for the wine promo would be:

	Meals	Wine	Total
Meal Sales (400 persons @ $5.50 average)	$2,200	0	$2,200
Variable Costs (food & beverage)	814	200	1,014
Contribution to Margin	1,386	⟨200⟩	1,186
Salaries			290
Income			$ 896

The projection for this promotion would be an increase of $353 in income. Contingency expenses in the kitchen are not considered here, and they can make the promotion a marginal experiment. A loss leader is needed to stimulate the sale of higher gross items.

(For these calculations, wine prices were doubled as opposed to using the profit-and-loss liquor cost percentage.)

A manager who knows in advance that the relative success of a wine giveaway is marginal can emphasize to his employees the critical need for the secondary sales effect. Selling appetizers, desserts, or any other items regularly on the menu will increase the probability of profit. Displays of items in the dining room to raise the check average will also be a factor contributing to profit.

Prior knowledge will better prepare you to make feasibility studies of any price-reduction merchandising plan. You can avoid disastrous consequences if you assemble as many facts as possible. The object of a promotion is increased profit, not just increased volume. Profit does not necessarily correlate with volume. Accurate records of past profit, costs, and sales are required to make correct profit decisions for the future.

Sales Profit Maximums

The next principle of economic strategy is a pricing graph for maximum item-contribution to margin of profit (see fig. 4-7). According to economic theory, the graph is based on:

1. An elasticity-of-demand theory: the lower the price, the more you will sell (estimated demand curve)
2. Average fixed cost per unit
3. Price based on sales line intersection with demand line
4. Assumption that variable costs (other than food) are uniform

The graph establishes a profit margin rectangle for each price. The rectangle above the fixed-cost-per-line (A) containing the most units of the per-unit-price axis and the total sales axis—that is, the rectangle with the largest unit-area—will give the operation the maximum pricing benefit.

The assumption above is correct except for one consideration: In the restaurant industry, the variable cost of labor fluctuates according to the item being presented on the menu; labor cost must be considered on individual items. If

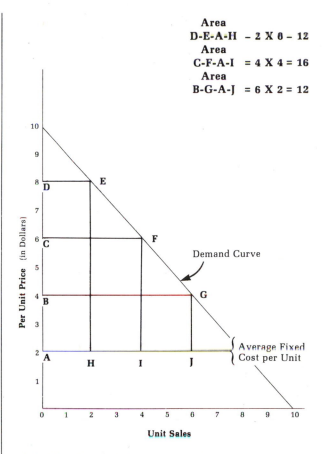

Area
D-E-A-H – 2 X 6 – 12
Area
C-F-A-I = 4 X 4 = 16
Area
B-G-A-J = 6 X 2 = 12

4-7. Elasticity-of-demand graph.

the graph is to be considered as correct, then labor on each item must be calculated into the average fixed cost per unit. To devise a realistic theory for the restaurant industry, sales mix and labor variables must be included in the formulation of maximum contribution to profit.

H. H. Pope, Jr., (president of Pope's Cafeteria Company) uses a basic formula of prime cost pricing that includes direct labor as one-third of the total labor cost. Direct labor is defined as labor that is used in the preparation and preparation of food. The other labor costs include support, service, and management. The obvious conclusion is that foods that do not require considerable preparation time can be priced lower. Or, if they are priced higher, they will make a much larger contribution to the profit margin.

Adapting the principle of actual labor cost to menu item pricing establishes the contribution-to-profit margin *after* the major controllable costs (variable costs of food and labor) of menu items have been calculated. Compare the following tables:

COST to OPERATION

Item	Raw Cost	Labor Cost	Total Cost	Percent Increase Due to Labor
Steak	$4.00	$ .35	$4.35	8.75%
Fried Chicken	1.20	1.10	2.30	91.67
Lasagna	1.25	.90	2.15	72.0

PROFIT to OPERATION

Item	Menu Price	Total Cost	Net Profit	Percent Contribution to Profit
Steak	$8.00	$4.35	$3.65	45.6%
Fried Chicken	4.00	2.30	1.70	42.5
Lasagna	3.60	2.15	1.45	40.3

A menu item with a low raw cost (such as lasagna) may have a proportionally high labor cost. The percent increase required by preparation is therefore large. Similarly, a high raw-cost item (such as steak) may require little preparation; the percent increase in its total cost required by labor is therefore small. As a result, the menu item with the low raw cost but a proportionally high labor cost may actually contribute less to the total profit than one with a high raw cost and a proportionally small labor cost. Labor cost and percent contribution to profit are critical to menu pricing. Because of them, the manager can reduce the price of a high-raw-cost, low-labor-cost item such as steak to have more appeal to the customer and still maintain a higher contribution to profit than he receives from the low-raw-cost, high-labor-cost item, lasagna.

Sales Mix

A fourth economic principle considers the sales mix of the various items sold. The calculations in the tables in the previous section indicate that approximately 2½ orders of lasagna would have to be sold to generate a profit equivalent to that made on the steak. A management projection or forecast is needed to determine an overall total contribution to variable margin:

FORECAST SALES AND PROFIT

Item	Forecast Unit Sales to Total Sales	Contribution to Profit (Variable Margin)
Steak	35%	45.6%
Fried Chicken	40%	42.5%
Lasagna	25%	40.3%

If, at the end of the accounting period, there is a deviation from the average contribution to profit, a detailed audit of actual cost and sales will determine what corrective action must be taken. The actual items can be evaluated and decisions can be made on continued marketing and menu pricing.

To determine the specific variations of the cost/sales/profit for each menu item, you can use the mix variation formula:

Sales Mix Variation (favorable or unfavorable) × Forecast Ratio of Contribution to Margin = Sales Mix Variation (favorable or unfavorable). If the sales mix is favorable, the total will be favorable. If the sales mix is unfavorable, the total will be unfavorable.

Cost Percentage Variation (favorable or unfavorable) × Forecast Sales Mix = Cost Variation (favorable or unfavorable). If cost is favorable, total will be favorable. If cost is unfavorable, total will be unfavorable.

Mix Variation × Cost Variation = Mix Cost Variation. If the mix variation is favorable, this compensates for any unfavorable cost variations and the total will be favorable. If both are unfavorable, then the total will be unfavorable.

Let's substitute hypothetical sales figures and say a restaurant had actual sales of 40 percent for steak instead of the 35 percent forecast and beef prices increased 48 percent instead of the 45.6 percent forecast.

Sales Mix Variation	5%	F × 45.6 = 2.28 F
Cost Variation	2.4%	F × 35 = .84
Mix Cost Variation		2.28% F × .84 = 1.9152 F

By adding favorable totals as positive numbers and unfavorable totals as negative numbers for each menu item, the specific variations of the cost/sales/profit can be located for each menu item.

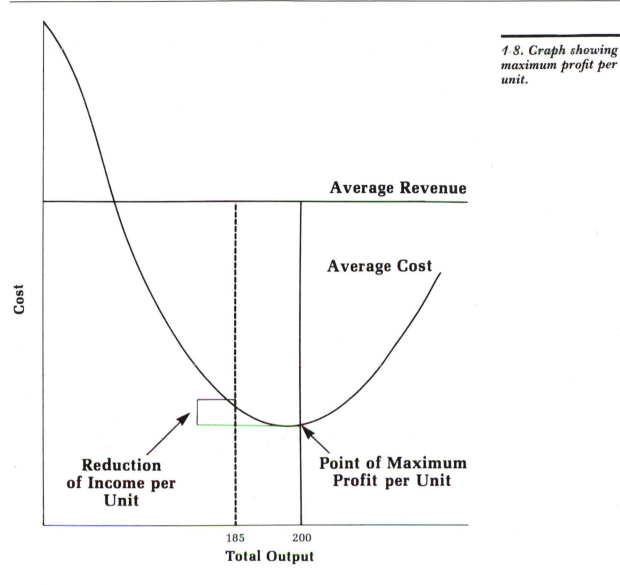

Diminishing Returns

The last economic consideration is the U-shaped curve. Simply stated, a graph is constructed to determine the average cost or expense per unit served (see fig. 4-8). This is important in pricing because, as has been mentioned, there is a point in every operation where profits are maximized and an increase in volume beyond that point will require an increase in expenses. This all has profound effects on the restaurant operation.

The law of diminishing returns enters in here. If equal increments of one input are added and the quantities of other inputs are held constant, the resultant increments of product will decrease. Thus, keeping constant a specified area of kitchen, dining space, and equipment, the operator can add labor in in-creasing amounts to the point of minimum average cost and maximum profits. If the volume then increases, space and equipment must be added to compensate for it.

Figure 4-8 is best explained by an experience of a local restaurant whose primary income is derived from wedding receptions. Past experience indicated to this owner that he could offer a complete package for a fixed price. Over a number of years, he served an average of 200 people per reception. This operation was very profitable and successful. During a recent year, the average attendance decreased by approximately fifteen people per event. Food quantities were decreased to reduce that variable cost, but orchestra, labor, and building fixed costs were not affected substantially by the smaller number of people. The total effect was a reduction in income that was not proportionate to a

4-9. The National Restaurant Association's breakdown of restaurant types, characteristics, and check averages. Courtesy NRA News, 1984.

Quick-service restaurants	Midscale restaurants	Upscale restaurants
Sandwich/varied menu*	Family style*	Varied menu*
Varied menu	Varied menu	Varied menu
Hamburger	Family style	Unclassified
Other sandwiches	Unclassified	
Retail		
Unclassified		
Specialty*	Specialty*	Specialty*
Fish/seafood	Fish/seafood	Fish/seafood
Chicken	Family steak	Steak
Pizza	Sandwich	Barbecue
Barbecue	Barbecue	Other
Other	Other	
Ethnic*	Ethnic*	Ethnic*
Mexican	Mexican	Mexican
Oriental	Oriental	Oriental
	Italian	Italian
Snack*	Hotel/Retail*	Hotel*
Ice cream	Hotel	
Donut	Retail	
	Cafeteria*	

* Restaurant subcategories reviewed in each quarterly *CREST Report*.

Quick-service restaurants	Midscale restaurants	Upscale restaurants
▪ Primarily fast-food establishments	▪ Includes restaurant types, such as family, cafeteria, and coffee shops	▪ Primarily white-tablecloth restaurants
▪ Usually do not offer table service	▪ Usually offer table service	▪ Offer full service
▪ Often offer take-out service	▪ Some offer wine and/or beer, but few provide cocktails	▪ Usually offer wine, beer, and cocktails and accept credit cards
▪ Check size averaged $2.41 in 1985.	▪ Check size averaged $4.05 in 1985.	▪ Many accept reservations
		▪ Check size averaged $8.73 in 1985.

possible reduction in cost. The solution for the catered events was a sliding-scale fixed price based on total attendance.

Market Share

The question most often asked in the restaurant industry is "How's business?" It reminds me of a well-known Henny Youngman joke. When he was asked, "How's your wife?" his comeback was, "Compared to what?"

A true response to "How's business?" is based upon an analysis of the market share of your restaurant in relation to the total market segment of similar operations. Market share is a percentage that indicates the relative strength of your restaurant versus that of your competition. It is determined by dividing the sales of your establishment by the total activity or sales of all similar operations. The resulting percentage is your individual market share.

$$\frac{\text{Your Sales Activity}}{\text{Total Industry Activity}} = \text{Individual Market Share}$$

Market share also can be calculated on the basis of volume in units, number of customers served, or any other measurement standard being used within the restaurant industry.

It can be difficult to determine the total sales figures of your area because of the many categories of restaurants and the variety of restaurants that are attempting to capture a part of the market, but it is important to make the effort. The major consideration in defining your market share is to identify your competition and the population base in which you are operating (see fig. 4-9).

Figures for calculating local restaurant activity are based on national statistics provided by the National Restaurant Association and the U.S. Census Bureau.

The first figure required is the total amount of money spent nationwide for food away from home. The National Restaurant Association, in its *1985 Foodservice Industry Facts,* estimated that $178 billion were spent for food and beverages away from home. (A study done in 1980 by the Hearst magazines showed that 17 percent of total income was spent on food and of that, 32 percent was spent on food eaten away from home.)

Zip code and census demographic statistics then can provide the average income per household within your market area. These income averages, used with the national percentages listed above and the restaurant categories and shares shown in figure 4-10, will show the amount of money available for eating out in your market area. (You can eliminate institutional-type foodservices from the calculations.)

If you have prepared a marketing plan, as described in Chapter 1, you will already know who your competitors are. This is essential information.

You may then assign a reasonable gross sales volume to each of these restaurants based upon National Restaurant Association statistics. (Figs. 1-1 and 1-2 provided such information.)

Next you can calculate the percentages to determine your market share in comparison to total market share.

At this point, your major objective should be

NUMBER AND PROPORTION OF RESTAURANT TYPES ACROSS THE U.S.

Restaurant type	Number of units	Proportion of total
Pizza	31,053	10.3%
Hamburger	26,585	8.8
Ice cream	18,104	6.0
Oriental	12,487	4.1
Family style	12,324	4.1
Mexican	11,851	3.9
Cafe	11,284	3.7
Chicken	10,879	3.6
Fish/seafood	8,531	2.8
Steak	7,751	2.5
Barbecue	5,228	1.7
Donut	4,771	1.6
Italian	4,096	1.4
Deli/bagel	4,076	1.3
Other sandwich	3,983	1.3
Sub	3,766	1.2
Coffee shop	3,584	1.2
Refreshment/snack	3,210	1.1
Cafeteria	2,624	0.9
Hot dog	2,526	0.8
Other specialty[1]	2,475	0.8
Grill	2,388	0.8
Other ethnic[2]	2,344	0.8
Diner	2,336	0.8
Luncheonette	2,303	0.7
Roast beef	2,150	0.7
Pancake/waffle	1,873	0.6
Upscale	1,751	0.6
French	1,285	0.4
Truck stop	763	0.3
Unclassified	94,456	31.2
Total	**302,837**	**100.0%**

[1] Includes: crêpe, natural/vegetarian, yogurt, potato, pretzel, soup, chili, biscuit and fondue restaurants.
[2] Includes: German, Spanish, Greek, Indian and soul food.
Source: RE-COUNT.

4-10. Market share and number of restaurant units in the United States. Courtesy **NRA News,** Feb. 1985.

to work to increase your market share. Fluctuations in population and food fashions can cause changes in your market share percentage, so vigilance—as recommended throughout this book—is critical to your success.

SUMMARY

Every principle discussed in this chapter merits your consideration in preparing a strategic profit plan. Calculations related to operating hours, discounts, and break-even cannot be based upon hunches. They must have a sound economic basis to have an impact on the overall profit. The formulas provided in this chapter, though not perfect, provide the opportunity for more realistic evaluations of what in the past has been based largely on guesswork.

CHAPTER FIVE

PRICING
SUPPORT
SYSTEMS

In the foodservice area, success is based on developing the right menu-pricing system. But before deciding on one of the seven or so methods of pricing (see chapter 6), it is crucial to establish support systems so that you will be able to document your pricing procedures and make profitable decisions based on them.

THE FOOD-COST BREAKDOWN

A basic support system for menu pricing is the food-cost breakdown to determine the value of each item. It is based on the investment that the operator has made in the item and its cost and risk. The return on investment, cost, and risk must ensure a satisfactory profit. At the same time, the customer must be assured sufficient value for his expenditure for the menu item. If he does not receive this value, he is not going to return.

The food-cost breakdown also depends on the ratios of food categories to each other and to the operation's food inventory. Price increases on commodity items can cause problems. The analysis of items for the menu will require knowledge of the percentage of each of these commodities purchased. (*The Uniform System of Accounts for Restaurants,* listed in the Bibliography, includes an inventory breakdown.)

Separating your food inventory and menu into categories will help a great deal in making a menu analysis, and will also reveal exactly what various foods are costing you and what food category cost-percentages are out of line (see fig. 5-1).

If your food cost is high, you must find out where it is high: dairy products? assorted groceries? Be thorough. Check all areas to find out how each rates.

Using the food inventory cost sheet (fig. 5-1), you can relate the daily or weekly dollar total of purchases to sales. Establish the number of food categories needed to obtain the information you require on cost breakdown; then categorize each purchase. Divide the total of each column by total sales to determine the cost ratio of purchases to sales.

After a short time, this system will indicate what the ratio (percent) of each category of purchases should be to sales at any given vol-

Date _____

Vendor and Item Purchased	Beef	Poultry	Fish/ SeaFood	Produce	Dairy	Frozen	Other
Total Categories Purchased							
Total Daily or Weekly Sales							
Ratio: $\frac{\text{Total Categories}}{\text{Total Sales}}$							

5-1. Food inventory cost sheet.

ume, and will enable you to see immediate exceptions to the established ratio. This breakdown determines your cost basis prior to making any adjustments in price or purchases.

Use the basic cost of goods to determine the selling price of menu items. Restaurant owners and managers have done so for many years and will probably continue to do so for a long time. But keep in mind that they are using only the cost of the raw food needed to produce the menu items that they sell. The entire pricing system is part of the purchasing system; categorizing both menu and purchased commodities can be controlled by your record-keeping.

Periods of volatile economic change are critical to cost; yet, foodservice operators historically have been reluctant to make menu price changes during these periods. Increases are not made even when reports from the field indicate that customers understand that steadily rising costs must be offset by higher menu prices. Conversely, customers are aware when inflation rates and other costs are low. Management must be attentive to general economic conditions in order to price menu items. When the economy is troubled, customers usually recognize that restaurant operators do not have a choice.

This customer attitude has not prevailed in every case, however. There have been reports that owner/operators have received more complaints when raising the price of coffee by ten cents than when raising the price of a steak item by $1.50. As an owner or manager, you have the discretion to choose what items to increase. Customer attitude will dictate what is acceptable.

Some restaurateurs feel that they should not increase prices. At a restaurant convention, Webb Lowe, former head of McDonald's and Bonanza restaurants, expressed the idea that, because of the economic conditions that existed, Bonanza restaurants had to try to keep from increasing prices in their units. He wanted them to stay where they were in price and market segment, and he felt that it was important to try to offer as much or more at the same prices as before.

Bonanza looks more at customer counts than at dollar volume. This seems to me a good practice. I am beginning to get more involved in analysis ratio—in counts of people and similar factors—to measure actual or anticipated profits than I am in food-cost percentage factors. The food-cost percentages do not always tell me quickly enough what I want to know about an operation to make operating adjustments. Many other indicators give much more information about a food operation than whether its food cost is running at the standard 40 percent. The final analysis is bottom-line profit, and I want to have indicators to guide me in making daily decisions to accomplish my profit objective. Such indicators include daily customer counts, the average check per customer, daily average purchases in food categories, and daily sales analysis to indicate trends of consumption. Equally important in this analysis is the review of geographic economic conditions. As economic conditions improve, the customer who formerly was in the top income group in your restaurant may move to a restaurant with higher status. When conditions deteriorate, the customer who was in the bottom income group may move to a restaurant of lower status, or he may not eat out.

Incidentally, there is a popular story about why a 40 percent food cost was chosen as the preferred operating figure. In the year 500 B.C., a man built a restaurant on the road to Rome. His first customer was an accountant who happened to stop to have dinner. When he finished, he said, "Say, I think you have a pretty good thing going. It looks as if this restaurant business may develop into something that will spread all over the world. How would you like it if I kept books for you?"

The restaurateur had no one working on his books, so he hired the accountant/customer to keep the books for his first month of operation. At the end of the month, the accountant came back to the restaurant operator and reported, "You have a 40 percent food cost."

The restaurateur asked, "Is that good?" The reply was, "That is very good." So, from that time forward, it has been accepted that all foodservice operations should maintain a 40 percent food cost.

ATTAINABLE FOOD COST

I do not believe that anyone would ever be so naive as to assume that food cost could be based upon the preceding story, but a formulation

Item	Raw Cost	Menu Price	Item Sales	Total Cost	Total Income

Raw cost = Standardized recipe cost
Menu price = Method used, one of seven
Item sales = Manual count or computer printout

Total cost = Item sales × raw cost
Total income = item sales × menu price

Attainable food cost is determined by dividing total cost by total income.

5-2. Form for calculation of attainable food cost.

for determining an attainable food cost must be devised by the restaurant manager/owner. You can frustrate yourself by trying to meet an objective that is impossible or impractical. The only accurate way to determine what your food cost should be is to do a calculation on attainable food cost. It is something of a chicken-and-egg situation.

The calculation is done by using the form shown in figure 5-2. On the form, list all items offered on the menu. Next you will need to determine a raw cost for each item. To do this, you will need to use an accurate cost sheet based on a standardized recipe. (More on how to devise a standardized recipe and prepare a cost sheet appears later in this chapter. The cost sheet includes no labor or overhead, only the per-portion raw food cost and garnish or accompanying items.) You can then establish a menu price (according to one of the methods outlined in chapter 6). Then you take an accurate count of the sales of the item. This can be a manual count or a computer printout from a point-of-sale register.

Using the raw cost, the menu price, and the item sales, you can determine the income from the sale of the item. The income is just the sales figure multiplied by the menu price. The cost of the item is determined by multiplying sales by the raw cost. The total for these two columns will give the total income and total cost for all items sold from the menu. By dividing the total income from sales into the total cost of the item, you can determine an attainable food cost for a given operating period.

The Margin, or Gross Profit

Another element in menu pricing is the margin, or gross profit. This is simply the difference between the cost of goods and the selling price. Margin, or gross profit, should cover your operating expenses and your profit as well, and it is a factor in menu-pricing systems. This term does not mean the bottom-line profit; it is used in retail establishments that also have foodservice operations, such as department store foodservice.

A major consideration of pricing for profit is operating expenses. Sometimes our approach in this area is similar to an example many of us were first introduced to in grammar school. If you buy six oranges for a nickel each and you sell them for a dime each, how much profit have you made? Obviously, the answer is you made a nickel on each one, or thirty cents profit. A number of operators have followed this same concept in pricing menu items. They have taken the position, as the public has for many years, that if you can buy a food item for $1 and sell it for $2, you are making a $1 profit.

Anyone who has been in the foodservice business for more than two days knows that is not true. Yet restaurateurs have also overlooked operating expenses, rent, taxes, interest on loans, repairs, salaries, supplies, telephone, allowance for shrinkage, depreciation, bad debts, heat, power, light, donations, insurance, and unclassified expenses. Yet all of these have to be considered because they all are part of the cost of the final menu item. There is no net profit if they are not covered by your pricing system.

THE STANDARDIZED RECIPE

As mentioned previously, an essential pricing support system is based on the standardized recipe (S.R.). A standardized recipe is one that has been checked and rechecked for all factors and will consistently produce a known quantity of food at a desired quality. The S.R. is a tool for managers of every type of foodservice establishment. I can envision no food establishment where this is not required. If the operator does not not know what goes into the food item and the cost of the ingredients, then the item cannot be priced realistically on the menu.

Management control requires the use of the S.R. For production control, known quantities of food are assigned to the manager and controlled by the manager's use of the S.R. The recipe takes the guesswork out of food production. The S.R. is the manager's production blueprint. It improves a manager's planning skill because it specifies portion size so that amounts can be correlated to the forecast.

The obvious advantages of standardized recipes are:

1. Consistency of product

2. A system of operation rather than dependency upon an individual
3. Improved cost control by forecasting and portion control
4. Recognition of deviation from the standard and the opportunity for immediate correction
5. Predetermined item cost
6. Provision of a plan of preparation and elimination of employee preparation decisions
7. An inventory list and purchase control of nonusable items

To develop your S.R. file, start with whatever recipes you are now using or beginning to write. Sources for recipes are offered continually by trade publications, food-manufacturing firms, quantity cookbooks, and your employees. Obtain your recipes from a reliable source and then adapt them to your operation. The recipe, regardless of the source, cannot be considered standardized until it has been tested in your kitchen. Recipe-testing procedures are:

1. Check the recipe for proper ingredient ratios.
2. Chech the preparation procedure for clarity.
3. Check the sequence of work.
4. Check your equipment to make sure it is appropriate for preparation.
5. Give measurements of dry ingredients by weight and liquid ingredients by volume.
6. Have a supervisor work with the production person and record any changes.
7. Prepare a small amount of the item for testing for standard.
8. Increase the amounts and retest for standard if the food is satisfactory.

When a recipe is accepted, implement it as you would in any training program:

1. Explain to the employees why the new recipe has been developed and the advantage of the new recipe.
2. Stress and detail any part of the recipe that may affect the final quality or a part where a problem may occur in the preparation process.
3. Work with and assist the employees in preparing the item.
4. Follow up on the item when it appears on the menu prepared without your assistance.

NAME OF PRODUCT

Formula No. _____

Method of Mixing and Comments	Ingredients Used in Order of Mixing	Weight of Ingredients		Mat'l Cost	Total Mat'l Cost	
		Lb.	Oz.	$	$	¢
Scaling Instructions:	Finished Weight of Mix	Lb.	Oz.	Batch Cost		
	Approx. Cost Per Lb. of Mix. $					
	Approx. Cost Per Oz. of Mix. $					
Baking Instructions:	Handling After Baking:					
Batch Information:						

5-3. Form for standardized recipe.

For evaluation of the product in the standardization test, use a panel of male and female employees of various ages. This procedure will stimulate the interest of the employees in the recipe program and will make them part of the program. Have the panel refrain from eating prior to the taste test; midday is an acceptable time for testing. Nonsmokers will have a finer sense of taste. Judgment of the final product should be based on the texture and temperature. Odor, visual impact, and size of portion will have an impact on the final rating.

If the item is accepted, write the recipe on a standardized-recipe form (see fig. 5-3) and place it in the standardized-recipe file. The file consists of one master copy of all recipes in the owner's or manager's office and individual recipes that are used in specific departments of the kitchen (such as pantry, range, pastry). A suggested file system is a three-digit number for each recipe. The first digit indicates the food group (such as beef, chicken, fish); the second digit, the classification within the group; and the third digit, the specific food item on the menu. For example, recipe 1–2–21 indicates Beef—1, Cubed—2, Swiss Steak—21. Recipe 1–4–5 indicates Beef—1, Ground—4, Meat Loaf—5. The form in which you present the recipe should be selected on the basis of what is most adaptable to your restaurant. Each form has its advantages and disadvantages. More important than the form is the actual information listed on the recipe. The information recorded should be detailed enough so that the person preparing the item needs to make no decisions.

Recipe Information

Below is the specific information that should be listed on the standardized-recipe form:

- **Name of product**
- **File number**
- **Yield.** The yield should specify a total quantity by weight, volume, or specific pan size after final preparation, as well as the number of individual servings.
- **Portion size.** The actual size served to the patron is given by weight, volume, or number of pieces. The portion may also be given by serving-utensil size or by the number of portions to be obtained from a specific pan size.
- **Garnish.** For a buffet or cafeteria operation, an amount of garnish per pan size should be specified. For individual-serving operations, an amount should be specified per portion. Plate size and type should be specified for individual orders.
- **Ingredients.** Ingredients are always listed in the order used. Any pre-preparation should be specified as the first step of the recipe. Quantities should be expressed in volume for liquids and weight for dry ingredients when more than one ounce is used. Less than one ounce may be expressed by volume, such as 1/4 tsp. All quantity abbreviations must be standardized on all recipes. Quantities must be listed in amounts that can be measured in standard measuring devices. For example, do not list 2/5 cup; use ounces or another standard measure. If the recipe can be standardized to current manufacturers' can sizes, these may be used as a measure, such as one no. 10 can. Give the physical state of the ingredient when added to the recipe: one cup flour sifted or one cup flour unsifted; one cup nuts chopped or one cup nuts

whole. If the quality of the finished product is dependent upon a specific brand or pack of product, then state this in the ingredients, such as whole, peeled tomatoes in purée.

- **Preparation.** List first any preparation for ingredients and preheating of equipment for the item. In the procedure section, list by groups of ingredients the method of combining them. Use the correct terminology: for combining, mix, blend, fold, or cream; for cooking, until reduced by one-half, or until thickened to syrupy consistency. List time and speed for mixing if applicable. Emphasize any special directions or precautions for the product.

- **Cooking.** Any special preparation of the cooking utensils should be written in the first part of the cooking section. The cooking temperature and length of cooking time should be specifically stated. Indications of doneness other than time may also be given, such as internal temperature or until a knife inserted comes out clean. Instructions for panning are also given in this section, such as the number of pieces, volume, or weight for specific-sized pans.

- **Handling.** State any finish that is to be given to the product after cooking, such as brushing with butter or cooling on a rack, as well as where, how, and at what temperature the product is to be held or stored until served.

- **Cost.** For accuracy in your menu pricing, every ingredient including garnish must be priced to obtain a total cost. A unit price for each ingredient is obtained from the purchase invoice. The unit price is converted into a recipe-ingredient cost. When a product is purchased at a price per unit that is different from the unit of measure in the recipe, the product must be converted into the recipe units. The recipe ingredient cost is multiplied by the amount required in the recipe to obtain a total cost per ingredient. Then the costs of all ingredients are totaled to obtain a total product cost. The total product cost is divided by the number of portions obtained from the recipe to get the cost per portion. Sample forms appear in Kotschevar's *Quantity Food Production* and Shugart, Molt, and Wilson's *Food for Fifty* (see Bibliography), or recipes can be written in measures that are the normal measuring units of purchase.

The standardized-recipe file is not static.

Changing eating habits, equipment, product development, and product cost, as well as many other factors, will require constant revision of the recipes. Change is required, even desired, but no changes should be made unless the item is reevaluated. No changes should be made on any recipe unless the change is made on all copies in the file. Every restaurant will have a different requirement for the amount of product to be prepared. The recipe should be standardized for the amount that best meets the quantity requirement.

Rapidly changing food prices require a review of recipe prices at least once every three months. Restaurant operators whose recipes are computerized will enjoy the advantage of instant reviews of any price change, and, with the correct menu strategies, can reflect in-creases or decreases in menu price within twenty-four hours.

The standardized recipe must be consistent in all factors of taste, quantity, quality, appearance, garnish, method of preparation, ingredients, style of service, and, most important, specific portion served at a specific price.

I recommend the preparation of costed standardized recipes, although I realize that it is a complex matter, since I have been through the procedures in more than one operation where we have had to standardize and cost all of the recipes. It is a very long, involved process. But it is worth the money, time, and effort required. One establishment where I helped to prepare such recipes moved from a position of operating at about $50,000 in the red to a profitable operation when we combined the use of

Item _____ Code _____

No. Portions _____

Portion Size _____

Garnish _____

Serving Piece _____

Ingredients	Quantities	Cost		Method
		Unit	Total	
(Ingredients are listed by groups or item, as used, separated by spaces.)				(The methods of preparation and/or procedure for each group or item are separated by spaces. This form shows the method for each group of ingredients or single ingredient and then the method for combining with the following ingredients.)

Total Cost _____

Cost per Portion _____

5-4. *Form for costed standardized recipe.*

ITEM: Chicken Fried Steak

PORTION: 50

4 oz. raw weight

GARNISH: Parsley/1 oz. sauce

SERVING PIECE: 12 by 20 pan—serve on 8-in. plate

RECIPE: 4-1-32
ST. LOUIS COMMUNITY COLLEGE
HOSPITALITY–RESTAURANT OPERATIONS

INGREDIENTS	QUANTITIES	COST	
	Amount served: 50	Unit	Total
Cube Steak (4/1 lb.)	12½ lb.	$2.00/lb.	$25.00
Flour	1½ lb.	$0.25/lb.	$ 0.375
Egg Mixture	4 cups	$0.15/cup	$ 0.60
Bread Crumbs	2 lb.	$0.35/lb.	$ 0.70

METHOD

1. Dip steaks into flour, then into egg mixture, then into bread crumbs. Make sure steak is completely covered with crumbs.
2. Lay steaks on a sheet pan until ready to cook.
3. Cook steaks in 375°F deep-fat fryer for 7 min. or until breading is golden brown.
4. Remove steaks from fryer baskets and place in 12×20 serving pans (25 per pan), overlapping steaks in pan.
5. Keep hot in warmer or low (200°F) oven for service.
6. Garnish pan with four sprigs of parsley before sending to serving line.
7. Portion sauce when serving.

NOTE: Do not bread steaks more than one hour prior to cooking.

Total Cost $26.675

Per 50-4 oz. portions

Per Portion $0.533

5-5. *Sample of costed standardized recipe.*

standardized recipes and careful portion control. Figure 5-4 shows a cost form and figure 5-5 is a hypothetical example.

An operation cannot do an accurate costing of items on its menus unless costed recipes are available that will tell the portion costs and portion sizes of the items. However, with the Texas Restaurant Association pricing system, you do not even have to update your recipes because you can calculate a percentage factor and use that percentage factor to update each recipe rather than having to recost the recipes completely. However, every six months you will have to evaluate your recipes to measure your profit.

SALAD BAR PRICING

A factor in the overall menu pricing is the cost incurred by the operation of a salad bar. Salad bar prices normally are based upon a competitor's price and adjusted when there is a general profit decline in the restaurant. The pricing of the salad bar is based upon several considerations.

A principal consideration is the cost of the items and their ingredients on the salad bar. This cost is related to the ABC inventory principle. The A items are expensive and should comprise 20 percent of the total number of items offered; B items are moderately priced and should comprise about 30 percent of the total number of items offered; C items are inexpensive and constitute roughly 50 percent of the items offered on the salad bar.

You should prepare a written "menu" for the selections on the salad bar so that the cost ratios of the offerings remain in the correct proportion. The specific items are not important, but the ratios are.

Another pricing factor is the arrangement and display of the ingredients on the salad bar. The size, shape, and arrangement may lead people to choose certain items. Accessibility of the item can increase or decrease the cost factor of the salad bar. The implement that you choose for serving each item will help to control the portion that the customer serves himself. Obviously, the smaller the implement, the more difficult it is for the customer to overportion. The width and depth of the container from which the product is eaten will determine the amount that the customer can place in his bowl.

The costs of the ingredients on the salad bar are determined by the actual cost of the amount of ready-to-eat foods. Determine the cost per servable pound or an actual cost by weight for foods that need to be cleaned and trimmed. This calculation is the original weight minus the waste, shrinkage, and trim to determine a usable weight (edible portions, or EP). Divide the original weight into the usable weight to determine a ratio of usable product.

2 lb. carrots (original weight)
1/2 lb. trim
1.5 lb. edible product
1.5 divided by 2 = a ratio of 75 percent for usable product.

Once the ratio is determined, the next step is to divide the market price by the ratio to determine a cost per servable pound.

Ratio = 75 percent
Cost per lb. = 50 cents (as purchased, or AP)
.50 divided by 75 percent = .666 cost per servable lb.

This formula can be used for the calculation of actual cost or you can use a food-purchasing book that lists product waste.

The costs of all items on the salad bar should be established on the basis of a standardized recipe that has been accurately costed according to the guidelines discussed earlier in this chapter. Once the cost has been established, pricing of the salad bar is a matter of inventory and monitoring.

The salad bar cost is determined and monitored with the calculations on a cost-and-use form (see fig. 5-6). The form consists of a beginning weight or count, any additions that are added during the meal time, minus an ending inventory, which will equal the total consumed. This total consumed, multiplied by a cost per unit or weight, will equal a total cost for each salad bar item. This total cost of all items, divided by the number of customers participating in the salad bar, will produce an average cost per customer. All calculations are simplified if the item can be determined and calculated on a weight rather than a count basis. Customer participation data are determined by manual count or a computerized system.

Item	Original Amount	Additions	Ending Inventory	Total Consumed	Cost per Unit/Wt.	Total

5-6. Cost-and-use form for monitoring salad bar pricing.

Item	Recipe Number	PORTION	Price	
			Date	
Beef Croquettes, sauce or gravy	56	2 2-oz. croquettes, 1 oz. saucc/gravy		
Swedish Meat Balls	72	4 1-oz. (raw) meat balls		

5-7. Sample page from price and portion book.

If salad bar costs become excessive, rearrange the items on the salad bar or increase the numbers of low- and moderate-cost items, or both. The key to salad bar profit is to maintain the integrity of record-keeping and to operate on an acceptable cost-per-portion basis.

PRICE AND PORTION

A procedure that I found to be very effective during the time I was in restaurant operations was a price and portion book. This book listed every item that appeared on the menu of the operation. The information contained in the book gave a stated portion size, price, and recipe number, and provided space for price revision (see fig. 5-7). The portion that appeared in the price and portion book was also the portion shown at the top of the standardized recipe in the space for portion size of that particular item.

Listing each menu item's portion size and price serves two purposes. The most obvious purpose is to document the price and portion of all items served. Second, it is a convenience to the management staff. Invariably, employees will approach any manager with the question, "How much do we serve and what do we charge for it?" The price and portion book is a ready reference for individual employees as well as management.

In any operation that has a portion control system, I recommend that only high school girls be hired as servers. They always seem to be on a diet and believe that everyone else should be. They always do a better job on portion control than high school boys, who can eat more than a combination of any three people on earth.

Portion control is the absolute responsibility of the management. Any device that you can develop and use to help you and your staff to control portions better is an obvious advantage. The price and portion book is an essential element of portion control.

CHAPTER SIX

MENU
PRICING
STRATEGIES

THEORY OF PRICING

One of the most monumental tasks that any restaurant owner or manager faces is the pricing of the menu. Many owners' pricing systems are a guess, at best. Some use what they say is a secret or special formula to arrive at prices. Pricing is, in fact, an art. The amount of money that is charged and received for the food sold is the sole source of revenue for the restaurant, so the price of the items on the menu will ultimately determine the success or failure of the restaurant.

The pricing of the menu is a profit-planning procedure. How much profit do you expect to make? Sales and profit are determined by the menu price of each item. Profit is defined as a return on the investment and a return on the effort that you spend in running the restaurant. As an owner or manager you must establish objectives for profit in your pricing policies. Both economic and strategic objectives should be pursued when prices are set. The price is related to the following three factors covered in chapter 1 about the menu marketing plan:

1. Clientele
2. Market conditions
3. Economic conditions

Menu prices are also governed by the curve of elasticity of demand, as we saw in figure 4-7. The market determines what the customer will pay. If the price is above the market, the customer will go elsewhere; if the price is below the market, you will suffer a loss. About once a year, and sometimes more often, owners or managers must stop to reassess the pricing of the menu and make any needed changes. A change of prices will have an effect on the volume. If there is a price reduction on a menu item and demand increases for that product, the item may be price-sensitive. If there is a price increase and the demand for that item drops, this is a clear indication of price-conscious demand for that menu item. Successful pricing means you have your product at a price that the customer will pay and where you produce a profit for the enterprise. Everyone looks for shortcuts in pricing, but there are none.

As discussed in chapter 5, the cost of the product limits what you can charge for it and also indicates whether or not you can profitably sell the product in the price range that you set.

The factor of perceived value of a product was covered in chapter 1. According to this concept, the base price of any item on the menu has a value in the mind of the customer and different items have different perceived values. In every market area, each item on your menu is going to be perceived differently by each customer. "Is the item worth it to me?" is really what is being asked. Quality and high perceived value are measured by the appearance of the food, the service, and the taste of the product. A higher menu price is more acceptable if you are creative in merchandising and serving the menu items.

To determine the menu price that you charge, the following factors should be considered:

1. Type of restaurant. I have classified restaurants as fast food, family type, or an "atmosphere" restaurant. There is a limit on what can be charged according to the type of operation.

2. Meal occasion. The time at which the person consumes the food (breakfast, lunch, or dinner) affects what the customer expects to pay.

3. Style and elaborateness of service. Whether the establishment is Russian, modified French, an "in" place, or an intimate bar, the style influences pricing.

4. Competition. Competition is extremely important, based on the laws of economics.

5. Customer mix. This is based on male–female ratio, expense accounts, occupations of the customers, and other demographic information. In all pricing systems, the customer will ultimately determine the amount that will be paid.

6. Profit objective.

Restaurant owners and managers suffer a great deal of frustration in trying to determine when to change the price of a menu item. I feel that price changes should depend on the elasticity of demand whether or not you are dealing with a price-sensitive group. If the clientele is sensitive to price changes, timing and the amount of change are crucial to success.

Price Increases

In most cases, foodservice operations wait too long before raising prices. They seem to be reluctant to do it and tend to postpone it. Often, the restaurant down the street becomes the spur for raising prices.

Some of the following approaches may make the price-raising process easier.

Make the price increase as bearable as possible. Change the size of portions—not noticeably, but enough to make up the necessary difference in the profit margin. Be sure you do not violate truth-in-menu regulations. Another approach that has been successful is to add something to a standard item to create a new package that can be sold for a slightly higher price. To a popular sandwich, add potato chips, which have a low cost factor, or two dill pickle chips on a little piece of lettuce, which also involve a low cost factor. You can increase the price, yet seem to be giving the customer added value for his money.

Be absolutely sure that your portion control system is effective. When your workers are told to serve 4 ounces, do they serve only 4 ounces? To improve portion control, you can set up a price and portion book, as discussed in chapter 5. But you will not know if the correct portion size is being served unless you check the portioning every day. This can be counted on to help keep profits up.

Some restaurantgoers equate high prices with higher quality and better service, although it is not necessarily true. Thus, there are certain destination restaurants where price is not a factor. Such operations are known for the quality of the product and the excellence of the service. People will go to such establishments and pay any price.

Try to avoid rapid increases over a short period of time. As mentioned, timing is very critical in increasing prices.

In the St. Louis area, there has been excellent media coverage about the fact that it is possible to eat out as cheaply as at home. Invite some of the media people to your restaurant and talk to them. They may very well be interested in having facts and figures to report that can develop a better understanding of the relative costs of at-home and away-from-home meals.

Continued maintenance of quality standards is essential after any price increase. The slightest decline in quality will instantly alter the customer's attitude. There is no substitute for food quality, there are no shortcuts for specified preparation methods, and there is no excuse for poorly presented foods. As a manager, be careful to pay attention to the smallest details to ease the shock of price increases.

The best time for any menu price increase (or decrease) is when the government announces the current cost-of-living figures or changes in the gross national product.

If at all possible, avoid increasing prices on the most popular of your menu items when they have reached one of the "magic numbers"—with a nine or a five as the last digit. (See Odd Cents Pricing, later this chapter.) When a dollar amount is changed on the menu, it is very noticeable to the customer and should be avoided. There will be occasions when you write a new menu and want to increase all the prices. Every customer will immediately notice this, so avoid across-the-board increases when you have new menus printed. Across-the-board increases are acceptable only in highly inflationary periods when customers expect regular price increases.

Select a format for the menu that makes price changes easy. A chalkboard, handwritten menus, table tents, and clip-ons make price changes easy, and any of these later can be incorporated into your menu. Let the menu reflect seasonal fluctuations. There are marked price differences for seasonal items, and these may be left unpriced on the menu and priced on daily quotes. If you make a price change, monitor the sales for changes in the quantities sold.

Edmund Yates, owner of the Highland Park Cafeteria in Dallas, Texas, computerized his recipes in 1979 and can make daily price changes of all menu items based upon market costs. Granted it is easier to make price changes in a cafeteria than on a restaurant's printed menu. Yates changes prices both up and down and most customers perceive the changes as fair.

Try to maintain price ranges that are generally within what you normally expect, and that, by check analysis, you have found your customers are willing to pay. Some restaurateurs suggest a price range in which the most expensive item on the menu would be no more than twice the amount of the lowest-priced item. Others suggest a price differential of $5 to $8 between the highest and lowest items. The price range must take into consideration the type of restaurant and make exceptions of daily high-priced items such as live lobster. The price range may be determined by a chart that analyzes check distribution or a *pro forma* budget of anticipated check averages.

SEVEN MENU-PRICING METHODS

The methods described here are currently in use throughout the foodservice industry. Only you, as the owner or manager of a restaurant, can make a judgment as to which is best. You can adapt, combine, or modify as your situation requires. If it works—use it.

Menu-Pricing Method 1—Nonstructured

This system is probably the simplest menu-pricing method in the world. You simply go to someone else's foodservice operation, take his menu away with you, and copy his prices. This may sound strange, but it has been done, probably by the same people who are advertising restaurants for sale in Sunday's paper, since conditions in any two types of foodservice operations are always different.

The only safe system of menu pricing is one developed by the owner/operator for his own establishment. To do this, you have to check the operational factors in your establishment that affect the prices on your menu. Do not be tempted to follow another operator's method of menu pricing, no matter how successful the operation seems. His may have operational factors of which you are not aware. He may own his own building and so may not be paying any rent. He may have fourteen children who work in the dining room and receive no pay except room and board. If you do not know the internal aspects of his operation, his system will not work for you. You must tailor your system to your own operation.

Menu-Pricing Method 2—Factor

The factor system has been in use a long time. To determine a menu sales price, the raw food cost is multiplied by an established pricing factor. You first establish the food cost you would like to have, 37 percent; then you divide this

into 100, and come up with 2.7 as your factor. The percentage you establish as your food-cost standard divided into 100 will always equal the multiplying factor. By multiplying the raw food cost by the multiplying factor, you will establish a menu price. The formula is:

Raw Food Cost × Pricing Factor
= Menu Sales Price

A second way to compute this is to divide the known or desired food cost percentage into the actual cost (taken from a standardized recipe) to determine a selling price.

$$\frac{.533}{.37} = \$1.44$$

Obviously, if you are satisfied with this profit, you can set prices by this method.

The factor system is popular in foodservice operations because most owner/operators are not mathematicians. It is probably also the easiest way to price a menu. This system has two aspects that should be given special consideration: (1) Based on the old, familiar belief in the 37 percent food cost, 63 percent of the income is to cover all expenses beyond food. But is 63 percent going to cover all other expenses? If it is not, you may need another system of pricing. (2) You are not going to know until the end of the month whether or not your other expenses will exceed 63 percent, so you may be pricing on a very unsound basis and not find this out until you have lost considerable profit.

Menu-Pricing Method 3—Prime Cost

The prime cost system was developed by H. H. Pope of St. Louis, who uses it mostly in cafeteria operations, where it appears to work quite well. In this system, a raw food cost is determined from the standardized recipe used. For example, a raw food cost of $0.533 plus a direct labor cost of $0.09 brings the total to a prime cost of $0.623. This prime cost includes direct labor—labor involved in the actual preparation of the item. It does not include any peripheral labor or management service, storerooms, clean-up or similar activities. Referring to your financial statement, you can determine your total labor cost, and one-third of that cost will be direct labor cost. Although this will not be a precise figure, it will be close enough in most instances.

Raw Food Cost in Dollars	$0.533
+ Direct Labor Cost in Dollars	0.090
Prime Cost Total	$0.623

When you have established the prime cost, multiply it by the factor you have set to get the menu price. To establish this factor, deduct the amount of direct labor from the total labor cost. Since we have been using a 37 percent food cost, let us arbitrarily set a 27 percent labor cost. You can make the assumption that one-third of your labor cost will be for direct labor.

Working from the 63 percent rounded-off margin, subtract 9 percent for your labor; you would then have a margin of 53 percent. The 53 percent margin divided into 100 gives you a factor of 1.88. (Some of these figures have been rounded off.) (Notice that this system is very similar to menu-pricing method 2.) Following this example to its conclusion results in a selling price or menu price of $1.171. Here is how it works:

Prime Cost Total × Factor = Menu Price

Prime Cost Total	$0.623
× Factor	× 1.880
Menu Price	1.177

Pope finds his system particularly satisfactory because he uses few convenience products and thus considers his direct labor cost a major factor of the pricing system. He says he has increased the menu prices in his cafeteria by only 20 percent since July 1971. He has accomplished this by using a very accurate system of pricing and measurement of product mix, as well as by using many other good management techniques.

For example, his managers are required to calculate what is needed for each meal on the basis of projected sales and forecast. Some of his recipes are written for four portions, some for twenty. Portion numbers are not standardized, in contrast to the form for costed standardized recipes shown in figure 5-4. This makes it necessary for each manager to calculate on a daily basis the recipe for the cook to use the next day. The foodservice worker follows the recipe as calculated by the manager when preparing the item.

With his system, Pope has reduced on-premise labor to the minimum. He is also giving his customer a better price value for his dollar. Pope keeps in constant touch with his thirty operations; he is in each one at least once a week. His managers turn in daily one-page reports containing enough information to show what each operation has done that day and to reveal immediately any of the exceptions to the principles of operation that he has set up.

Pope operates on the "management by exception" philosophy: If profit is running the way it should, leave the operation alone; when an exception appears, whether it is on the high or low side, do something about it. His system is essentially the factor system with a built-in direct-labor factor, but he knows what is occurring and can handle any deviation immediately. With this system, you can increase or decrease the direct labor cost, depending on the labor involved in a product.

People in operations using a considerable amount of direct labor might need a higher factor than 10 percent, and should keep in mind that the 10 percent figure is simply a rule of thumb and not applicable to all types of operations. A sandwich shop might have a much higher percentage of items requiring more direct labor, although there may be specific items that have little or no direct labor.

To summarize, direct labor cost is roughly one-third of the total labor cost: by deducting one-third of your labor cost from the labor cost on your profit-and-loss statement, and then deducting the remainder from your gross profit, you arrive at the percentage that you will need to divide into 100 to find your own factor.

Menu-Pricing Method 4—Actual Cost

The actual pricing method accomplishes the goal of any menu-pricing system: to include profit as part of every price on the menu. A menu-pricing system always develops to a point where all the cost factors and profit have been established and covered. Using the actual pricing method, you are beginning to develop a complete system, but you are not doing it to the degree that it *should* be done.

In setting up the actual pricing system, the first step, once more, is to establish a food cost; we will use $0.37. For this example, we will use a total labor cost of $0.26; this is not direct labor, but the total labor cost, including management. This then gives us a total food and labor cost of $0.63. You can arrive at this labor cost by a time-and-motion study or by determining the percentage of the labor cost from your profit-and-loss statement.

Next, use the profit-and-loss statement to get the variable cost, fixed cost, and profit. The two principal variable costs, food and labor, have been covered by the food and labor amounts used above. Any other variable costs are picked up as percentages from the profit-and-loss statement and used in the formula. Now we add our fixed cost percentage and, finally, a profit percentage.

We calculate the dollar amount of $0.63 by costing the standardized recipe and calculating a percentage per dollar of the cost of each menu item for total labor. Then we determine a percentage for all other costs and profit by dividing sales into the recorded costs of each additional profit-and-loss cost item and profit. When these figures have been established, we can set up an algebraic equation.

ACTUAL COST METHOD
Raw Food Cost (dollars)
+ Labor (dollars)
+ Variable Cost (percentage of sales)
+ Fixed Cost (percentage of sales)
+ Profit (percentage of sales)
―――――
= Menu Price

The two parts of the procedure are as follows:

PART 1. DETERMINATION OF COST — Costs from P&L Statement

Food Cost	.37	Variable Cost*	= 11.05% of sales
Labor Cost	.26	Fixed Cost	= 20% of sales
		Profit	= 10% of sales
Total Food & Labor	.63	Total	= 41.05%

* Other variable costs not including food and labor

PART 2. CALCULATION

1. Selling Price = X or 100%
2. Fixed and Variable Costs and Profit = 41.05%
3. Food and Labor = .63
4. Food and Labor = 100% − 41.05% = 58.95%
5. .5895 X = .63
6. X = .63 ÷ .5895
7. X = $1.069 Menu Price

In the above calculations, the menu price is established as 100 percent or X; the fixed and variable costs plus profit are 41.05 percent; food and labor total $0.63. So menu selling price equals 100 percent, minus 41.05 percent, giving us a percentage of 58.95, representing food and labor. In other words, 58.95 percent of our selling price is equal to $0.63.

Menu-Pricing Method 5—Gross Profit

The gross profit method of menu pricing is designed to determine a specific amount of money that should be made from each customer who comes into the operation. It is based primarily on past financial statements, customer counts, and guest-check analyses. Here is how it works. A foodservice operation has:

$100,000 Sales (Food)
−40,000 Food Cost
―――――
$ 60,000 Gross Profit Serving 20,000 Covers (Customers)

These figures are based on a one-year operating period. A careful customer count has been kept, which makes it easy to determine the gross profit per check or an average gross profit per customer. The gross profit is divided by the number of customers, and an average gross profit of $3 is established. Keep in mind that this is not net profit. It is profit after the raw product was paid for, but nothing else.

Having established this figure, this system requires adding any extra meal items and the gross profit to the price of the food to arrive at a selling price for each menu item. Referring to the menu, we determine the extra items that will be served and price these to find out their total cost.

EXTRA MENU ITEMS
$0.20 Salad Bar
0.10 Baked Potato
0.10 Bread and Butter
0.05 Plate Garnish
0.05 Coffee
―――――
$0.50 Total cost of the non-entrée items

A complication may occur in using this system if the owner/operator runs a salad bar, whether it is a large salad bar or a limited one. Probably the best solution is to use the highest cost on the salad bar per person rather than to try to find out an average cost. (See chapter 5 to calculate the price per person for the salad bar.)

All of the extra menu items that are included in the total meal should also be included in the menu price. The next procedure is to determine the cost of the entrée item from the standardized recipe. In our sample problem, we will use chicken, steak, and lobster. The cost of each entrée item is calculated as follows: half-chicken, $0.75; steak, $2.50; lobster, $3.50. List the entrée cost and then add the cost for the extra menu items, previously determined as $0.50; then add the average gross profit of $3.00 from the previous year.

	Entrée Cost	Extra Menu Items	Gross Profit	Menu Price
Half-Chicken	$0.75	$0.50	$3.00	$4.25
Steak	2.50	0.50	3.00	6.00
Lobster	3.50	0.50	3.00	7.00

It is interesting to compare this with selling prices below based on a 40 percent food cost, using the 2.5 factor, to determine what the difference would be in the menu prices.

Selling Price Based on 40 Percent Markup

Chicken	$ 3.15
Steak	7.50
Lobster	10.00

With the gross profit method of menu pricing, the higher-priced entrée items are brought down to a lower price. This system largely benefits the customer who tends to choose from the expensive menu items. It penalizes the customer who is looking for the less expensive items. This system uses figures based on past financial records, a *pro forma* budget, or budget forecast, and it assures the owner/operator that he is going to make a predetermined sum of money on every customer.

This system is currently in use in a steakhouse with a predetermined gross profit factor for appetizers, entrées, desserts, and accompanying items. The gross profit factor for each of the menu categories is worked out. This system has predetermined that for each item sold on the menu, the restaurant will receive a specified gross profit. The individual items are priced according to a required gross profit figure.

A principal consideration in the gross profit pricing method is that each customer will share equally in all of the cost associated with the serving of the meal. The method assigns a portion of all fixed and operational costs to the pricing system. The costs are assigned a share; the determination of a share is based upon the history of the operation, taken from the profit-and-loss statement. The system is easily adapted and can be used advantageously to price banquets or other catered events. The gross profit system lends itself well to the costing and determination of a sales price where known customer counts are predetermined.

The gross profit method is probably more adaptable to an institutional operation, such as a hospital foodservice, where it is essential to ensure a certain return for each participant every time a meal is served. The costs of operating change less rapidly in the institutional area, and records are more accessible. In some commercial operations, where the profit could easily be worked out for each category of item, and where these categories are not presented as part of an inclusive menu, this method is also applicable. A gross profit would have to be set up on each of the categories of items.

The problem with this system is that it is hard to adjust for any serious decline in business or for major price fluctuations. It breaks down unless the operation runs at a pretty steady level, because it must be based on a projection of total number of customers if the operator is to get the amount of money he is going to need in income.

The gross profit method is a good system; it will work except where rapid and drastic price and/or customer changes are encountered. These distort the actual cost, or expense, since food cost is not the important concern in this system. Gross profit is the important factor; it assures continued net profit for the operation.

Menu-Pricing Method 6—Base Price

The base price method is a system in which, as the first step, the base price establishing the

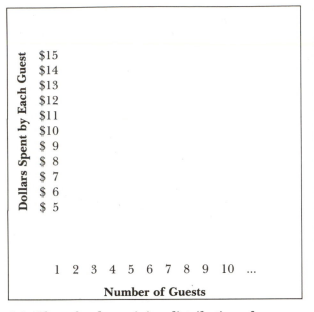

6-1. Chart for determining distribution of customer check expenditures.

entrée cost is developed from a customer-check distribution graph. This is a system in which the menu items are priced at a certain level to satisfy the market. For example, the "beef and beverage" specialty operations frequently find their market to be the $10 check group.

The first question then becomes, "What can be served for $10?" This system starts with the menu price and then works backward to the profit. It is very much like the actual pricing method but done in reverse; the amount that can be spent on raw product is established last.

The $10 figure simplifies the example; whatever other figure represents the desired price to be paid by the customer can easily be substituted. The figure used should be what is actually spent per customer in the operation. A distribution curve of all checks must be made to determine the average check; then a statistical analysis is made to find out what that check is (see fig. 6-1).

The answer can also be obtained from a forecast or a projection of the preferred type of customer. How much income or how many dollars should be spent by the customer? Whether it is established by check distribution, the statistical analysis of checks, or by predetermining the desired type of customer, the average or the median can be established. In our example, it is the customer who will pay $10 for his meal. This customer will have to be provided with an entrée or a meal that is going to run about $10.

With this method, there must be a known market, because the selling price is designed for that market. Using this information, the owner/operator can go from the selling price to the point where he knows how much he can spend on the raw product and still maintain his required net profit. Price value relationship and customer perceived value are critical points to the success of this pricing system.

The profit-and-loss statement or *pro forma* budget will establish average percentages of the desired profit, and, using a projection, forecast, or the information from the profit-and-loss statement, the percentage of profit can be set. In this example, it is a 10 percent profit. Since 10 percent of $10 is $1, that becomes the profit goal. The overhead figure is established next. If the rate is 27 percent (of $10), the overhead figure is $2.70. If labor is running at 26 percent (of $10), labor cost is $2.60. These figures, derived from the profit-and-loss statement, provide a total of the amount of money to be spent for items other than food.

From the profit-and-loss statement, calculate the following:

Profit = 10% × $10, or $1.00
Overhead = 27% × $10, or $2.70
Labor = 26% × $10, or $2.60

The same percentage requirements for profit, overhead, and labor as previously stated can also be derived from the forecast, budget projection, or actual records of past operation. Subtracting $6.30 ($1 + $2.70 + $2.60) from $10 shows that $3.70 could be spent on raw product.

In other words, any costed standardized recipe with a raw product that costs less than $3.70 can be served and will provide a standard profit while meeting the necessary overhead and labor costs. Information from the check distribution chart will show what price level the operator should not go above or below. Also, he can determine the number or percent of each price range for entrées by dividing the total in each range by the total number of guests.

Menu-Pricing Method 7—Forced Food Cost

The final pricing method to be considered is an extension of a system first developed by the

1 **MEDIUM MARKUP**	2 **LOW MARKUP**
− & +	− & −
HIGH VOLUME HIGH COST OR RISK	HIGH VOLUME LOW COST OR RISK
3 **HIGH MARKUP**	4 **MEDIUM MARKUP**
+ & +	+ & −
LOW VOLUME HIGH COST OR RISK	LOW VOLUME LOW COST OR RISK

6-2. Sales matrix for menu markup.

Texas Restaurant Association. This system seemed impressive at the beginning, but it became clear, after a considerable period of use, that it did not provide some of the essential information needed to price the menu. After further study and use of this system, it was established that the amount set forth as the menu price is really determined by the market.

This system is based, first of all, on the following considerations: Operators have to charge enough to stay in business. They must also, as the risk of loss or spoilage increases, make sure they are making a reasonable profit. As the risk goes up, it is only right to charge more for the product. The increase in risk may be, for example, spoilage or no sale for an item, but, whatever it is, be sure you have provided for enough profit to cover it.

Volume takes care of a lot of ills and a lot of operating errors as well. However, the opposite is also true. The lower the volume, the higher the markup needed. The pricing system markup is based on some elementary laws of economics. In any competitive industry:

1. The amount set for any price is determined by the market.
2. To charge more than the price acceptable to the market will cause customers to go elsewhere for the product.
3. To charge less than the price acceptable to the market will cause a loss to the enterprise.
4. As the risk of loss or spoilage increases, the more essential it is for the foodservice operator to take a higher markup.
5. As the risk of loss or spoilage decreases, the foodservice operator may take a lower markup.
6. The higher the volume, the lower the markup can be.
7. The lower the volume, the higher the markup needs to be.

Taking the Texas Restaurant Association method outlined here one step further requires an analysis of the menu. Every item on a menu can be fitted into one of the four categories that make up the following matrix (See also fig. 6-2).

> High Volume—High Cost
> High Volume—Low Cost
> Low Volume—High Cost
> Low Volume—Low Cost

Or, stated another way:

> Popular—Not Profitable
> Popular—Profitable
> Not Popular—Not Profitable
> Not Popular—Profitable

Ideally, every item on a menu would be a high-volume, low-cost item, but real menus do

MENU ITEM	Cost/Risk		Sales		Markup or Profit
	High	Low	High	Low	

6-3. Form for classification of items in the menu matrix.

not work out that way. However, the proper category should be determined for each menu item (see fig. 6-3).

The Texas Restaurant Association has used its computer system to develop certain percentages of markup for all of the items on a menu. They are based on a consensus of the state's leading operators as to what their average markups are. However, their classifications do not permit you to take advantage in your pricing of such basic economic rules as: the higher the risk, the more right the operator has to a profit; the lower the sales, the higher the markup should be.

After further work with this system, it was concluded that this system of pricing required a range of percentages rather than a standard, static percentage for an item. It is only by using the range that the system will work. The range was developed as follows:

Menu Categories	Profit Markup Range Percentage
Appetizers	20%–50%
Salads	10%–40%
Entrées	10%–25%
Vegetables	25%–50%
Beverages and Breads	10%–20%
Desserts	15%–35%

Basing the pricing approach on the previously stated economic laws, the matrix of the items, and a range of percentages turned out to be a most workable variation of the forced food cost system. It is reasonably simple to apply this system in an operation.

The forced food cost system bases sale price on the required profit on individual menu items. It permits the food cost percentage to float to the level required for the right profit on each item.

The basics of this system of menu pricing are a well-planned budget broken down into operating (overhead) costs, raw food costs, labor costs, and the markup that gives the desired percentage.

This food-cost formula is developed in just six easy steps:

1. Determine your operating (overhead) cost per dollar volume.
2. Budget your labor cost.
3. Determine the desired profit (markup) percentage per dollar of business.

4. Add operating (overhead), labor, and profit-wanted percentages to arrive at your cost without food percentage.
5. Subtract your cost without food from 100 points, the value of the dollar in cents.
6. Determine the raw food cost from the standardized recipe and add the raw cost of extra trimmings. Divide the answer by your raw food cost to find the value of each food point. Then multiply the 100 points by the value of each food point, and you have your menu (selling) price.

	Percentage of Dollar
Operating (overhead) Cost	27%
Labor Cost	26%
Desired Profit (markup)	+ 15%
Total Cost Without Food	68%
Value of Dollar in Points	100 points
Total Cost Without Food	−68
True Raw Food Cost	32 points

Using the costed standardized recipe example given in Figure 5-5, we can do the following calculations to determine raw food cost and menu price:

Chicken Fried Steak

Meat	$0.500
Flour	.007
Egg	.012
Bread Crumbs	.014
	$0.533

$$32 \text{ points} \overline{\smash{)}\ \$0.533} = \$0.0167$$

$0.0167 per point × 100 points = $1.67
Menu price: $1.67

There may be other factors involved in a particular operation that would keep the markup percentage from coming out even. Based on conditions of the operation, your discretionary decisions may indicate that a specific menu item could fall at any point on the continuum for profit markup range; you may have a mid-high or a mid-low rather than an absolute high, medium, or low. While a medium reading is acceptable, the high end, or near it, is preferable. (See fig. 6-4.)

	Sales		Cost/Risk		Item	Markup or Profit
	High	Low	High	Low		
1		X	X		Apple Pie	H
2	X		X		Shrimp Cocktail	M
3		X		X	Strip Steak	M
4		X	X		Lobster Tail	H
5	X			X	French Fries	L
6	X		X		Hamburger	M
7		X	X		Club Sandwich	H
8	X			X	Milk Shake	L
9		X		X	Fried Chicken	M
10	X		X		Rib of Beef	M

6-1. Example of profit markup form. Markup is indicated as high (H), mid-range (M), or low (L).

You have to work this out for your menu items in your own foodservice operation. You determine what markup is needed based on the cost/risk factor and on volume. In a recent exploration of this method, ice cream was used as an example. Ordinarily, ice cream, since it is kept frozen, does not involve a risk. However, one operator was having so much trouble because of the potential for pilferage in his ice cream service that it was one of the highest risk items on his menu.

PRICING DECISION

As I have mentioned, there are no absolutes and no shortcuts in menu pricing, but one valuable aid to making decisions is a pricing system comparison chart (see fig. 6-5).

On this form you list the pricing system used on each of the menu items. (The example shows three of the methods just discussed.) There is also space to make comparisons with the competitors that you consider most likely to share the same market. A check of the competition should include prices, food quality, and dining circumstances to give you some idea of the range of prices that can be charged. The assumption is that quality of product, service, and ambiance is the same in your restaurant as that of the competition.

The last column covers what I refer to as "gut feelings." This is the value judgment that you make about the price, related to sales and

profit. We all use such nebulous elements in pricing a menu, no matter how unscientific this may be.

ODD CENTS PRICING

In *The Cornell Quarterly*, August 1982, Lee M. Kreul and Anna M. Stock published an article called "Magic Numbers." The article could very aptly have been named "Odd Cents Pricing" or "The Psychological Impact of Prices on the Consumer." Odd cents pricing generally uses a nine or five as the last number in the price of the item. There is no guarantee that menus priced by this method will be effective, but they seem to appeal to some intangible consumer behavior. Many of the pricing methods used in the industry are somewhat obscure, and odd cents pricing fits into this category. It has been used effectively for years in retail systems. It is an attempt to maximize profit and psychologically affect the customer. The "magic numbers" supposedly stimulate the consumer to buy.

Kreul and Stock point out that there are three methods practiced in odd cents pricing:

1. The price ends in an odd number.
2. The price ends in a number other than zero.
3. The price is just below zero.

The best explanation for odd cents pricing is that the price creates an illusion of a discount

MENU ITEM	FACTOR	GROSS PROFIT	FORCED FOOD COST	COMPETITOR A	COMPETITOR B	FINAL MENU PRICE	VALUE JUDGMENT

6-5. Chart for comparison of pricing systems.

and reduces the buyer's resistance. A second explanation is that there are different perceptions of prices in upscale and moderate-priced restaurants. Odd cents pricing is for people who *eat* out, not people who *dine* out. The primary appeal of odd cents pricing is to a customer group that is price-conscious. One perception is that prices ending in a nine indicate a lower quality of service or a fast-food operation.

Another consideration in the psychology of pricing is that the consumer regards the first digit as the most significant. The number of digits in the price creates an image of the expense of the item. The customer attracted by psychological pricing has a tendency to round to the nearest dollar, up or down: 39 cents is generally rounded down, 40 to 79 cents is rounded to 50 cents, and 80 cents or above goes to the next full dollar.

Psychological pricing is common in the restaurant industry. It is just assumed that everyone is looking for a bargain. The validity of such an assumption is questionable, but there certainly is a relationship between the item choice and the purchase price.

CATERING PRICING

Current articles in trade publications are giving a great deal of exposure to the plight of the independent restaurateur regarding "no-shows" for reservations. The caterer, whether on- or off-premise, has always faced this problem. If you have worked in catering, you know that the first head count of guests for a function is always substantially higher than the number who attend. There is a point at which the operator cannot overcome certain costs associated with doing business based on a quoted price, and not all operational costs will decrease as the head count decreases.

A catering pricing system was devised by Lee Zesch, who was my partner in Blayney Catering Company in St. Louis. His formula was used extensively in the operation of the company, which we owned and operated for twelve years. The system is based upon the principle of maximization of profits (which was shown in figure 4-8), the gross profit pricing system (discussed earlier in this chapter), and the profit/volume ratio (discussed in chapter 4).

1. Total food cost	$200
2. Prepreparation salary	$100
3. Fixed expenses (10% of total of 1 & 2)	$ 30
4. Profit (total of 1, 2, & 3 times 50%)	$165
Total (add 1, 2, 3, & 4)	$495
5. Possible additions	$ 20
6. Food attendants: Multiply the hourly wage by the number of attendants by seven (seven-hour minimum time) for the total	$175
7. Beverage attendants: Multiply the hourly wage by the number of attendants by seven (seven-hour minimum time) for the total	$140
8. Rental equipment	$ 50
9. Total	$880

Note: The total divided by number attending equals the proposed cost per person.

6-6. Worksheet for pricing catering services.

With the Zesch system, a catering pricing worksheet (fig. 6-6) is completed to obtain a total cost. This total is divided by the number of persons slated to attend to obtain a price per person for the contracted event.

The system is predicated on a break point at every ten guests. The caterer's only controllable factor for these ten persons is the actual cost of the food, and the only saving from a decrease in number will be food not purchased or served for the ten people. As a caterer, you cannot substantially reduce fixed costs, equipment rental, or personnel needs until there is a decrease of more than ten people.

Follow the procedure below to calculate a cost per person when there is a decrease in attendance. (The amounts are based on the example in figure 6-6.)

Total cost $880
No. attending   50
Cost per person attending $17.60
Cost of raw food per person $4
10 persons × $4 = $40 cost of food for 10 fewer persons

In this case, there is a savings of $40 in the food cost for 10 persons, resulting in a new total cost of $840. The cost per person is $21.

If the cost per person based on 40 is $21 and the cost per person based on 50 is $17.60, the difference is $3.40.

Divide $3.40 by 10 persons to get a price-increase factor of 34 cents per person. Therefore, for 49 persons, the price per person is $17.94 and for 48 persons, the price per person is $18.28.

This pricing system is contrary to what one normally considers in menu pricing; as the number goes down, the price increases. You are passing on to the consumer those costs that cannot be absorbed by the caterer based on fixed and nonreducible costs. When you reach the forty-person level, you recalculate to determine a new price per person and the change in price on the sliding scale from forty to thirty persons. At forty persons, the price per person is $21.

This pricing system was developed for the protection of the caterer. If you use it, you must explain to the client that price changes are based upon attendance. The catering contract should be written on a price-per-person basis.

SUMMARY

The February 1985 issue of *The Cornell Quarterly* ran an article by David Hayes and Lynn

Huffman entitled "Menu Analysis: A Better Way." It states that there are currently three recognized methods for menu analysis and gross profit contribution of menu items being used in the restaurant industry. Thus, the authors acknowledge that there are several routes to profitability, many pricing methods by which an owner profits from food item sales.

Although there is no purely mathematical formulation that solves all pricing problems, a totally theoretical approach is not practical either. Despite what we theorists of menu pricing and profit would like you to believe, there is a great deal of assumption and guessing about what menu items are good for sales and good for profit. Keep in mind that when any one of the "fixed variables" is changed—such as a new item on the menu, the rearrangement of menu items, a change of menu copy, or a change of prices, the probability of choice by the customer will be affected. There is no solid way to predict what the effect will be. Nothing succeeds like continuing profit, so, "If it ain't broke, don't fix it."

One final point on menu-pricing strategy: If your strategy works to make your customer think you are giving him a perceived value, he is going to be happy; he is going to come back, and he will tell his friends about your place. If your menu pricing includes a proper profit, you can count on being repaid for your risk and effort.

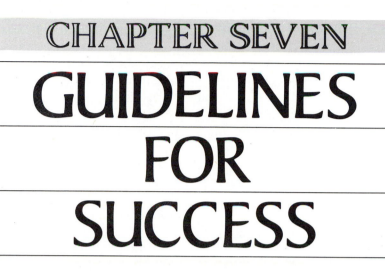

CHAPTER SEVEN
GUIDELINES FOR SUCCESS

FIFTY TIPS FOR A SUCCESSFUL MENU

A profitable operation hinges on a successful menu, but every operation is different. So what works in one restaurant may not work in another. As I have said before, "If it works, use it." In the operational cost control and menu-development seminars that I have led over the years, the following fifty ideas have been discussed as techniques for increasing sales and profit through the menu.

1. Establish budgets for comparison of forecasted sales to actual sales. Deviation of sales mix and costs at the end of an accounting period may cause a significant variation in the month-end totals. The budget is really a score card, so you can compare where you are to where you should be.

2. Increased prices are inevitable. There is a point, however, when customers will not accept the increase if it is not properly timed. The government is constantly announcing cost-of-living price increases or specific-product price climbs. Time a menu-price increase to national or regional publicity about raw-product price increases.

3. Determine what you are doing that is different or better. Many restaurants are serving less-than-spectacular food in an environment and with service that make them very successful. Many others are serving well-prepared, quality food in a less-than-spectacular environment and with mediocre service, and they are successful. Price may not be a major customer consideration for food that is unique, food that has high quality standards, or for an environment that is unusual.

4. Keep records as your road map for the future. The details of your record-keeping should enable you to isolate specific areas that are exceptions to your established standards. A high-food-cost percentage provides you with little information, but records indicating high cost for a specific commodity zero in on the target.

5. You may classify yourself in any price range you choose, but too wide a price range will tend to make your clientele stereotype you. Provide a range, but establish it by the clientele you hope to attract—high-, medium-, or low-priced. The wide range will tend to increase volume at the lower menu prices and will not give an equitable price spread. Range the prices within each of the classifications.

6. To control profit, establish systems for continuous monitoring of sales mix and recipe cost. The fluctuation of product cost makes it important to review prices and pricing methods a minimum of once per quarter. Any deviation from forecasted sales mix is to be analyzed as quickly as this on the basis of the total cost/sales/profit relationship.

7. Your prices need not necessarily relate to the prices of restaurants surrounding you. The cost of overhead, labor, and product may vary considerably, and prices must be based upon what you need to charge for profit.

8. Consider an à la carte pricing system. Many restaurants have gone to this system. A number of customers surveyed have indicated that excessive amounts of food are served by restaurants. A la carte menus permit the individual to order the amount of food he wants and reduce waste.

9. Today's patron is more sophisticated than in the past and recognizes items of value on the menu. Failure to change prices as product and labor costs change may encourage patrons to take advantage of prices advantageous to them or to avoid high-priced menu items that they consider to be a poor value.

10. It is foolish to maintain the listing of any item that is not profitable to the operation only to increase volume. The loss-leader item must stimulate the additional sales of profitable items or the theory of loss leader is destroyed, and the item becomes a loss-of-profit item. Analyze secondary sales to validate the original intent of using a loss leader.

11. Some less profitable items will always be on the menu. Do not list or arrange the menu in any way that will assist in the sale of these items. Hide them to decrease sales. Make no effort to advertise the items and recommend a policy of "No Suggestion" of the item by service persons.

12. Investigate purchasing procedures and policies. After thorough analysis, be positive that your restaurant is obtaining the best-quality product at the lowest available price for the intended use of the product. Make price comparisons, do some specification-bid buying, and check prices for contract purchases.

13. Reduce the portion size. The best way, if

you are positive of quality control, is to survey what is not consumed. Considerable costs are incurred because of excessive portions. The portion may be intentionally or unintentionally large. In either case, a size reduction is appropriate.

14. Written preparation methods should be periodically reviewed; intended preparation methods and actual methods may vary considerably. Yields on many menu items are dependent upon cooking and preparation methods. Improper procedures often cause food waste and higher costs.

15. Serving personnel will not usually do suggestive selling. However, if you can use table tents, buttons, or menu copy to cause the patron to ask the service person a specific question requiring a direct answer, suggestive selling may result. Get serving people to recommend high-profit items. Customers welcome suggestions.

16. Modify current recipes by the use of extenders or less-expensive ingredients—more potatoes, more crumbs, more pasta—but do not misrepresent the item as it is listed on the menu.

17. If yours is a cycle or combination static–cycle menu, use expensive, low-profit items less frequently on the menu. Such an item may become a once-every-two-weeks item instead of a weekly one.

18. By combining a lower-cost item with higher-priced items, you may decrease the portion of the high-cost product. The customer perception of value will be there because of additional food, but the actual cost will decrease. In some instances, a price increase can be made because more food is being served.

19. Redesign the menu to increase the sales of high-profit items. Use primacy and recency in the list of menu items offered for sale. (If you are operating a cafeteria, relocate items so the most profitable ones are in the first two entrée openings.)

20. A natural tendency on the part of an employee is to overgarnish a plate. Write a specification for garnishes and garnishment of every item. Calculate the cost of garnish into the menu price. Food must look attractive, but cost must be considered in total pricing. As a manager, you control the cost.

21. Eliminate holdover food on expensive or low-profit items. Forecast for a run-out time of holdover foods that are not cooked to order. Preparing food a second time is expensive. The second preparation and second-cooking shrinkage will almost double the cost per portion.

22. Instead of adding new items, emphasize a new method of preparation of an entrée so that your pricing can effectively incorporate the change. The product cost of the ingredients of the new method is minimized and the total cost slightly increased. Emphasizing the preparation of the entrée adds value perception by the patron and improves sales of high-profit entrées. Sales at a slightly higher price will greatly increase the contribution to margin.

23. Purchasing products from local suppliers or manufacturers may offer you the opportunity to reduce the raw cost of foods. If quality standards are established, then use of locally manufactured products of the expected quality will reduce shipping and handling costs and ultimately will result in a price decrease.

24. Restaurant managers in every section of the country have indicated that any item listed on a chalkboard as the daily special will sell. Take advantage of holdover food, banquet overproduction, or special purchases to promote high-profit food items as chalkboard specials.

25. When a price increase is effected, the impact on your customer may be reduced by a change in the appearance or packaging of the product. Cutting sandwiches into three pieces instead of the current two-cut method, serving them open-faced, placing the food on the plate differently, or using a different-sized plate may all help reduce the impact on your customer.

26. A contradiction to two other methods previously mentioned is the fixed-price (or *prix fixe*) meal. For this, calculate a price that includes appetizer through dessert. Analysis of customer eating habits can determine the refusal percentage of categories of foods offered. The advantage is that, although the item is included in the price, it is not consumed by the guest.

27. An obvious way to increase profit is to sell more mixed drinks. Actually, to sell more beverages of any type will increase profits. If the alcoholic beverages are going to be merchandised, develop special house drinks. Fruity limited-alcohol drinks have tremendous appeal to many drinkers. Wine is an excellent promotion because of the national publicity given wines. Promote nonalcoholic beverages as well.

28. The concept of one-stop shopping is not new to restaurants, but the thought is frightening to most persons in the industry. Vendors are willing to bid lower on the guarantee of a known volume of purchasing for a specified time period. Concentration of dollar volume creates considerable price leverage.

29. Inventory items can be segregated into three groups. Group A, sometimes called the critical few, will comprise about 20 percent of the total inventory items but will amount to approximately 70 percent of the dollar value of the inventory. Focus attention where the money is being spent. Consider overproduction, overportioning, decline of quality by aging, and pilferage. Isolate items where you have your large dollar usage and control the purchase of these items.

30. Preparation waste control is a major factor of total cost. Conduct a study to decide whether to make or buy an item. In many instances, buying prepared or partially prepared products may substantially reduce total cost. Specific trim loss for products should be determined and spot-checked on a random basis.

31. Conduct tests of yield amounts based on grade comparison. Often, lower-grade and lower-priced items will test to a higher plate cost per portion than a high-quality item with a smaller amount of trim. The final profit hinges on what it costs to put the item on the plate.

32. Continually explore for new products to improve labor and/or food cost. Utilize salesmen, employees, and your own eating experiences to explore for new products or improved methods of preparation and presentation. Never let your past experience limit your vision for improvement.

33. Eliminate menu items that are not selling from your menu listing. These items require dollars of investment and will deteriorate from age to an unusable state because of lack of sales. Establish a sales standard or goal for each menu item and, if there is no justification for below-standard sales, delete the items that are nonsellers.

34. Provide all production employees with the equipment for the correct preparation of the food item according to the recipe procedure. Calibrate on a specific time interval the temperature setting on all cooking equipment. Purchase and install timing devices wherever practical in the cooking or preparation process. Use mechanical devices and automation to assist in cooking.

35. Make portioning equipment available and train employees to use it. Standardize the utensils and serving pieces to the specified portion size. Standardize bowl and plate size or capacity to no more than the specified portion size.

36. Use a price and portion book. Every item on the menu should have a specified amount to be served for a specified price. The amount of the portion served should be cross-checked against the stated portion size on the standardized recipe. Conduct random audits on the accuracy of portions being served by your employees.

37. Staying within the bounds of prevailing sanitation and health regulations, you may be able to salvage some items from the table. Any food product that would be reasonable to rescue should be rescued and reused in the same or different form. Individual foil-wrapped butter pads, for instance, can be removed from the table, rechilled, and used again.

38. Until the manager takes command of production forecasting, the cooks will set their own production requirements. This usually means cooking all that is available. Decide and enforce the production schedules and amounts to be prepared based on past sales records and anticipated increases or decreases in sales.

39. Determine how much food is wasted, destroyed, or unacceptable because of bad timing by your employees. Cold, overcooked, unattractive, or undercooked food will not be accepted, consumed, and paid for by your customers. Customize and systematize the timing of preparation and service to lessen the loss factor of improper timing.

40. Spoilage is a major cost factor for many operations. Have each department supervisor or head person complete a weekly report of loss from spoilage. Careful investigation and follow-up should indicate the responsibility for the loss. Take action to correct the cause and prevent a repeat of the loss.

41. High-risk and high-cost items should be

on a continuous-count inventory system. Use visual checks or a physical count. High-cost merchandise needs a daily accounting to permit immediate action to be taken.

42. Poverty may be one of the best production-utilization teachers there is. Ask some of your employees how they would use some of the things you are throwing away. Survey your garbage for trim and underutilization of raw product.

43. Determine how much you are paying for the packaging of your product. A major cost factor of all products is the wrapper or container. The national average of labor productivity is 40 percent. Are there products that you are using that could be purchased in bulk and repackaged for better labor utilization and lower product cost?

44. If you do not receive merchandise you cannot sell it. Set up a system of auditing and cross-checking for invoice payment. Require approval from two or more persons or systems before the invoice is paid.

45. Use a system of guest-check and cash-register recording devices that is self-auditing. Every food product that leaves the kitchen is recorded and balanced against a cash/charge sales record and is balanced or audited on a regular basis.

46. Control free food to employees and guests. The authority to void checks should be vested in the manager on duty. Employees are entitled to specified food benefits, but the benefits should be controlled by a recording system. Surveillance of your food giveaway should be monitored carefully.

47. When you increase the menu price of an item, determine the point where the customer says no. But remember that there is also a point when all that is humanly, physically, and mentally possible has been done to control the price, yet the price still must be increased.

48. If an item is in an unfavorable corner of the sales matrix, and if the situation cannot be corrected, remove the item from the menu.

49. Close the restaurant entirely. This is the ultimate solution to cost control.

50. If you are unwilling to close, fire the manager. Somehow, owners always think this will increase profit and boost the volume.

Obviously, the last two suggestions are facetious. The object of the fifty menu strategies is

an attempt to make suggestions to have every menu item in the high sales–low cost corner of the pricing matrix. Some suggestions may be impractical or invalid for your specific operation. Creativity and flexibility are certainly criteria for successful business operation. These ideas on menu management are offered to stimulate your own creativity for adapting any one of them to increase the profitability of your menu.

MENU SELF-EVALUATION

Menu self-evaluation is a continuing procedure that you can use to compare your menu with the theories of menu development. The form that follows will help you perform such an evaluation. Some of the points may not be applicable to your operation. In this instance, if your menu meets your requirements of service, rate yourself five points. For example, if you operate a limited-menu, fast-service operation, the point of menu variety does not apply, so rate yourself five points. No standard scores of excellent to poor have been established, but a perfect score of 200 points means you can establish your own standard. Any score of less than 100 should give you considerable cause to suspect your menu and to give major consideration to redesigning and reorganizing it. Note that a column is provided for a plan to improve what you are now doing. Set a time schedule for yourself and begin a systematic program to improve what you are doing and so improve volume and profit.

The influence of the computer is beginning to be felt in the restaurant industry in the selection of menu items, in their costing, and in the analysis of sales. Consumer dining trends are charted on the computer. The design of menus ultimately will be affected by the computer. As a result, the menu is in a state of transition along with the continuously changing habits of a mobile society. Be prepared for change—it is the key to your restaurant's success.

		Your Menu Score (Poor to Excellent)	Plans for Change and Improvements
1.	Menu presents a contrast in the flavor, consistency, and color of foods listed.	1 2 3 4 5	
2.	Ample and correct types of equipment are available in the kitchen for preparation of items on the menu.	1 2 3 4 5	
3.	There is an even distribution of raw cost of the items offered on the menu.	1 2 3 4 5	
4.	Menu items do not involve excessive time or high skill level to prepare.	1 2 3 4 5	
5.	There are not too many items prepared by the same method of cooking (fried, baked, broiled).	1 2 3 4 5	
6.	There are few seasonal items that would cause an excessive raw cost.	1 2 3 4 5	
7.	The foods listed on the menu are readily available on the local markets.	1 2 3 4 5	
8.	Many of the menu items require special equipment or skill to serve.	1 2 3 4 5	
9.	A sales analysis has been done to determine that each menu item is selling its proportionate share.	1 2 3 4 5	
10.	Sales prices of menu items are varied enough to appeal to all of your customers.	1 2 3 4 5	
11.	Menu items that the customer may not be familiar with or may not understand are explained in the menu copy, and nonsellers are removed.	1 2 3 4 5	
12.	The basic menu copy is honest in its description of the item, its quality, and its size.	1 2 3 4 5	
13.	Special menus are utilized to take advantage of special patrons, events, or slack times.	1 2 3 4 5	
14.	There is enough light in the restaurant so the menu can be read easily.	1 2 3 4 5	
15.	With the static menu, at least one daily special (complete luncheon or dinner) is included on the menu for variety.	1 2 3 4 5	
16.	The menu has a unique shape to emphasize the history, location, or name of the restaurant or area.	1 2 3 4 5	
17.	If daily special items are added as menu clip-ons, none are repeats of menu items already listed.	1 2 3 4 5	
18.	The menu items offer variety to the customer but still minimize the inventory (combinations, sauces, preparations).	1 2 3 4 5	
19.	Menu items are listed by price or in order of your preferred sales, with higher-profit items getting a bolder treatment.	1 2 3 4 5	
20.	When complete dinners are offered on the menu, the price is advantageous to the customer.	1 2 3 4 5	
21.	Menu items or prices have been crossed out and changed.	1 2 3 4 5	

		Your Menu Score (Poor to Excellent)	Plans for Change and Improvements
22.	Menu items that are known to be loss items still remain on the menu.	1 2 3 4 5	
23.	Menu prices are competitive with those restaurants around you that you consider to be your competition.	1 2 3 4 5	
24.	Items on the menu interfere with or restrict the production of other, higher-profit items.	1 2 3 4 5	
25.	The menu is changed to take advantage of seasonal or plentiful foods.	1 2 3 4 5	
26.	The workload is evenly distributed among all the kitchen employees.	1 2 3 4 5	
27.	Convenience foods are used as labor- or equipment-saving devices.	1 2 3 4 5	
28.	There is an unusual design, copy, color, or logo to reflect the individuality of the restaurant.	1 2 3 4 5	
29.	The color, design, and material of menu construction are appropriate to the theme and decor of the restaurant.	1 2 3 4 5	
30.	The food produced and served by your employees is consistent with any color illustration used on the menu.	1 2 3 4 5	
31.	Categories of menu items are separated by headings, illustrations, or pictures.	1 2 3 4 5	
32.	Items are arranged to give the best listing to highest-margin items, or some symbol to catch the eye is used to point out the item.	1 2 3 4 5	
33.	A variety of easily readable type is used in the menu copy.	1 2 3 4 5	
34.	Descriptive copy complies with the basic requirements of accuracy-in-menu or truth-in-menu laws.	1 2 3 4 5	
35.	Space on the menu is used to give information about the restaurant.	1 2 3 4 5	
36.	Space on the menu is utilized to inform guests of other restaurant facilities and service (catering, meeting space, take-out foods).	1 2 3 4 5	
37.	Menu prices have been analyzed and changed up or down to reflect changes in product, labor, and overhead costs in the last three months.	1 2 3 4 5	
38.	Size of the menu is appropriate to the style and decor of the restaurant and accommodates all listings so they are read easily.	1 2 3 4 5	
39.	Printing is professionally done with clear, sharp letters on a paper or stock that is practical and durable.	1 2 3 4 5	
40.	Clip-ons are of the same paper quality and same type of print as the menu and do not cover any menu copy.	1 2 3 4 5	

CHAPTER EIGHT
SAMPLE
MENUS AND
COMMENTS

This chapter consists of menus selected from St. Louis area restaurants as well as restaurants in other areas that best exemplify the theories and principles discussed in the preceding chapters. They all have one or more features of a well-developed and well-designed menu.

Certain menus best illustrate the use of the institutional copy of quality pledge, historical significance, and family involvement in the operation. There are also examples of the advertising that can be included on the menu cover.

Others demonstrate in layout and design the principle of spotlighting signature items for which the restaurants have become known or items that are particularly profitable. Some illustrate classical descriptive copy. One menu is a prime example of theme development in the item names and the design.

Although none of the menus follow every theory offered in this book, all are included here to show what can be done in marketing and merchandising.

BORDELLO RESTAURANT

HANNIBAL, MISSOURI

My wife, Anita, always told me that any textbook I write should include a centerfold or something on sex to increase the sales. My reply was always, "How can I do that in a book entitled *Menu Pricing and Strategy*?" I found the solution when I had dinner at the Bordello Restaurant in Hannibal, Missouri (see fig. 8-1).

I was intrigued the first time I saw the menu and excited about the operation of the restaurant. Its menu incorporates many of the recommendations included in this book.

The front cover of the menu is a graphic representation of the building itself and includes the boilerplate information of the address and phone number. The back cover includes an advertisement for a bed-and-breakfast facility now offered at the Bordello. Included in the institutional copy is a brief history of the building as an old house of ill-repute and some material on the reclamation and refurbishing of the building.

The menu item names are suggestive and most appropriate for the theme of the restaurant. For some items, a brief description explains the name. The prices are written in script, which diminishes the impact of the amount. The boxing of the special filets directs customer attention to these items.

I met the owner, Richard Turner, at a seminar I conducted the day after we had dinner. He told me that one of the most interesting aspects of the development of this menu was the staff meeting called to decide on names for all of the menu items. Turner said that good taste and discretion kept them from using many of the names that were suggested. Considering the names that *are* on the menu, I can just imagine some of the ones that were rejected.

The menu design and item names never deviate from the theme of the restaurant. The menu fulfills so many requirements of the qualities of a good menu and the development of a theme type of restaurant that it deserves special commendation.

BORDELLO LTD.

RESTAURANT · LOUNGE

BED 'N BREAKFAST

.111 BIRD.

Not Quite What It Used To Be,...But You Can Still Buy A Great Dish Here!

FOR RESERVATIONS, WRITE OR CALL:
111 BIRD STREET, HANNIBAL, MO 63401
314-221-6111

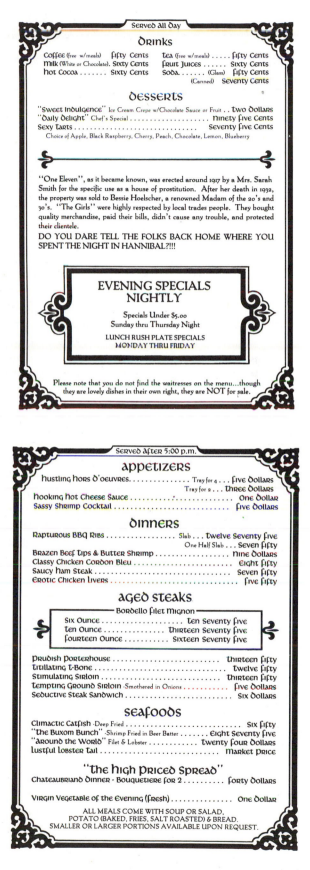

Served all day

Drinks

Coffee (free w/meals)	Fifty Cents	Tea (free w/meals)	Fifty Cents
Milk (White or Chocolate)	Sixty Cents	Fruit Juices	Sixty Cents
Hot Cocoa	Sixty Cents	Soda (Glass)	Fifty Cents
		(Canned)	Seventy Cents

Desserts

"Sweet Indulgence" Ice Cream Crepe w/Chocolate Sauce or Fruit . . Two Dollars
"Daily Delight" Chef's Special . . . . Ninety Five Cents
Sexy Tarts . . . . Seventy Five Cents
Choice of Apple, Black Raspberry, Cherry, Peach, Chocolate, Lemon, Blueberry

"One Eleven", as it became known, was erected around 1917 by a Mrs. Sarah Smith for the specific use as a house of prostitution. After her death in 1932, the property was sold to Bessie Hoelscher, a renowned Madam of the 20's and 30's. "The Girls" were highly respected by local trades people. They bought quality merchandise, paid their bills, didn't cause any trouble, and protected their clientele.

DO YOU DARE TELL THE FOLKS BACK HOME WHERE YOU SPENT THE NIGHT IN HANNIBAL?!!!

EVENING SPECIALS NIGHTLY

Specials Under $5.00
Sunday thru Thursday Night

LUNCH RUSH PLATE SPECIALS
MONDAY THRU FRIDAY

Please note that you do not find the waitresses on the menu...though they are lovely dishes in their own right, they are NOT for sale.

Served Before 5:00 p.m.

BRUNCH

"Mae West's Morning After" . . . . Three Twenty Five
2 Eggs w/Bacon, Sausage or Ham & Potatoes or Grits & Toast
"The French Affair" . . . . Two Twenty Five
French Toast (4 Slices French Bread)
"Turn a Trick" . . . . Three Dollars
3 Egg Omelet with 2 Ingredients & Toast
With Hash Browns . . . . Three Fifty
Other Ingredients . . . . Forty Cents Each
"Red Light Special" . . . . Three Dollars
"Fill & Thrill" crepes (2)
½ Order (1) . . . . Two Dollars
"Silk Stocking Special" Quiche . . . . Three Fifty
Served w/Spinach Salad or Tossed Salad
Happy Hooker Soup du Jour   Cup . . . . One Dollar
                               Bowl . . . . One Fifty
"Garter Variety"
Chef's Salad . . . . Three Fifty
½ Order . . . . Two Twenty Five
Popeyes Prowess Spinach Salad . . . . Four Dollars
½ Order . . . . Two Fifty

Madam's Sandwiches

Served w/Choice of Chips, Fries or Potato Salad

"The Rise of John Dillinger" . . . . Two Twenty Five
Bacon, Lettuce & Tomato
"Valentino's Virtue" . . . . Two Seventy Five
Ground Sirloin (¼ lb.)
"Don Juan's First Love" . . . . Two Fifty
Grilled Ham & Swiss
"Humphrey Bogart's Ecstasy" . . . . Two Twenty Five
Grilled Cheese w/Bacon or Tomato or Both
"Rabbi Reuben's Weakness" . . . . Three Dollars
Corned Beef, Swiss Cheese and Sauerkraut
"Errol Flynn's Touch" . . . . Three Dollars
Hand Breaded Pork Tenderloin
"The Working Girls Dream" . . . . Three Twenty Five
Open Faced Turkey or Ham Sandwich. w/Bacon and Cheese Sauce

SALAD DRESSING: 1000 Island, Catalina, Ranch, Italian, Garlic, Ranch-Blue Cheese or Dry Roquefort.

Served after 5:00 p.m.

Appetizers

Hustling Hors d'oeuvres . . . . Tray for 4 . . . Five Dollars
                                        Tray for 2 . . . Three Dollars
Hooking Hot Cheese Sauce . . . . One Dollar
Sassy Shrimp Cocktail . . . . Five Dollars

Dinners

Rapturous BBQ Ribs . . . . Slab . . . Twelve Seventy Five
                                   One Half Slab . . . Seven Fifty
Brazen Beef Tips & Butter Shrimp . . . . Nine Dollars
Classy Chicken Cordon Bleu . . . . Eight Fifty
Saucy Ham Steak . . . . Seven Fifty
Erotic Chicken Livers . . . . Five Fifty

Aged Steaks

Bordello Filet Mignon	
Six Ounce	Ten Seventy Five
Ten Ounce	Thirteen Seventy Five
Fourteen Ounce	Sixteen Seventy Five

Prudish Porterhouse . . . . Thirteen Fifty
Titillating T-Bone . . . . Twelve Fifty
Stimulating Sirloin . . . . Thirteen Fifty
Tempting Ground Sirloin -Smothered in Onions . . . . Five Dollars
Seductive Steak Sandwich . . . . Six Dollars

Seafoods

Climactic Catfish -Deep Fried . . . . Six Fifty
"The Buxom Bunch" -Shrimp Fried in Beer Batter . . . . . . Eight Seventy Five
"Around the World" Filet & Lobster . . . . Twenty Four Dollars
Lustful Lobster Tail . . . . Market Price

"The High Priced Spread"

Chateaubriand Dinner - Bouquetiere for 2 . . . . Forty Dollars

Virgin Vegetable of the Evening (Fresh) . . . . One Dollar

ALL MEALS COME WITH SOUP OR SALAD,
POTATO (BAKED, FRIES, SALT ROASTED) & BREAD.
SMALLER OR LARGER PORTIONS AVAILABLE UPON REQUEST.

8-1. Menu, Bordello Restaurant.

THE PIRATES' HOUSE

SAVANNAH, GEORGIA

There is always some controversy among restaurant owners as to whether or not to have a children's menu. The Pirates' House has always used a clever children's menu and will continue to do so (see fig. 8-2). The front of the menu is a pirate mask that children can punch out and wear. The children are also offered a treat from the "Big Treasure Chest" in the restaurant lobby. The menu items are compatible with the regular offerings but are smaller portions and priced proportionately.

Special consideration should be given to menu design for children, because their likes and dislikes can have a big effect on where the parents eat.

Development of a children's menu offers a great deal of room for innovation and creativity in the naming of the items. Children particularly enjoy offbeat names, so a traditional item with an exotic name can have considerably more appeal to a child.

This menu has a design that permits the child to play, to use the menu at the restaurant, and to take it home. It also may be a part of a package of materials specially developed for the child at the restaurant. To a child, the value of the special menu may be in the gift and the physical form of the menu as opposed to the food. The child may consider these a very important part of dinner out.

A children's menu should have a limited number of items and stick to standard food that children enjoy. The language should be straightforward and easily understandable for a child. A child of reading age should be able to read the menu. When I designed a menu for the Dow Hotel years ago, we listed the items under "kinda hungry," "pretty hungry," and "real hungry." Terms like these are familiar to children and work better on menus designed expressly for children.

Welcome to
Herb Traub's Nationally Famous

Pirates' House

in beautiful Savannah, Ga.

MOCKTAILS
SUPER DELICIOUS NON – ALCOHOLIC THIRST QUENCHERS FROM OUR RAIN FOREST BAR

Blackbeard's Boot
A Festive Blend of 4 Fruit
Juices and Grenadine... and
We gladly give you the
fancy Glass Boot! **2.75**

Frozen Rainbow
Strawberries, Peaches,
Pineapple, Coconut,
Fruit Punch and Grenadine
...All Frozen Together! **3.00**

Good Scout (Boy or Girl!)
Sprite and Grenadine
A Scout can drink ALL of this
and still walk the
straight and narrow! **.75**

First Mate's Menu   For Little Pirates Under 12

❶

Long John Silver
Always Eats a Delicious
HAMBURGER
or
CHEESEBURGER
(Tell Us What You Want On It!)
Special P.H. Steak Fries
Tea · Coke · Milk
3.15

❷

Tough Captain Flint
Loves Our Golden Crisp
FRIED CHICKEN
(2 Pieces)
Served with Your Choice of
Any 2 from the Vegetable—Salad List
Homebaked Bread & Butter
Tea · Coke · Milk
3.50

❸

Bold Billy Bones
Would Surely Order
FRIED FILET OF FISH
OF THE DAY
Served with Your Choice
of Any 2 From the
Vegetable—Salad List
Homebaked Bread & Butter
Tea · Coke · Milk
3.50

Vegetables and Salads
STEAK FRIES • SAVANNAH RED RICE • VEGETABLE OF THE DAY
ORANGE CANDIED YAM CIRCLES (AFTER 5:30) • BAKED POTATO (AFTER 5:30)
TOSSED SALAD, CHOICE OF DRESSING • MIXED FRESH FRUIT SALAD
CONGEALED FRUIT SALAD

BE SURE TO SAVE ROOM FOR ONE OF OUR H.L.D.'S
[HUGE LUSCIOUS DESSERTS]

Merry-Go-Round Sundae
Vanilla Ice Cream Surrounded with
Animal Crackers and Topped with a
Tiny Umbrella that Really Works! **.95**

Ice Cream Or Sherbet
Sprinkled All Over with
Little Candy Jewels! **.75**

Blazing Atomic Sundae
Order One and Be Surprised.
It's Really
Supercalifragilisticexpialidotious!!! **1.25**

Sensational Do-It-Yourself Sundae
A Tremendous Dish of Ice Cream
plus TWO Lazy Susans Loaded with
Assorted Toppings, Whipped Cream,
Nuts and Cherries! **4.75**

And don't forget! If You're VERY Good and if You Eat ALL of Your Dinner, Billy Bones
Will Have a Swell Treat Waiting for You in His Big Treasure Chest in the Lobby!!!

8-2. Children's menu, Pirates' House.

HOFAMBERG INN
ST. LOUIS, MISSOURI

Each time I do a class or seminar on menu design and development, I discuss the menu of the Hofamberg Inn (see fig. 8-3). This menu represents a classic in the maximum utilization of space and advertising copy on a menu. The front cover of the menu is used for institutional copy about this restaurant owned by the Schneithorst family. This copy includes the Schneithorst family history in the restaurant business and a statement pledging quality based on family involvement. This is excellent institutional copy.

The back cover of the menu carries an advertisement of the restaurant's catering facilities and meeting function rooms. Through this menu promotion as well as other advertising, the restaurant has an excellent catering business that supplements the profits. In addition to this restaurant, the family owns and operates a coffee shop next door. Promotion of this operation is also done on the back cover of the menu.

The interior of the menu is done in a classic column style of a two-panel layout. The lettering and graphic design are used to attract the patrons to the items that they desire to sell and the specialties of the restaurant. The copy, black lettering on a beige background, is relatively easy to read, although I still recommend black on white. With the items subdivided into various categories, the eye moves very well through this menu. In addition to the static menu, the restaurant offers a market insert for both lunch and dinner, which is placed in the center of the menu. This combination keeps the guest interested by adding variety and adds new customers to the many restaurant regulars.

Where necessary, this menu gives brief descriptions of the ingredients and methods of preparation for all of the menu items. The menu also specifies the foods that accompany each menu item, and the price is stated for each item.

The Weinskeller Lounge, advertised in the bottom left-hand corner, has received national recognition for its architectural design and the construction of its vaulted stone ceilings. This advertisement, as part of their menu, is another example of the excellent utilization of space in promoting another dimension of the operation.

SINCE 1917

The Schneithorst restaurants began with a young man's dream at the turn of the century. That was when Arthur B. Schneithorst, aged seventeen, began his restaurant career as a silver steward in the famous old Planters Hotel in downtown St. Louis and dreamed of owning his own fine restaurant. In the years that followed, the dream grew. Long-time St. Louisans will fondly recall the Benish Restaurant and the popular Rock Grill, owned by Mr. Schneithorst. Through the 1940's and early 1950's, Schneithorst's Bevo Mill and Airport Restaurant were two of St. Louis' favorites. Today, there are two Schneithorst's restaurants in the St. Louis area, each of which commands the respect of gourmets from all over the nation.

Probably the most famous of the two is the Schneithorst's Hofamberg Inn. Seating more than 600 guests, it offers three public and nine private dining rooms. The most popular is the Hofamberg Room, in which antiques, massive beams, polished woods and authentic designs from the corners of the world have created an atmosphere of old-world Bavarian charm.

The Hofamberg Inn takes its name from Schneithorst's Hofamberg Farm (Hofamberg means "house on the hill") at Clarksville, Missouri.

Guten Apetit!

meeting rooms

The Hofamberg Inn features nine private meeting rooms for groups of 2 to 250. Speaker systems and screens are available, and we will arrange for other equipment, if needed.

The Bavarian Room, with its large fireplace, cathedral ceiling, chandeliers and private service bar, takes you back to the manor dining halls of Bavaria, with seating up to 175 people.

The Walnut Room, with seating up to 16, is paneled in soft Walnut and features the Schneithorst family collection of hunting and gun prints.

The Pike Room, seating up to 25, is paneled in soft Pecan and features the Schneithorst family collection of riding accessories and original prints of the St. Louis World's Fair buildings. The Pike Room's long layout is perfect for presentations, board meetings and other small groups.

kaffee haus

The Kaffee Haus is the perfect place for casual dress or a quick luncheon, dinner or snack while shopping, or anytime your schedule won't permit the more relaxed, luxurious atmosphere of the Hofamberg Inn dining rooms.

WINES

By the Bottle
CALIFORNIA PREMIUM
Burgundy - Chablis - Vin Rose
Full Bottle 6.95
Half Litre 3.95
Glass 1.95

appetizers

HOT
SOUP OF THE DAY ...... Cup 1.75
Made kettle-fresh everyday   Bowl 2.25
from our own recipes.
Mushrooms en Skillet 2.95
Toasted Ravioli (with meat sauce) 2.95
Sauteed Shrimp Scampi
in Garlic Caper Butter 4.50
COLD
Oysters on the Half Shell (in season) 4.95
Chilled Shrimp Cocktail 4.95
"Peel & Eat" Shrimp (¼ lb.) 5.95
Marinated Herring in
Sour Cream with Onions and Capers 3.95

for the little baron

(Children under 12)
Choice of Chopped Beef Steak, Fried Sole, Fried Shrimp or
Fried Chicken Leg and Thigh, served with Potato,
Jello Dessert and a Beverage
5.50

THE WEINSKELLER LOUNGE
An authentic Bavarian Cellar
with vaulted ceilings and walls.

BRAISED SHORT RIBS OF BEEF

served with Fresh Garden Vegetables
and Whipped Irish Potatoes
9.95

SAUERBRATEN

Two Special Cuts of Hofamberg Beef marinated in
Vinegar and Spice Brine and then braised
to a juicy goodness in rich Wine Sauce.
With German Potato Pancakes
and Applesauce
10.95

Above Entrees Served with Tossed Green Salad

special dinner salads

Additional, when substituted for Tossed Green Salad.
FRESH SPINACH SALAD 1.50*
With hot bacon dressing.
HEARTS OF PALM AND ARTICHOKES .. 1.50*
On bibb lettuce with vinaigrette dressing
SCHNEITHORST'S SPECIAL SALAD ... 1.50*
Crisp Romaine lettuce with croutons
topped with our special creamy
anchovy-based dressing.
IMPORTED ROQUEFORT DRESSING 1.50
Imported from Europe, this Roquefort Cheese is the
only one in St. Louis awarded the French Red Sheep Seal
for genuine excellence. Marinated and tossed
at your table. Additional on all Salads.

the lighter side

HAUPT SALAD BOWL 7.25
Julienne of Turkey, Baked Sugar-cured Ham,
Swiss Cheese, Tomato Wedges, Hard-boiled Egg,
and fresh June Garden Peas tossed with Mixed
Greens and 1000 Island Dressing.
CLUB HOUSE SANDWICH 6.50
With Potato Chips.
HAM AND EGGS 6.95
With Hash Browned Potatoes
THE CLAYTONIA 6.95
Chopped Beef Steak on Toasted Bun with Broiled
Onion, French Fried Potatoes, and Relishes.

steaks

K.C. SIRLOIN STRIP STEAK .. 15.50
FILET MIGNON 15.50
CHATEAUBRIAND FOR TWO . 39.00
Served with Vegetables.
THE LINDBERGH 13.50
A Petite Sirloin Strip Steak.
Fresh Mushrooms en Skillet 2.95
French-fried Onion Rings 2.75

ROAST PRIME RIB OF BEEF 14.95
A generous Cut of Aged Beef roasted slowly
to preserve all the natural juices.
BAVARIAN PLATTER 10.95
Roast Loin of Pork, Pan-fried Bratwurst and
Knackwurst served with Sweet-Sour Red
Cabbage.
WEINER SCHNITZEL A LA HOLSTEIN .. 13.50
A Tender Cut of Choice Veal Steak, breaded
and Pan-fried to a Golden Brown, garnished
with Country-fried Egg, Lemon Wedge,
Anchovy on a bed of zesty Tomato Sauce.
BARON'S SPECIAL 8.95
Broiled Chopped Hofamberg Beef on crusty
Vienna Bread topped with Molten Cheese
Rarebit Sauce and crisp Bacon and
brightened with Onion Rings.
SAUTEED FRESH "PROVINI" VEAL
LIVER 10.50
With Sauteed Onions.
COUNTRY FRIED CHICKEN 8.25
Or if you prefer - Broiled.
BREAST OF CHICKEN A LA KIEV 10.95
SAUTEED MEDALLIONS OF
PORK TENDERLOIN 9.95
With Glazed Apples.

seafoods

FRESH FILLET OF BOSTON SCHROD .. 10.95
Broiled or Sauteed
GENUINE CAPE SCALLOPS 12.95
CHANNEL CATFISH – Pan-fried 9.95
JUMBO SRIMP 11.50
Fried, Broiled or Sauteed.
With Tartar or Cocktail Sauce.
FILLETS OF FRESH LEMON SOLE 11.50
Broiled or Sauteed
SHRIMP DELIGHT 11.50
Steamed Shrimp on Broccoli Spears
with Hollandaise Sauce.
STUFFED FLOUNDER 10.95
Stuffed with Crabmeat Dressing and
topped with Hollandaise Sauce.
FRIED FILLET OF SOLE 9.95

desserts

HOT APPLE STRUDEL 1.95
With Brandy Sauce.
Philadelphia Cream Cheese Pie .. 2.25
Homemade Apple Pie 1.95
With a Wedge of Cheese.
German Chocolate Cake 1.95
Or Select From Our Dessert Tray

Above Entrees served with:
Tossed Green Salad – Vegetable du Jour or Baked Idaho Potato
with Choice of Sour Cream or Butter.

8-3. Menu, Schneithorst's Hofamberg Inn.

PIRATES' HOUSE
SAVANNAH, GEORGIA

This cocktail menu (fig. 8-4) is an excellent example of a list of house drinks developed by the owner or staff. The drink menu and the marketing thrust are directed to high-margin cocktails that are specials of the house. If you decide to print drink menus or list cocktails on your menu, the best marketing strategy is to imitate the Pirates' House. Space and advertising are given to the items for which the management wants to be known: their own house specials. Lists of commonly known drinks are not a good utilization of menu space. House drinks can be marketed at a higher profit margin and can help build a reputation as well.

Note that some special drinks also include the option of keeping the glass in which the drink is served. Having the glass as part of the price reminds the patron of the Pirates' House and serves as a conversation piece to bring up the restaurant's name.

The names of all of the special drinks are in keeping with the theme of the restaurant—a classic example of one of the marketing principles covered in this book. With the names of the drinks and brief descriptions, the management hopes to create a demand for specialty drinks at premium prices.

In addition to its cocktail menu, the Pirates' House has created a wine list that was a winner in the National Restaurant Association's Great Menu Contest.

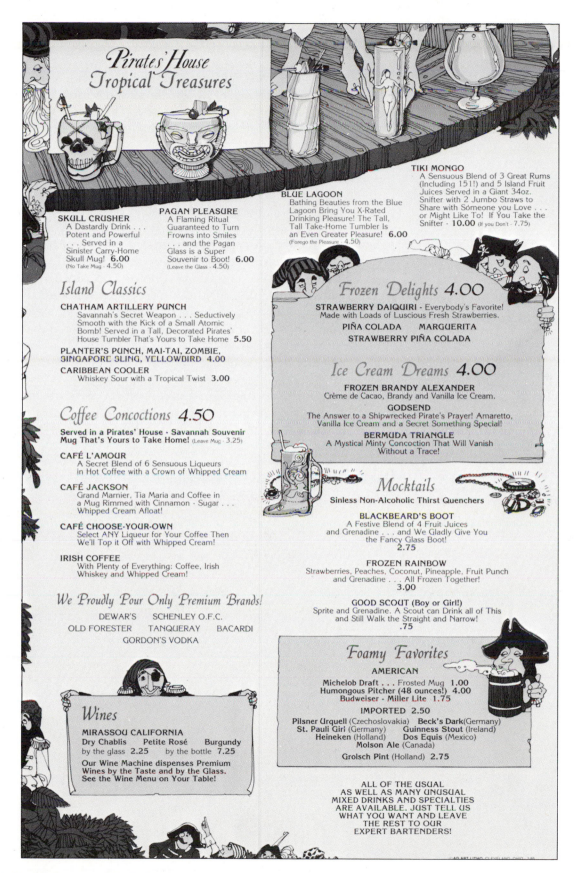

Pirates' House Tropical Treasures

TIKI MONGO
A Sensuous Blend of 3 Great Rums (Including 151!) and 5 Island Fruit Juices Served in a Giant 34oz. Snifter with 2 Jumbo Straws to Share with Someone you Love . . . or Might Like To! If You Take the Snifter · **10.00** (If you Don't · 7.75)

BLUE LAGOON
Bathing Beauties from the Blue Lagoon Bring You X-Rated Drinking Pleasure! The Tall, Tall Take-Home Tumbler Is an Even Greater Pleasure! **6.00**
(Forego the Pleasure · 4.50)

SKULL CRUSHER
A Dastardly Drink . . . Potent and Powerful . . . Served in a Sinister Carry-Home Skull Mug! **6.00**
(No Take Mug · 4.50)

PAGAN PLEASURE
A Flaming Ritual Guaranteed to Turn Frowns into Smiles . . . and the Pagan Glass is a Super Souvenir to Boot! **6.00**
(Leave the Glass · 4.50)

Island Classics

CHATHAM ARTILLERY PUNCH
Savannah's Secret Weapon . . . Seductively Smooth with the Kick of a Small Atomic Bomb! Served in a Tall, Decorated Pirates' House Tumbler That's Yours to Take Home **5.50**

PLANTER'S PUNCH, MAI-TAI, ZOMBIE, SINGAPORE SLING, YELLOWBIRD 4.00

CARIBBEAN COOLER
Whiskey Sour with a Tropical Twist **3.00**

Coffee Concoctions 4.50
Served in a Pirates' House - Savannah Souvenir Mug That's Yours to Take Home! (Leave Mug · 3.25)

CAFÉ L'AMOUR
A Secret Blend of 6 Sensuous Liqueurs in Hot Coffee with a Crown of Whipped Cream!

CAFÉ JACKSON
Grand Marnier, Tia Maria and Coffee in a Mug Rimmed with Cinnamon - Sugar . . . Whipped Cream Afloat!

CAFÉ CHOOSE-YOUR-OWN
Select ANY Liqueur for Your Coffee Then We'll Top it Off with Whipped Cream!

IRISH COFFEE
With Plenty of Everything: Coffee, Irish Whiskey and Whipped Cream!

We Proudly Pour Only Premium Brands!
DEWAR'S   SCHENLEY O.F.C.
OLD FORESTER   TANQUERAY   BACARDI
GORDON'S VODKA

Wines
MIRASSOU CALIFORNIA
Dry Chablis   Petite Rosé   Burgundy
by the glass **2.25**   by the bottle **7.25**

Our Wine Machine dispenses Premium Wines by the Taste and by the Glass. See the Wine Menu on Your Table!

Frozen Delights 4.00
STRAWBERRY DAIQUIRI - Everybody's Favorite! Made with Loads of Luscious Fresh Strawberries.
PIÑA COLADA   MARGUERITA
STRAWBERRY PIÑA COLADA

Ice Cream Dreams 4.00
FROZEN BRANDY ALEXANDER
Crème de Cacao, Brandy and Vanilla Ice Cream.
GODSEND
The Answer to a Shipwrecked Pirate's Prayer! Amaretto, Vanilla Ice Cream and a Secret Something Special!
BERMUDA TRIANGLE
A Mystical Minty Concoction That Will Vanish Without a Trace!

Mocktails
Sinless Non-Alcoholic Thirst Quenchers

BLACKBEARD'S BOOT
A Festive Blend of 4 Fruit Juices and Grenadine . . . and We Gladly Give You the Fancy Glass Boot!
2.75

FROZEN RAINBOW
Strawberries, Peaches, Coconut, Pineapple, Fruit Punch and Grenadine . . . All Frozen Together!
3.00

GOOD SCOUT (Boy or Girl!)
Sprite and Grenadine. A Scout can Drink all of This and Still Walk the Straight and Narrow!
.75

Foamy Favorites
AMERICAN
Michelob Draft . . . Frosted Mug **1.00**
Humongous Pitcher (48 ounces!) **4.00**
Budweiser - Miller Lite **1.75**

IMPORTED 2.50
Pilsner Urquell (Czechoslovakia)   Beck's Dark (Germany)
St. Pauli Girl (Germany)   Guinness Stout (Ireland)
Heineken (Holland)   Dos Equis (Mexico)
Molson Ale (Canada)
Grolsch Pint (Holland) **2.75**

ALL OF THE USUAL AS WELL AS MANY UNUSUAL MIXED DRINKS AND SPECIALTIES ARE AVAILABLE. JUST TELL US WHAT YOU WANT AND LEAVE THE REST TO OUR EXPERT BARTENDERS!

8-4. Cocktail menu, Pirates' House.

J. R. Federhofer's Restaurant & Bar
St. Louis, Missouri

J. R. Federhofer's Restaurant opened in 1984 with a traditional three-fold menu (see fig. 8.5). The menu is designed with attractive graphic representations of items. In the center of the middle panel are boxed items that are the house specialties and the prime marketed items.

Prime space has been given to a peanut butter and jelly sandwich and a bottle of Asti Spumante for two. There has been only about one order per month for this outrageous item, but word-of-mouth advertising has accomplished its purpose. Advertising, not sales. And little inventory is needed for the item.

The J. R. Recommendation in the upper right-hand panel has special emphasis to call customers' attention to the item. It is an excellent way of pointing out a house special.

The libations are listed without price to provide some flexibility. Considerable space is given to desserts on this menu. The restaurant owner is connected with Federhofer's Bakery and uses the restaurant as an outlet for desserts and breads. The acceptance of desserts by the patrons has been outstanding because of the bakery's reputation.

The *J. R.* logo (which also appears on the back of the menu and on the front flaps) serves to identify the restaurant. This logo is continued in the matches and other amenities of the restaurant.

The menu was revised three times in the first year. Careful attention is given to price fluctuation of the raw product and changes in eating habits of the clientele. The menu continues to reflect the items that are most popular and profitable within the targeted market area.

Caffè Espresso

SUCH A TEMPTATION

SHRIMP COCKTAIL $1.99
(Las Vegas style) Tiny native shrimp, boiled, chilled in a parfait glass, topped with lemon slice and cocktail sauce.

FLORETS OF FRESH TENDER BROCCOLI .. $4.25
Encased in cheese, battered dipped and deep fried.

TOASTED RAVIOLI $2.95
Toasted golden brown dusted with parmesan cheese and served with our tangy tomato sauce.

CRISP FRIED MUSHROOMS $2.95
Dusted with parmesan cheese and served with our own tomato sauce.

FRIED MOZARELLA CHEESE STICKS $3.95

TWICE BATTERED ONION RINGS $2.25
Deep fried until crisp, served pipin' hot.

JR'S VEGI PLATTER $3.95
Cauliflower, broccoli, carrots, and zucchini. Cold with dip or steamed with cheese sauce.

THREE ALARM CHICKEN WINGS $3.95

DEEP FRIED ZUCCHINI $2.95
Lightly breaded, served with tangy tomato sauce.

STUFFED MUSHROOM CAPS
Mushroom Caps Stuffed with Crabmeat $4.25
Mushroom Caps Stuffed with Italian Sausage . $3.95
Topped with cheese.

ESCARGOT $4.95

CHEESE GARLIC BREAD $1.50
Federhofer's Bakery Famous garlic bread topped with melted cheese.

GARLIC BREAD $1.25

TO ACCOMPANY

FRENCH ONION SOUP $2.00
Lightly sauteed onions served in a hearty broth that is covered with a crust of bread, melted parmesan and mozzarella cheese.

SOUP DU JOUR .... Cup $1.25 Bowl $1.95
Our chef takes pride in conjuring up a new and exciting soup everyday. One we are sure you will enjoy!

CLAM CHOWDER .... Cup $1.75 Bowl $2.25
Every Friday.

LETTUCE ENTERTAIN YOU

CAESAR SALAD $4.25
Romaine lettuce and croutons, topped with our delicate caesar dressing.

CHEF'S SALAD SUPREME $4.25
Tossed greens with julienne sliced ham, peas, two kinds of cheese, turkey, hard cooked egg wedges, and tomato wedges. Served with choice of dressing.

SEAFOOD SALAD $5.25
Tossed greens with a seafood mixture, guaranteed to tantalize and satisfy that seafaring taste.

DINNER SALAD $1.95
Tossed greens with tomato wedges and cheese.

LIBATIONS

ST. LOUIS' SUNSET
Champagne, vodka, orange juice and a dash of grenadine ...

CREAMSICLE
Orange juice, cream and Amaretto ... Place in blender and beat with good humor...

GRAND AM
Grandmariner and Amaretto ... served over ice. Great for after dinner.

PRIME RIB OF BEEF

PRIME RIB OF BEEF 14-oz. $12.95
Accompanied by a zesty horseradish sauce.

MODEST CUT 10-oz. $10.95

SIMPLY SIRLOIN

STEAK ON A STICK $8.95
One skewer of charbroiled beef and vegetables marinated in light fruit juices, just the right spices to tantalize your palate. Served over rice.

FILET MIGNON 8-oz. $11.95
The aristocrat among fine steaks.
MODEST CUT 6-oz. $9.75

KC STRIP 12-oz. $10.95
A hefty portion, cut for the steak lover with a big appetite

PEPPER STEAK 12-oz. $11.95
An old Southside favorite. KC strip steak charbroiled to perfection with fresh cracked pepper.

LARGER CUTS AVAILABLE UPON REQUEST.

ENTREES EXTRAORDINAIRE

LONDON BROIL $9.95
Charbroiled filet, marinated sliced and topped with our famous Aujus.

STEAK OSCAR $13.95
Twin medallions of beef tenderloin, topped with Lobster meat, and asparagus spears under Hollandaise sauce.

CHICKEN PARMIGIANA $7.25
A real favorite, lightly breaded and topped with mozzarella, dusted with fresh parmesan cheese and nestled in rich red marinara sauce.

CHICKEN MARSALA $7.55
Boneless breast of chicken sauteed in marsala wine, mushrooms and green peas.

CHICKEN PICCATTA $7.25
Boneless breast of chicken sauteed in white wine and lemon butter.

CHICKEN KIEV $8.95
Boneless breast of chicken stuffed with JR's special stuffing. Served on rice with a rich and creamy sauce.

FRIED CHICKEN $6.95
Floured, battered and pan fried to a golden brown texture. Just like homemade.

CHICKEN PRIMAVERA $7.95
Boneless breast of chicken served over rice, topped with fresh vegetables, and white wine lemon butter sauce.

CHAMPAGNE &
BATTER FRIED LOBSTER $16.95

VEAL LOBSTER $13.95
Provimi white veal sauteed and topped with Lobster meat, and asparagus spears under light sherry wine sauce.

VEAL PICCATA $10.95
Provimi white veal sauteed in white wind and lemon butter.

VEAL PARMIGIANA $10.95
The all time favorite prepared as it should be. Lightly coated in a seasoned breading, sauteed and topped with mozzarella cheese, dusted with parmesan cheese on a bed of bright red marinara sauce.

— ALL ENTREES INCLUDE —
CHOICE OF SOUP OR SALAD AND POTATO OR VEGETABLE.

THE BEST OF BOTH WORLDS

PBJ & ASTI $21.95
A platter of Peanut Butter & Jelly Sandwiches and a bottle of Asti Spumante for Two.

STEAK STICK AND
CHARBROILED SHRIMP $12.95

THE ODD COUPLE .... priced daily
Combination of Lobster Tail and Filet Mignon.

HOUSE WINES

Chablis   Rose'
Burgundy   Rhine

IMPORTED FRENCH WINES

White
Red

SEAFOOD SENSATION

SCAMPI $11.95
Jumbo scampi sauteed in butter, lemon and garlic.

CHARBROILED SHRIMP $10.95
Charred to perfection and served with lemon butter sauce, or our own tomato sauce.

FRIED SHRIMP $9.95
An old standard done with a different twist, served with a choice of tangy hot tomato sauce or tartar sauce.

FRESH BAKED WHITE FISH $7.95

SOLE PARMIGIANA $8.95
A New Favorite - Fillet of sole lightly breaded, pan fried, topped with mozzarella cheese, dusted with parmesan cheese, on a bed of marinara sauce.

CATFISH $7.95
Lightly breaded and pan fried to golden brown.

LOBSTER TAILS .... priced daily
Broiled Lobster Tails ready to eat with butter.

BABY FROG LEGS $11.95
A Gourmet's Delight - lightly breaded and charbroiled. Topped with a lemon, butter and garlic sauce.

PERFECT PASTAS

ALLA RAMAGNA $5.95
Prosciutto ham, and fresh broccoli sauteed in sauce of wine, butter, and cheese.

LINGUINI TUTTO MARE $6.95
A delicate seafood sauce.

PRIMAVERA PASTA $5.25
Fresh spring vegetables tossed in sauce. Served with a Capellini.

FETTUCINE CARBONARA $5.95
A sauce of prosciutto ham, cream and cheese.

FETTUCINE ALFREDO $5.25
A sauce of fresh cream ricotta cheese, and parmesan cheese.

RAVIOLI WITH MEAT SAUCE $5.25
A St. Louis favorite.

LINGUINE WITH CLAM SAUCE $6.95

TORTELLINI PIZZILI $6.95
Fresh mushrooms, peas, and a cream sauce.

CAVETELLI CON BROCCOLI $5.95
Fresh broccoli, mushrooms, tomatoes, and a cream sauce.

CAPELLINI CAULIFLOWER $5.95
Fresh cauliflower, mushrooms and a cream sauce.

BAKED SPAGHETTI & MEAT BALLS $4.95

BAKED CANNELONI & CREAM SAUCE $5.95

BAKED CANNELONI & TOMATO SAUCE $4.95

JR RECOMMENDS

SHRIMP JR $11.95
A favorite recipe from JR's private file... Jumbo Shrimp rolled in seasoned bread crumbs, sauteed in a white wine, butter, garlic, and tomato sauce.

Pizza my Heart

	14"
CHEESE	$4.95
ONION	4.95
SAUSAGE	6.25
PEPPERONI	6.25
HAMBURGER	6.25
BACON	6.25
CANADIAN BACON	6.25
MUSHROOM	5.95
BLACK OLIVE	5.95
GREEN PEPPER	5.95
ANCHOVY	6.25
SHRIMP	6.95
JR's SWEETHEART	7.95

Sausage, bacon, mushroom, green pepper, onion, and hamburger.

EXTRAS	1.00

SWEET DREAMS

CHOCOLATE FONDUE $5.95
A Pot of the finest bittersweet chocolate fudge ... warm and fragrant ... surrounded by cubes of angel, pound, and devils food cake. Maraschino cherries and seasonal fresh fruits ... All waiting to be dipped and devoured! How can you resist?

BONITA'S DELIGHT $2.95
Two slices of old fashioned pound cake, lots of ice cream, a special carmel sauce, topped with whip cream, and a cherry. Warning: Can be habit forming!

SUICIDE SUNDAE $3.95
(For those who like to live dangerously) You'll get a tremendous dish of ice cream plus a lazy susan loaded with assorted toppings, whipped cream, nuts and strawberries. From then on it is up to you!

BIT OF HEAVEN $2.95
A thick slice of light-as-a-cloud angel cake topped with a super scoop of vanilla ice cream. Then strawberries ... then whipped cream ... then nuts ... then a cherry ... then tomorrow we diet!

THE LITTLE DEVIL'S DELIGHT $2.25
A thin slice of devils food cake topped with a small scoop of vanilla ice cream, hot fudge, and a bit of whipped cream, and a few nuts. To satisfy the little devil in all of us.

FRESH FRUIT FLAMBÉ for two $5.25
Delicious fresh fruit sauteed to perfection. Flamed tableside. Served over french vanilla ice cream.

8-5. Menu, J. R. Federhofer's Restaurant & Bar.

BUFFALO CHIPS
SANTA MONICA, CALIFORNIA

This menu (fig. 8-6) was a winner in the 1985 National Restaurant Association Great Menu Contest. It is designed as a horizontal letter-fold menu. It incorporates several historical photographs to emphasize the mood of nostalgia. The entire feeling of the menu is one of informality, very appropriate to the primary restaurant offering of hamburgers. The menu is designed in such a way that size, quality and garnishment are immediately stated on the menu.

The beverage section is apparent when the menu is first opened. Directly above this section are the four principal burgers on the menu. The other items are visible when the menu is unfolded further. The menu very effectively uses clip-art to draw attention to other items on the menu. The back cover is designed so it can be mailed as an advertising piece and can be a souvenir for those who have dined at Buffalo Chips.

The judging of the 1985 Great Menu Contest occurred when all restaurant associations were calling for the restriction of happy hours. Buffalo Chips was the first restaurant that I observed making a point of being a club for drivers who are not drinking. The menu is as effective in creating an atmosphere, in merchandising and sales development, as any of those entered in the 1985 contest.

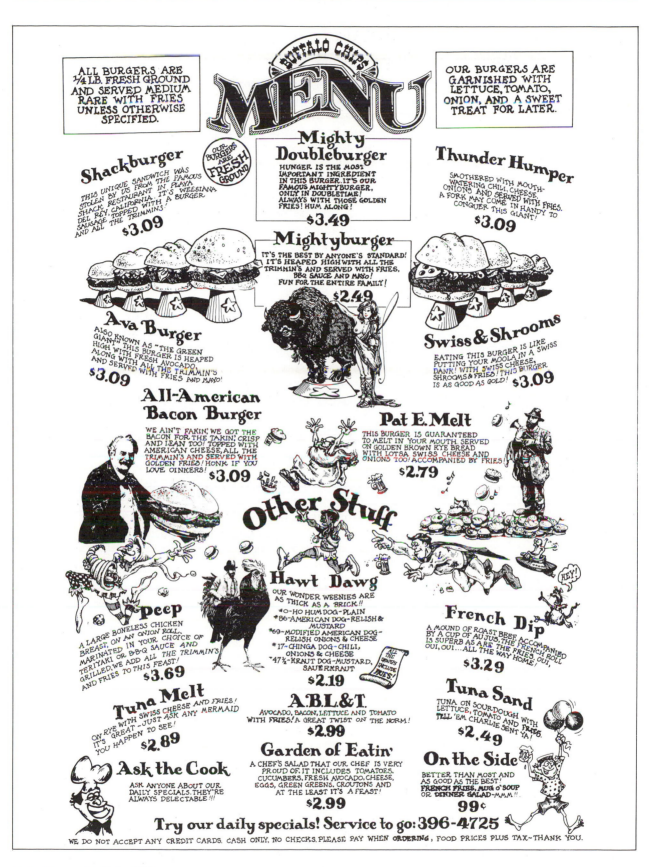

8-6. *Menu, Buffalo Chips.*

NOAH'S ARK
ST. CHARLES, MISSOURI

After the publication of the first edition of this book, in which I included the Noah's Ark menu, the restaurant evolved through a series of changes in management. Each manager made changes in the static menu. It became multipaged and offered items not typically associated with a steakhouse. A small decline in customer counts accompanied each change. It was a classic example of a restaurant that lost sight of its market and the desire of its customers within that market.

The most recent manager has restored the menu to a classic static menu for a steakhouse (see fig. 8-7). Although some new items have been added, the menu remains virtually the same as the original one. As a result, customer counts continue to increase and the restaurant has again identified its market segment.

The menu layout is done on the advertising principle of primacy and recency. The high-gross items are located in sequence so that patrons will be most likely to order them. Noah's Ark signature items—the cauldron of chowder and the salad bar—receive special attention on the menu. An analysis of sales indicates a reasonably equitable distribution in the sales of all menu items. Note that the accompaniments are listed with the entrées. The menu is printed on serviceable stock so it can be reused for a period of time.

Noah's Ark has separate dessert and drink menus. Management has elected not to use any of the regular menu space to merchandise these items. This decision requires the service personnel to recommend desserts and beverages to the guest. Requiring the service personnel to announce items or to offer a separate menu is an excellent way to increase the sale of these items.

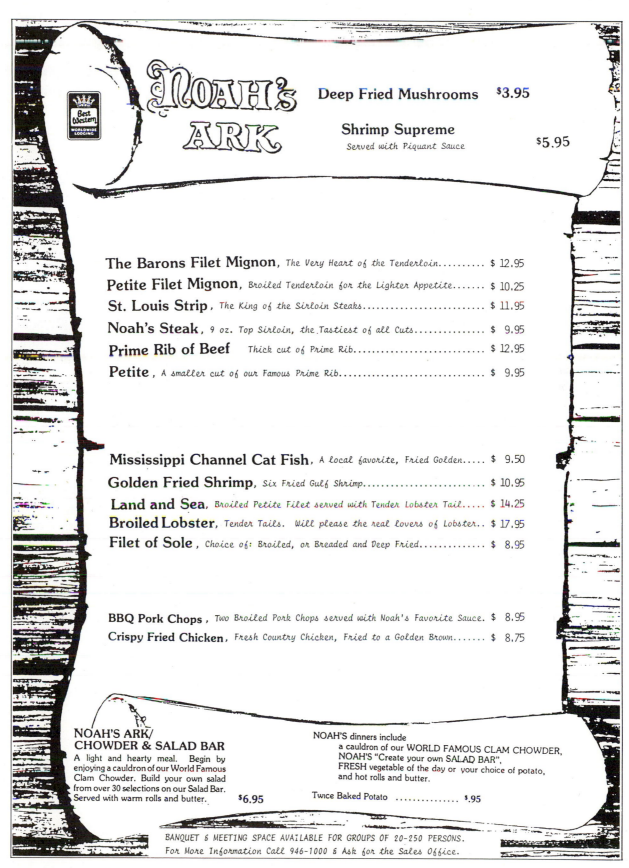

NOAH'S ARK

Deep Fried Mushrooms $3.95

Shrimp Supreme $5.95
Served with Piquant Sauce

The Barons Filet Mignon, *The Very Heart of the Tenderloin* .... $ 12.95

Petite Filet Mignon, *Broiled Tenderloin for the Lighter Appetite* .... $ 10.25

St. Louis Strip, *The King of the Sirloin Steaks* .... $ 11.95

Noah's Steak, *9 oz. Top Sirloin, the Tastiest of all Cuts* .... $ 9.95

Prime Rib of Beef *Thick cut of Prime Rib* .... $ 12.95

Petite, *A smaller cut of our Famous Prime Rib* .... $ 9.95

Mississippi Channel Cat Fish, *A local favorite, Fried Golden* ..... $ 9.50

Golden Fried Shrimp, *Six Fried Gulf Shrimp* .... $ 10.95

Land and Sea, *Broiled Petite Filet served with Tender Lobster Tail* ..... $ 14.25

Broiled Lobster, *Tender Tails. Will please the real lovers of Lobster* .. $ 17.95

Filet of Sole, *Choice of: Broiled, or Breaded and Deep Fried* .... $ 8.95

BBQ Pork Chops, *Two Broiled Pork Chops served with Noah's Favorite Sauce.* $ 8.95

Crispy Fried Chicken, *Fresh Country Chicken, Fried to a Golden Brown* .... $ 8.75

**NOAH'S ARK/
CHOWDER & SALAD BAR**
A light and hearty meal. Begin by
enjoying a cauldron of our World Famous
Clam Chowder. Build your own salad
from over 30 selections on our Salad Bar.
Served with warm rolls and butter. **$6.95**

NOAH'S dinners include
a cauldron of our WORLD FAMOUS CLAM CHOWDER,
NOAH'S "Create your own SALAD BAR",
FRESH vegetable of the day or your choice of potato,
and hot rolls and butter.

Twice Baked Potato .... $.95

*BANQUET & MEETING SPACE AVAILABLE FOR GROUPS OF 20-250 PERSONS.
For More Information Call 946-1000 & Ask for the Sales Office.*

8-7. Menu, Noah's Ark.

PIRATES' HOUSE
SAVANNAH, GEORGIA

The dessert menu from Herb Traub's Pirates' House (fig. 8-8) is a modified three-fold menu, one of my preferences for the menu fold-out. I am particularly intrigued by this menu because the descriptions of the offerings comply totally with the truth-in-menu philosophy. I have eaten a selection from the Pirates' House dessert menu, and the most outstanding aspect of it is that you get exactly what is described. The manager meets the criteria he has established in the written descriptions with all desserts sold. At the Pirates' House, "what you read is what you get."

The names that have been developed for the desserts are merchandisers in themselves. They spur customers to order these extra items and thus add to the checks.

The Pirates' House has always taken the attitude that if the dessert can be sold by menu description, it is an additional source of income. The advent of American Cuisine and regional cooking has increased the sale of desserts in all restaurants. They continue to constitute a high percentage of total sales. *Nation's Restaurant News* recently carried an article on the dramatic increase of total sales brought about by merchandising and the display of desserts. In addition to dessert items, after-dinner drinks can be listed on the dessert menu to merchandise selected specialty items.

Of special interest to me on the dessert menu, as well as on the luncheon and dinner menus at the Pirates' House, is Traub's promotion of the city of Savannah. He has used the back cover of his menu not just to merchandise and promote the Pirates' House but also to describe Savannah's historical significance, its impact on the economy of Georgia, and its significant location in the Southeast.

Traub has used the space on all his menus very well. For good reason, the menus have been chosen to receive the Great Menu Award given annually by the National Restaurant Association.

8-8. Dessert menu, Pirates' House.

JOHNNY'S CAFE
OMAHA, NEBRASKA

The Johnny's Cafe menu (fig. 8-9) is the traditional two-fold style, but the interior is designed like a three-fold menu, as recommended in this book. The front cover of the menu makes a statement about the historical significance of the restaurant and the back cover is used for a children's menu.

The history and location of Johnny's make it appropri-ately a steakhouse operation, so their steaks have prime positions on the menu. The descriptive copy is very limited but adequate for this type of restaurant. Knowing their reputation and having had the opportunity to dine at Johnny's, I do not believe that a lengthy description of the steak is necessary. Their quality statement is made at the beginning of the steak listings and at the end of the menu. The listing of a hamburger as

"steak trimmings" is a novel merchandising device and more accurate than "ground sirloin steak." The menu also includes the restaurant's definitions of "doneness" of the various steaks.

The brown ink on a beige background suits the steakhouse motif. The cattle brands that form the menu border carry out the restaurant theme.

COCKTAILS or MOCKTAILS
"Sip into something delicious"

– BLOODY MARY
– PINA COLADA
– MARGARITA   1.95
– DAQUIRI – Strawberry or Banana
– MAI TAI

HEARTY SOUP

Beef and Fresh Vegetable		
Soup Du Jour	CUP .95	BOWL 1.15

APPETIZERS AND SIDE ORDERS

Shrimp Cocktail	3.95	Cheese Toast	1.90
Cold Shrimp You Peel'm	7.50	Garlic Toast	1.80
Potato Skins	3.95	Fresh Hash Browns	1.00
Chicken Liver Pate	3.00	American Fries	1.00
Relish Dish	1.95	Whipped Potatoes	1.00
Marinated Herring	1.95	Onion Rings	1.80
Rooster Fries	3.95	Cole Slaw	.65
Tomato or V-8		Buttered	
Juice Cocktail	.80	Mushrooms	2.60

DINNER SALADS

Johnny's Famous Salad Bowl	1.25
Wedge of Lettuce Salad	1.35
With Roquefort	
Shrimp Salad	5.10
Chilled Sliced Shrimp on Bed of Crisp Greens, Tomato Wedge and Hard Cooked Eggs, Choice of Dressing	
Chef's Salad	4.35
Crisp Mixed Greens with Julienne of Turkey, Ham or Cheese, Tomato Wedge, Hard Cooked Eggs, Choice of Dressing	

Johnny's ... Since 1922
Omaha's Original Steak House

"Three generations of the Kawa Family assuring you the finest in the Mid-west dining tradition."

ROAST PRIME RIB OF BEEF	9.95
– EXTRA CUT	12.45
– EXTRA EXTRA CUT	14.95
BROILED RIB EYE STEAK	9.95
STRIP STEAK	10.95
Omaha Cattleman's	
TOP SIRLOIN	9.95
Some call this a CLUB STEAK	
PETITE TOP SIRLOIN	7.95
STEAK TRIMMINGS	6.95
Ground and hand formed	
PORTERHOUSE	14.95
First two premium cuts past the pin bone	
T-BONE	12.95
PETITE FILET	8.95
FILET	11.95
The tenderest	

CHATEAUBRIAND (FOR TWO)	27.95
Hand carved at your table	
LOBSTER AND PETITE FILET	17.95

ALL DINNERS INCLUDE:
– House Salad with Johnny's Dressing
– Choice of Potato
– Fresh Baked On-premises Bread and Rolls with Whipped Butter and Seasoned Cottage Cheese

A 62 YEAR TRADITION OF INDIVIDUALLY SELECTING, ON-PREMISES AGING AND HAND CUTTING EACH AND EVERY STEAK.

BROILING DONENESS DEFINITIONS:

– RARE	Red and Cool	– MEDIUM WELL . . . . . No Pink
– MEDIUM RARE	Red Center	– WELL DONE . . Not responsible
– MEDIUM	Pink Center	

TREASURES FROM THE SEA

FRENCH FRIED LOUISIANA SHRIMP	8.95
ICED GULF SHRIMP	8.95
NORTHERN CHANNEL CATFISH	6.95
ROCKY MOUNTAIN RAINBOW TROUT	7.30
HALIBUT, Broiled or Breaded	8.50
DEEP FRIED FROG LEGS	7.50
BROILED AFRICAN	
ROCK LOBSTER TAIL	Market Price

SEAFOOD CATCH OF THE DAY
YOUR SERVER WILL MAKE TODAY'S CATCH AVAILABLE TO YOU. ALL SEAFOOD IS SUBJECT TO SEASON, –WEATHER– AND FISHING LUCK!

DINNERS

DEEP FRIED HALF OF SPRING CHICKEN	5.75
CHICKEN LIVERS	5.45
BROILED CENTER CUT PORK CHOPS	6.95
HAM STEAK	6.95
GRILLED YEARLING LIVER, Onions or Bacon	5.50
VEAL SWEETBREADS, Breaded or Broiled	6.10
CHICKEN FRIED STEAKS, two	6.95

DINNER SANDWICHES
Includes Fresh Fries and Johnny's Salad

STEAK SANDWICH	4.95
PRIME RIB SANDWICH	6.95
CHOPPED STEAK BURGER	3.95
Cheese Choice – American or Swiss	
TURKEY CLUB	4.95
REUBEN	4.95

DESSERTS

Cheese Cake	1.50
Fruit Pies	1.00
Cream Pies	1.00
Creme de Menthe Sundae	.85
Wine Sundae	.85
Custard Cup	.85

BEVERAGES

Coffee	.45
Sanka	.50
Milk	.60
Tea	.45

8-9. Menu, Johnny's Cafe.

Welcome to Johnny's Cafe
Omaha's Original Steak House
Since 1922

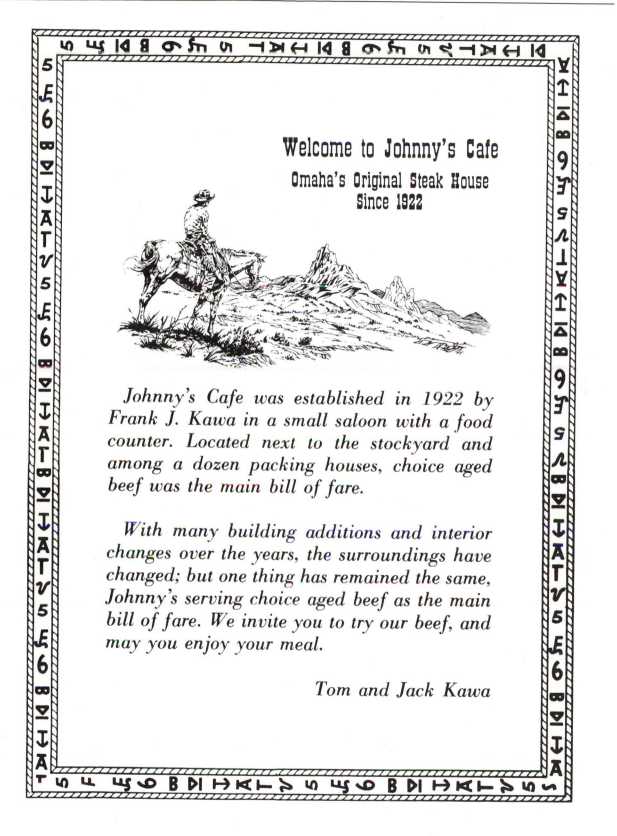

Johnny's Cafe was established in 1922 by Frank J. Kawa in a small saloon with a food counter. Located next to the stockyard and among a dozen packing houses, choice aged beef was the main bill of fare.

With many building additions and interior changes over the years, the surroundings have changed; but one thing has remained the same, Johnny's serving choice aged beef as the main bill of fare. We invite you to try our beef, and may you enjoy your meal.

Tom and Jack Kawa

TONY'S

St. Louis, Missouri

In my classification of restaurants, Tony's rates as a destination restaurant. If you are ever fortunate enough to attain the classification of *destination restaurant,* you can throw away the book on menu design. (See fig. 8-10.)

This classification is unique to the restaurant industry in that the quality of food and status of service are superior to that of all the competition within the market area. The consumer group represents a high check average. Price is not a major consideration for the patrons, but food and service are. Many of the customers have predetermined their choices before entering the restaurant. The service person is responsible for considerable verbal presentation and descriptions of menu items as well as specials. This is effective with the professional waiters at an establishment such as Tony's.

The menu is revised annually to take advantage of current food trends and to offer new items that have been developed by the staff and by the owner, Vince Bommarito. The quality of the products served is never compromised, so the menu sells itself.

The restaurant is an Ivy Award winner and has consistently been given a well-deserved 5-star ranking. The menu is included as an example from one of America's outstanding restaurants.

Primi Piatti

Agnolotti 5.50
Cannelloni 5.50
Fettucine, Romano or Meatsauce 5.50
Cappellini Carbonnara 5.50
Cappellini Primavera 6.50
Cavatelli Brocalli 5.50
Fusilli Pesto 5.50
Penne Meatsauce 5.50
Capelli d'Angelo, Marinara 5.50
Linguine, Fresh Clams 6.75
Soups 5.00
Manicotti of Eggplant 5.50

Insalata

Tony's Salad 5.00
Tomato, Red Onions, & Anchovies 5.00
Special Green Bean Salad 5.00
Bibb Lettuce, Artichokes, Hearts of Palm 5.50
Spinach, Avacado, Crumbled Roquefort 5.00

Secondi Piatti

Seafood
Fresh Seafood Mediterranean 18.50
Fresh Dover Sole 18.75
Grilled Fresh Salmon 16.50
Fresh Trout, Almond-Pecan Butter 16.50
Red Scampi, Adriatic 18.50
Lobster Albanello 16.95
Lobster Tails 22.50

For Tonight's Fresh Seafood Special
See your waiter

Entrees
Tournedos of Beef 16.75

Veal Marsala, Wild Mushrooms 17.50
Veal Piemontese 17.50
Veal Piccatta 16.75
Veal with Eggplant alla Parmigiano 16.75

Roasted Quail on Angel's hair nest 16.50
Boneless Chicken Breast, Peppercorn Sauce 13.50
Boneless Chicken Breast, Fresh Fruit Sauce 13.50
Chioppino of Chicken 15.50

From the Grill
Veal Chop, Truffel Sauce 22.50
Prime Sirloin Steak 18.75
Prime Sirloin Steak, Sicilian Style 17.95
Prime Sirloin Steak Diavola 17.95
Filet Mignon 16.95
Beef Tenderloin and Mushrooms,
Skewer, Wild Rice 16.50
Lamb Chops 18.50
Prime Rack of Lamb 38.00
Chateaubriand 36.00
Linguine Con Pesce 13.75

For other Pasta Entrees consult your waiter

8-10. Menu, Tony's.

CHAPTER NINE

ACCURACY
IN
MENUS

The glowing descriptions—*homemade; corn-fed; ground sirloin;* and other similar phrases—are gone from our menus forever unless they are the truth. Several years ago, it was said that, "If you think consumerism is a gun in your back today, it is going to be a knife at your throat in the future." Accuracy-in-menu legislation has thrust the restaurant industry into that future.

THE RESTAURANT OPERATOR'S OBLIGATION

Government regulation at all levels of the restaurant industry is cause for alarm. The industry does not need any additional laws or reviewing agencies to restrict its free-enterprise operations. Without regulations being imposed on us, we have the opportunity to police ourselves and to take actions that will not require laws and inspection agencies. Every restaurant owner or manager and every person involved in developing menus must assume a personal obligation to total accuracy and truthfulness in the copy that describes food offered for sale.

Traditionally, the menu has been our vehicle for appealing to our customers' senses with verbal descriptions of menu items. Fortunately, there were only a few isolated—and usually unintentional—occasions when menu copy had no relationship to what was prepared and served to a guest. The intent of menu writing always was to stimulate the guest's desire for a specific food by using the most appetizing and appealing words available. It was always assumed that most people did not know the difference between a bay and a sea scallop anyway. The more extensive the copy, the better the food had to be—or at least that was the premise.

Suddenly, with the appearance of a widespread consumer movement, people became more knowledgeable and sophisticated about the food they were eating. They reacted. "You are not telling us the truth about your food. If you are not willing to do this of your own accord, we will have laws passed to force you to have honest descriptions on the menu." California's resulting truth-in-menu legislation made every menu writer accountable for his output. The National Restaurant Association and California's restaurant association, viewing the situation with alarm, decided to try to assist operators to design self-controlled programs.

First the associations adopted a policy for accuracy in menus. (A copy of the *Accuracy in Menu Language Guidelines for the Food Service Industry (AIM)* appears in the Appendixes.) The policy's objectives are to assure consumers that the descriptions of the menu items are accurate and honest; to inform menu writers what is correct for descriptions, specifications, and standards for foods; and to describe common terms and descriptions used in the industry that could be misleading.

The Missouri Restaurant Association has instituted a major program for education and self-policing of *AIM.* A committee of restaurateurs, food vendors, and state officials has been appointed to review menus for accuracy. After a menu is certified as accurate in its description of items, the AIM logo may be affixed to the menu. This alternative to a government regulating and inspection agency is certainly to the advantage of the industry. Based on my own observations, I believe that customers as well as the government are willing, even anxious, to have the industry achieve this kind of accuracy on its own. Self-improvement of menus, education in definitions, and prevention of misleading copy are in the best interest of every restaurant, because they give the consumer confidence that the food served is as represented on the menu.

ACCURATE MENU-WRITING GUIDELINES

Inaccuracies do exist on menus. These inaccuracies are not meant to deceive the consumer; they result from long-term use of industry terminology. As mentioned earlier, "what you read is what you get" is the guideline for modern menu writing. Poetic license is no longer permissible in menu writing. Basic, simple, honest copy is a must. The menu is a kind of catalog that implies a contract between the foodservice establishment and the consumer. Manufacturers of food equipment list specifications for all of the items in their catalogs, and when you buy the equipment, you know what you *expect* to receive. If your expectations are not met, or if the equipment is different than you specified, then you return the merchandise. The foodservice consumer has the same expectations. He reads in your catalog (menu) what you have specified about each item (*prime,*

12 oz., fresh) and has a right to reject an item if it is not prepared or served as represented. Take action now with your menu. Make it an honest catalog and a dependable contract.

Customer satisfaction and prevention of government intervention depend on truthful menus. Take care that all written and spoken words are substantiated with product, invoice, or label.

Representation of Quantity

Proper operational procedures should preclude any problems with misinformation on quantities. Steaks are often merchandised by weight, and the generally accepted practice is to describe the precooked weight.

Obviously, double martinis are twice the size of the normal drink, and if jumbo eggs are listed, the terms have exact meanings—jumbo is a recognized egg size. *Petite* and *supercolossal* are among the official size descriptions for olives. The use of terms such as *extra large salad* or *extra tall drink* may invite problems if they are not qualified further, but there is no question about the meaning of *three-egg omelette* or *all you can eat*. Also remember the implied meanings of words: A bowl of soup, for example, contains more soup than a cup.

Representation of Quality

Federal and state grades for standards of quality exist for many restaurant products, including meat, poultry, eggs, dairy products, fruits, and vegetables. Terminology used to describe grades includes *prime, grade A, good, no. 1, choice, fancy, grade AA, and extra standard*.

Exercise care in preparing menu descriptions with these words. In certain uses, they can imply certain standards. An item described as *choice sirloin of beef* connotes the USDA choice grade of sirloin. One recognized exception, however, is the term *prime rib*. *Prime rib* is a long-established, well-understood, and accepted description for a cut of beef (one of the primal ribs, the sixth to twelfth ribs) and does not represent the grade quality, unless the USDA abbreviation is used in conjunction with the description.

Because of the volume of the industry's use of ground beef, it is best to remember that the USDA definition of ground beef is just what the name implies: No extra fat, water, extenders, or binders are permitted. The fat limit is 30 percent. Seasonings may be added as long as they are identified. These requirements apply only to products ground and packaged in federal- or state-inspected plants.

Representation of Price

If your pricing structure includes a cover charge, service charge, or gratuity, these must be brought to the attention of customers. If extra charges are made for requests such as "all white meat" or "no-ice drinks," these must be stated to the customer at the time of ordering.

Any restrictions placed on the use of a coupon or premium promotion must be defined clearly. If a price promotion involves a multi-unit company, the units that are participating must be indicated clearly.

All menus should accurately state the total price of menu items.

Representation of Brand Names

Any brand of product that you advertise must be the one served. A registered or copyrighted trademark or brand name must not be used generically to refer to a product. (For example, do not advertise Coca-Cola and then serve other cola drinks instead.)

Your own house brand of a product may be so labeled even if it is prepared by an outside source, as long as it was manufactured to your specifications. Containers of condiments and sauces placed on a table must hold the product that appears on the container label.

Among brand-name restaurant products are Coca-Cola, 7-Up, Swift's Premium Ham, Star-Kist tuna, Jell-O, Heinz Tomato Ketchup, Kraft Cheese, Ritz Crackers, and Miracle Whip.

Representation of Product Identification

Because of the similarity of many food products, substitutions often are necessary because of nondelivery, nonavailability, merchandising considerations, or price. When such substitutions are effected, be certain the changes are reflected on your menu. Be sure to make the distinctions in such cases as the following: maple syrup and maple-flavored syrup; veal cutlet and chopped and shaped veal patty; ice milk and ice cream; ground beef and ground sirloin of beef; whipped topping and whipped cream; turkey and chicken; cream and half-and-half; nondairy creamers and cream; Roquefort cheese and blue cheese; and mayonnaise and salad dressing.

Representation of Points of Origin

Potential errors can occur in the description of the point of origin of a menu offering. Be sure you can substantiate claims by packaging labels, invoices, or other documentation provided by your supplier. Of course, mistakes are possible due to shifting sources of supply and availability of product.

Following are some common assertions of points of origin: Idaho potatoes, Maine lobster, bay scallops, Gulf shrimp, Florida orange juice, Wisconsin cheese, Colorado brook trout, Alaskan king crab, and Colorado beef.

Many geographic names are used in a generic sense to describe a method of preparation or presentation. Such terminology is readily understood and accepted by the customer, and no restrictions are necessary on the use of these names. Examples are: French toast, Denver sandwich, french fries, German potato salad, Russian dressing, English muffins, Manhattan clam chowder.

Representation of Merchandising Claims

A difficult area for making the distinction between right and wrong is the use of merchandising claims. "We serve the best gumbo in town" is understood for what it is—boasting for advertising's sake. However, "We use only the finest beef" implies that USDA prime beef is used.

Advertising exaggerations are tolerated if they do not mislead. Advertising a "mile-high pie" would lead a customer to expect a pie heaped with meringue or a similar fluffy topping, but advertising a "foot-long hot dog" and serving something smaller would mislead the customer and be wrong.

Mistakes are possible in properly identifying steak cuts. Use the industry standards that are

provided in the National Association of Meat Purveyors' *Meat Buyer's Guide*.

Home-style, homemade-style, or *our own* are accepted terminology—rather than *homemade*—to describe menu offerings prepared according to a home recipe. Most foodservice sanitation ordinances prohibit the preparation of foods in home facilities.

Use of any of the following claims should be verifiable: fresh daily, flown in daily, kosher meat, aged steaks, finest quality, own special sauce, and low calorie.

Representation of Means of Preservation

The accepted means of preserving foods are numerous, including canned, chilled, bottled, frozen, and dehydrated. If you choose to describe your menu selections with these terms, be sure they are accurate. Frozen orange juice is not fresh, canned peas are not frozen, and bottled applesauce is not canned.

Representation of Food Preparation

The means of food preparation is often the determining factor in the customer's selection of a menu entrée. Absolute accuracy is a must. Customers will readily comprehend if you specify that items are charcoal-broiled, deep-fried, smoked, prepared from scratch, roasted, mesquite-grilled, grilled, or barbecued.

Representation of Visual and Verbal Presentation

When your menu, wall placards, or other advertising contains a pictorial representation of a meal or a platter, the picture must accurately portray the actual contents. Examples of visual misrepresentations include: whole strawberries pictured on a shortcake when sliced strawberries are used; a single thick slice of meat pictured when numerous thin slices are served; six shrimp pictured when five shrimp are served; vegetables or other extras pictured with a meal when they are not included.

Servers must also provide accurate descriptions of menu items. Verbal misrepresentation occurs when a service person asks, "Would you like sour cream or butter with your potatoes?" when an imitation sour cream or margarine is served. It is also wrong to say "The pies are baked in our kitchen," when in fact they were baked elsewhere.

Representation of Dietary or Nutritional Claims

Accuracy is essential when representing the dietary or nutritional content of food. Foods listed as salt-free or sugar-free must be exactly that to protect customers who are under particular dietary restraints. When using terms such as *high fiber, low fat, low sodium,* or *low cholesterol,* be prepared to answer questions and to quantify *high* and *low.* Low-calorie claims must be backed by specific data.

The importance of accuracy in this area should be stressed to all restaurant employees. All employees should have a thorough knowledge of ingredients and preparation of foods so that they can respond intelligently and accurately to patrons' questions.

APPENDIX ONE

NATIONAL RESTAURANT ASSOCIATION POSITION STATEMENTS

STANDARDS OF BUSINESS PRACTICES

The following is a position statement of the National Restaurant Association that was adopted in 1985:

As a member of the National Restaurant Association and in keeping with the spirit of the highest standards of public service and business responsibility, we pledge to:

Food	Provide the optimal value of wholesome food to our customers.
Service	Maintain courteous, attentive, and efficient service in a pleasant atmosphere.
Health	Protect everyone's health by operating clean, safe, and sanitary premises.
Employment standards	Establish performance standards for personnel, based on education and training, and provide equitable wages and attractive working conditions.
Citizenship	Contribute to community life by participation in civic and business development through association and cooperation with responsible authorities.
Fair competition	Engage in fair and open competition, based on truthful representation of product and services offered.
Competitive purchasing	Purchase goods and services only from reputable purveyors on a competitive basis.
Industry development	Contribute through service to the public toward the growth and development of the foodservice industry.
Reasonable profit	Maintain the ability to earn a reasonable profit for service rendered.

Accuracy in Menu Offerings

The following is a position statement of the National Restaurant Association that was adopted in February 1977:

The foodservice industry has long recognized the importance of accuracy in describing its products on menus and through visual or oral representation, both on ethical grounds and from the standpoint of customer satisfaction. The National Resturant Association incorporated standards of accuracy in all representations to the public in its "Standards of Business Practice," originally adopted by the association in 1923. We reaffirm and strongly support the principles therein expressed.

"Truth in dining" or "truth in menu" laws and ordinances have been proposed and in some cases adopted in some government jurisdictions in the belief that representations on restaurant menus present a unique problem in consumer protection. The National Restaurant Association believes that such legislation is unnecessary as federal, state, and many local governments have laws and regulations which prohibit false advertising and misrepresentation of products and provide protection from fraud. In an industry such as ours, where economic survival depends upon customer satisfaction, misrepresentation is most effectively regulated by the severe sanctions of customer dissatisfaction and loss of patronage.

To be equitable, the complexity of such legislation would be staggering. It is conceivable that standardized recipes for each menu listing would be required if regulatory refinement followed its logical course. The problems of enforcement and proof if due process is observed would be monumental if not impossible.

The "truth in dining" movement is not confined to the proposition that restaurant menus be absolutely accurate in the representations. Legislation and ordinances have been proposed that would require identification of a specific means of preservation, method of preparation, or statement of food origin. Such requirements could unjustly imply that certain foods, processes, or places of origin are unwholesome or inferior.

Government action must be confined to problems where its intervention can be effective and at a cost commensurate with the benefits to be gained.

Note: These statements are reprinted with the permission of the National Restaurant Association.

APPENDIX TWO

ACCURACY IN MENU LANGUAGE

(U.S. GOVERNMENT GUIDELINES)

MENU LISTING	ACCURATE DESCRIPTION	IMPROPER USAGE
FRESH	Denotes timeliness or recency of production as in freshly baked bread. A product which has not been frozen. A product as grown or harvested which is not canned, dried or processed. Contains no preservatives to extend shelf life.	Serving a commercially baked or processed food product. Substituting a frozen juice, seafood, and vegetable. Salads made with commercially packed fruit sections which contain a preservative to extend shelf life.
HOMEMADE	A product which is prepared on the premises.	Serving products which have been commercially baked, cooked or processed.
OUR OWN or HOUSE BRAND	Food which is prepared on the premises. Food which is commercially prepared to exclusive recipe or specification. A product which bears your label or name.	Substitution of commercially prepared (baked, cooked or processed) foods or brand name products.
IN SEASON	A product which is readily available in the fresh state.	Substitution of a frozen or processed food product.
GEOGRAPHIC ORIGIN	A product which is grown, harvested, processed or packed at the location specified on the menu. Recommend the word *imported* be used in lieu of a specific country unless there is an assurance of continued availability of the product from a specified country. Further recommend the use of geographic area designation for domestic products in lieu of listing a specific state, e.g., "Gulf Coast Shrimp" in lieu of "Louisiana Shrimp." This provides a degree of flexibility and assures menu accuracy if the product should originate from Florida. *Note:* Since the consumer perceives products advertised by geographic origin may represent a desired quality and value, it is essential that the product served be as advertised.	Serving a product from a different geographic origin than stated on the menu.
CREAM	A product derived from milk and contains a minimum of 18% milkfat.	The substitution of half-and-half (contains approximately 12% milkfat) or nondairy coffee blends.
FRENCH ICE CREAM	Ice cream that contains egg yolks and which meets the D.C. standard of identity for frozen custard.	Serving ice cream to include a premium or high quality line which is not labeled French.
MAPLE SYRUP	A natural product obtained from the sap of the maple tree.	The serving of imitation flavored maple syrup or blends known as table syrup.

MENU LISTING	ACCURATE DESCRIPTION	IMPROPER USAGE
ROQUEFORT CHEESE	A semi-hard cheese which derives its name from the village of Roquefort, France. Usually made from sheep's milk but goat's milk may be used. Looks like blue cheese but has a stronger flavor.	Making a substitution with blue cheese or serving a product which is not labeled Roquefort.
KOSHER STYLE	A product flavored or seasoned in a particular manner which has no religious significance.	
KOSHER	Those products which have been prepared or processed to meet the requirements of the orthodox Jewish religion. They are usually identified by the presence of Hebrew lettering or symbols on the tag, label or product wrapping.	Substitution of a non-kosher or kosher *style* product.
AGED MEAT (TRADITIONAL METHOD)	Storage of select primal cuts of meat for a period of 3 to 6 weeks under controlled temperature and humidity. Meat is tenderized through enzymatic action and it acquires a characteristic flavor as a result of this aging.	Substitution of meats which have not been aged by the traditional method.
PRIME	A product which is first in quality excellence or value. Highest quality grade assigned to meat products by the USDA. Prime denotes a USDA grade of meat *except when it precedes the word* rib.	Serving choice, "house grades" or ungraded meats for prime.
CHOICE	The second highest quality grade assigned to meat products by the USDA.	Serving "house grade" or ungraded meats as choice.
PRIME RIB	A primal cut from the forequarter which contains 7 ribs (6th through 12th inclusive). This beef cut adjoins the anterior portion of the loin in a side of beef. When the word *prime* precedes *rib* on the menu, it denotes the generic name of the cut and not the USDA grade.	Advertising Rib of Prime Beef and serving USDA choice or an ungraded beef rib.
BEEF LOIN	That portion of a hindquarter remaining after removal of the round. It is comprised of the short loin and the sirloin.	
SIRLOIN	The posterior of the beef loin. It is comprised of the sirloin butt (top and bottom) and the butt tenderloin.	Serving roasts or cuts derived from the beef round.
CLUB STEAK	A steak cut which is obtained from the anterior portion of the short loin. It precedes the T-bone and is noted by lack of a tenderloin. May also be a boneless cut from the strip loin.	Substitution of steaks from the top of bottom sirloin butt.

MENU LISTING	ACCURATE DESCRIPTION	IMPROPER USAGE
TENDERLOIN (FILET)	The most tender boneless meat cut obtained from the loin of animals.	Serving miscellaneous boneless meat cuts as tenderloin or filet.
GROUND BEEF	A product comprised of small pieces of meat from boning and trimming operations or non-specific cuts and combinations thereof which is ground. Product may be prepared to varying degrees of leanness. There is no USDA quality grade associated with this product unless the product is so labeled or is prepared exclusively from graded (USDA) meats. This product may be advertised as chopped beefsteak (nondescript).	Representing the product as being obtained from specific cuts, steaks or a USDA quality grade, i.e., chopped sirloin, ground sirloin, sirloin steak, chopped round, prime chopped sirloin, etc.
CHOPPED/ GROUND SIRLOIN	A product labeled in this manner or derived from grinding of trimmings/ portions of meat from the beef loin.	Product labeled ground beef or derived by grinding meat which is not from the loin.
CHOPPED/ GROUND ROUND STEAK	The product labeled in this manner or prepared by the exclusive grinding of a cut of round steak.	Using a product which is not ground round steak.
VEAL	The product of a bovine animal which is slaughtered between 3 and 6 weeks of age and seldom over 3 months. The USDA designates whether product is veal when the product is graded.	
CALF	Mature veal slaughtered between 3 and 10 months of age. Identified as calf by USDA on graded product.	Serving this product as milk-fed veal.
VEAL CUTLET	A single slice of veal obtained from the veal round.	Substitution with veal steaks or patties.
VEAL STEAK	A slice or slices of veal obtained from other areas of the carcass. It may consist of slices which have been formed.	Substitution with veal patties.
VEAL PATTIES	This is a ground formed product which primarily consists of veal.	Serving this product as a veal cutlet or veal steak.
BAKED HAM	A ham which has been heated in an oven for a specified time. The product may exhibit a crust and have a residue of syrup or a caramelization of sugar apparent on the surface.	Serving ham which is not labeled "baked," or a product which has not been oven baked.
COUNTRY HAM	A dry cure ham prepared in the country.	Serving "canned," "smoked," or "fully cooked" hams.
VIRGINIA HAM	A dry salt cured ham from Virginia which is cured from 1 month to over a year. This product is not smoked.	Making a substitution with "Virginia style" or "country ham."
VIRGINIA STYLE HAM	Ham which is cured in the same manner as a Virginia ham but it is not from Virginia.	
SMITHFIELD TYPE VIRGINIA HAM	A dry cure ham which has been smoked.	Serving "Virginia style" or "country ham."

MENU LISTING	ACCURATE DESCRIPTION	IMPROPER USAGE
SPRING LAMB	Those lambs born during early winter and slaughtered between March and early October. These carcasses are identified and stamped "Spring Lamb" by the USDA when they are graded.	Lamb not identified as "Spring Lamb" by the USDA.
CAPON	A surgically unsexed male chicken usually under 18 months of age. It is tender meated and has soft, pliable, smooth-textured skin.	Serving other classes of chicken as capon.
CHICKEN SALAD	A mixture containing chicken as the primary ingredient with spices, dressing and possible inclusion of vegetable(s).	Prepared from turkey in lieu of chicken.
FISH FILLET	Fillets are the sides of the fish cut lengthwise away from the backbone. Usually they are boneless.	Representation of other than this market form as a fillet.
FISH PORTION	Are uniform shaped (generally square) pieces cut from frozen fish blocks made from fillets (not minced fish). Portions must weigh more than 1½ ounces a piece and are at least ⅜ of an inch thick.	Representation of portions as fish fillets are economic fraud.
SALMON	Members of the family Salmonidae are found in many waters of the world. The U.S. fisheries is centered in the Pacific Northwest and utilizes the following species:	
Chinook, King, Spring	This species, *Oncorhynchus tshawytscha*, is usually sold as canned and steaks.	Substitution of any species or market form for a more expensive species or market form would be considered fraudulent.
Blueback, Red, Sockeye	This species, *Oncorhynchus perka*, is usually sold as canned.	
Coho, Cohoe, Medium red, Silver	This species, *Oncorhynchus kisutch*, is usually sold as steaks, dressed, and some canned.	
Pink	This species, *Oncorhynchus gorbuscha*, is usually sold as canned.	
Chum, Keta	The flesh of this species, *Oncorhynchus keta*, ranges from pink to almost white. They are sold as canned and as steaks.	
Masou, Cherry	This species, *Oncorhynchus masou*, is found only around the Asian coast. It closely resembles the Chum in appearance, but is generally considered superior. Seldom canned, sold in the Orient as fresh, frozen or salted.	

MENU LISTING	ACCURATE DESCRIPTION	IMPROPER USAGE
SOLE and FLOUN-DER	This category includes a number of species of flatfish. Flatfish are those that have both eyes on one side of the head. They are found in waters around the world and most species are considered very edible. The following are some of the most common commercial species:	Inaccurately representing specific species of sole or flounder would be a misrepresentation.
Sole	*Parophrys vetulus*—English sole *Glyptocephalus cynoglossus*—Gray sole *Eopsetta jordani*—Petrale sole *Pseudopleuronectes americanus*—Lemon sole *Lepidopsetta bilinesta*—Rock sole *Psettichthys melanostictus*—Sand sole	
Dover Sole	A flatfish of the species *Microstomus pacificus* that can reach 10 pounds. It is found in waters off of Washington, Oregon, California and Alaska. Approximately sixteen million pounds of fillets per year are produced by the U.S. fisheries.	The representation of lesser value sole, domestic or imported, as the very popular "Dover Sole" would be a serious misrepresentation.
Flounder	*Pseudopleuronectes americanus*—Black back flounder *Limanda ferruginea*—Yellowtail flounder *Hippoglossoides platesscides*—Dab, Plaice *Paralichthys dentatus*—Fluke *Platichthys stellatus*—Starry flounder	
TROUT		
Rainbow	A fresh water relative of the Salmon. The species, *Salmo gairdnetii,* is found naturally in rivers and streams throughout the United States, but wild rainbows are *not commercially fished.* Those found in the market are hatchery reared and many are imported from Denmark and Japan and should be marketed as such.	The representation of hatchery reared trout as "wild" or "naturally occurring" would be considered fraudulent. Imported trout listed as native would also be a misrepresentation.
Brook	This fresh water fish, *Salvelinas fontinalis* is found naturally in Maine, Labrador to the Saskatchewan, South in the Alleghenies and has been introduced into waters west of the Mississippi. It is dark gray or olive with small round gray or red spots. It is *not fished commercially.* The brook trout found in the market are hatchery raised. Some are imported from foreign countries.	

MENU LISTING	ACCURATE DESCRIPTION	IMPROPER USAGE
CRUSTACEANS		
Blue Crab	Crustaceans of the species *Callinectes sapidus,* which is about 7 inches across the back. Found in the waters off the Atlantic and Gulf Coasts. Marketed whole and as picked meat (flaked, lump and claw). It is usually more marketable on the east coast than Dungeness Crab.	Substituting a lesser value crab or crab meat for a more expensive one.
Dungeness Crab	Crustaceans of the species *Cancer magister* (9 inches across the shell) fished in the Pacific from northern California to Alaska. Marketed whole and picked meat (body and leg meat). It is usually more marketable in the west coast than Blue Crab.	
King Crab	Crustaceans of the species *Paralithodes camtschatica, Paralithodes brevipes,* and *Paralithodes piatypus* found in the waters of Alaska as well as north and south of the Aleutian Islands. They are 3½ to 4 feet from the tip of the leg to tip of the leg. King Crab meat is sold both picked body meat and leg sections. It is usually more expensive than Snow Crab.	Substitution of the Snow Crab for the usually more expensive King Crab. Substitution of picked or body meat of either species for legs.
Snow Crab	Any crustacean of the species *Chinoecetes* spp. which is 2½ feet from tip of leg to tip of leg. Fished in the Pacific Coast waters off Oregon, Washington, Alaska, Bering Sea and the Aleutian Islands. Snow Crab meat is sold as picked body meat and leg sections.	
North Atlantic Lobster	Crustacean of the species *Homarus americanus* found off the coasts of New England and Canada. It has pincers and is usually sold live and sometimes as picked canned meat.	Substitution with picked meat of a lesser economic value.
Spiny or Sea Crayfish Lobster	This lobster has no pincers and is usually sold only as frozen tails. The tails are sold by size with larger ones less expensive per pound than the medium size. This crustacean, *Panularis argus,* is found in waters from Beaufort, North Carolina, to Brazil and is a close relative to *Panularis interuptus,* which is found on the West Coast of Africa, New Zealand and Australia.	Substituting a warm water tail for the more expensive cold water tail.
Danish or Dublin Bay Prawn Lobster	This crustacean is of the species *Nephrops norvegicus* and is the size of a large U.S. shrimp. They are found off the coasts of Britain, France, Iceland, Spain, Ireland and Denmark.	Representation of Danish lobster tail as a spiny lobster tail.

MENU LISTING	ACCURATE DESCRIPTION	IMPROPER USAGE
Breaded Shrimp	The tail portion of shrimp of accepted commercial species, i.e., *Pineaus*. These crustaceans complete their life cycle in brackish and salt water. The tail portion of shrimp of commercial species must comprise 50% of the total weight of the finished product labeled "breaded shrimp."	
Lightly Breaded Shrimp	The shrimp content is 65% by weight of the finished product.	Any misrepresentation of the various market forms.
Imitation Shrimp	The shrimp content is less than 50% by weight of the finished product.	
Round Shrimp	Round peeled shrimp with tail segment attached.	
Fantail or Butterflied Shrimp	Prepared by peeling the shrimp except the tail fins remain attached, then splitting the shrimp meat on its long axis.	Any representation of a lesser value size as a more expensive size.
Shrimp Pieces	Pieces or parts of peeled shrimp without tail segments.	
Shrimp Size	Usually the smaller the size shrimp the less the cost.	
Prawns	Applied to a number of shrimp-like crustaceans which complete their life cycle in fresh water.	Representing prawns as shrimp.
MOLLUSKS		
Soft Shell Clams (Long Neck, Mananose, etc.)	Bivalves of the species *Mya arenaria* are taken from the Atlantic Coast waters of North America from South Carolina to the Arctic Ocean. Size determines cost and use (large-chowder, medium-fryers, and small-steamers).	Substitution with clams of lesser market value.
Hard Clams (quahog, quahoug)	Bivalves of the species *Venus mercenaria* taken from the Atlantic Coast waters of North America from Cape Cod to Texas. The smaller the size the more expensive. "Chowders" are often chopped up for wholesale marketing. Shell size determines cost and use (chowders 4″ and larger, medium 3″ to 4″, cherry stone 2.25″ to 3″, little necks 2″ to 2.25″.)	Substitution of large sizes for more expensive smaller sizes.
East Coast or Cove Oysters	Mollusks of the species *Ostrea virginica* found in the waters off the eastern U.S. and Gulf Coast. Oysters of this species are often given names which include the area in which they are cultured. These specially identified oysters have some market characteristic which demands a high price, i.e., size, shape, flavor, or color.	

MENU LISTING	ACCURATE DESCRIPTION	IMPROPER USAGE
Bluepoint Oysters	Planted and cultivated at 4 months in the waters of Great South Bay on Long Island. Brings a higher price than the common oyster.	
Chincoteague Oysters	Planted and cultivated in Chincoteague Bay waters located on the seaside of the Eastern shore of Maryland and Virginia. Brings a higher price than common oysters.	Substitution of common East Coast oysters.
Maurice Cove	Planted and cultivated in the waters of Maurice Cove in the Delaware Bay off the New Jersey coast. Brings a higher price than common oysters.	
Cotuit Oyster	Planted and cultivated in the waters of Cotuit Bay off Nantucket Sound in Massachusetts. Brings a higher price than common oysters.	
Lynnhaven Oyster	Planted and cultivated in Lynnhaven Bay waters off Lynnhaven, Virginia. They have a larger size and elongated shape—brings a higher price than common oysters.	
Count sizes for East Coast Oysters		
Extra Large	This size commands the higher price, with the smaller sizes varying proportionate to size. One gallon contains not more than 160 oysters. One quart of the smallest oysters from the gallon contains not more than 44 oysters.	The substitution of smaller sizes for larger.
Large (Extra Selects)	One gallon contains from 160 to 210 oysters per gallon.	
Medium (Selects)	One gallon contains from 210 to 300 oysters.	
Small (Standards)	One gallon contains from 300 to 500 oysters.	
Very Small	One gallon contains more than 500 oysters. The least expensive size.	
Olympia Oysters	Mollusks of the species *Ostrea lurida* which are only from the waters of Puget Sound. These tiny oysters number 2,200 meats per gallon and demand a very high price.	The substitution with small oysters of any other species.
Pacific Coast Oysters	Mollusks of the species *Ostrea gigas* which are found in the waters off the West Coast of the U.S. These oysters are larger than the East Coast variety, but are not usually marketed on the East Coast.	

MENU LISTING	ACCURATE DESCRIPTION	IMPROPER USAGE
Count size for Pacific Coast Oysters		
Large	One gallon contains not more than 64 oysters and the largest is not more than twice the weight of the smallest oyster therein.	Substitution with smaller sizes for larger.
Medium	One gallon contains from 64 oysters to 96 oysters.	
Small	One gallon contains from 96 to 144 oysters.	
Extra Small	One gallon contains more than 144 oysters.	
Bay Scallops	A ridge shelled bivalve mollusk *Pectin irradians*, taken from the bays and the sounds from Massachusetts to the Gulf of Mexico. They are ½ to ¾ inch in diameter (much smaller than sea scallops), and run 500 to 850 meats per gallon. Bay Scallops are usually more expensive than Sea Scallops.	Substitution with Sea Scallops.
Sea Scallops	A smooth shelled bivalve mollusk, *Placopecten grandis*, taken from depths of 1 to 150 fathoms. Much larger than Bay Scallops with 110 to 170 scallops per gallon—found from New Jersey to Labrador.	Advertising the product as fresh or from domestic sources when they are imported.
FROG LEGS	Are the skinless hind legs of any of the members of the family Ranidae. Those mostly marketed are *Rana catesbiana* or common bullfrogs. Few commercial frog farms exist in the U.S. Most frog legs on the market are imported from India, Indonesia, Bangladesh, and Japan as frozen products.	
STATED PORTION	Product listed on the menu by size or weight.	Serving portions smaller than stated.

Reprinted by permission of the Environmental Health Administration—Government of the District of Columbia, from *Accuracy in Menu Language Guidelines for the Food Service Industry*.

APPENDIX THREE

ACCURACY IN MENU LANGUAGE

(CALIFORNIA STATE GUIDELINES)

The California Restaurant Association has printed and distributed to its membership a most comprehensive Special Report explaining the labeling and advertising requirements of the California Business and Professional Code for food items served by restaurants. The Special Report is designed to educate restaurant owners and operators by clarifying the existing requirements under California law. The report is designed as an information piece on the subject of accuracy in menus. It is not to be considered as an absolute interpretation of law, but rather background and clarification of the requirements of the California Truth in Menu Law.

This 1982 revision of the Special Report is reprinted here with the permission of Stan Kyker, Executive Vice President, California Restaurant Association, 3780 Wilshire Boulevard, Los Angeles, California 90010.

Most county health departments, in conjunction with the California Department of Health Services, have established enforcement programs relative to menu misrepresentations by restaurants. Setting the pattern for most of these programs was the Los Angeles County Department of Health Services with its "Truth-In-Menu" enforcement policy and guidelines issued September 27, 1976. These guidelines, and all other county and health department enforcement policies, are based on California's Business & Professions Code and the Sherman Food Drug & Cosmetic Law (California Health & Safety Code), and were established to ensure that food items served by restaurants are properly labeled and advertised.

The California Restaurant Association, as part of its own membership services, has conducted a 'truth-in menus" program for more than 20 years advising members of their responsibility to see that the menu does not mislead the consumer about items served. Only since the mid-seventies, however, have county health departments and the Attorney General's office declared an official "crackdown" on menu misrepresentations, indicating that they do not intend to allow the restaurant operator to shirk his responsibility. *Caution:* Included as violations are inaccurate oral statements by employees regarding products served or substituted whether in response to customers' questions or simply volunteered by the employee.

This paper is designed to provide members with additional background on the subject and clarification of enforcement policy guidelines.

THE LAW/PENALTIES

The various portions of the Business & Professions Code and Health & Safety Code, which are the basis for this enforcement program, are as follows:

1. *Business & Professions Code.* Section 17500, False or Misleading Statements Generally.
   "It is unlawful for any person, firm, corporation or association, or any employee thereof with intent directly or indirectly to dispose of real or personal property or to perform services, professional or otherwise, or anything of any nature whatsoever or to induce the public to enter into any obligation relating thereto, to make or disseminate or cause to be made or disseminated before the public in this State, in any newspaper or other publication, or any advertising device, or by public outcry or proclamation, or in any other manner or means whatever any statement, concerning such real or personal property or services, professional or otherwise, or concerning any circumstance or matter of fact connected with the proposed performance or disposition thereof, which is untrue or misleading and which is known, or which by the exercise of reasonable care should be known, to be untrue or misleading, or for any such person, firm or corporation to so make or disseminate or cause to be made or disseminated any such statement as part of a plan or scheme with the intent not to sell such personal property or services, professional or otherwise so advertised at the price stated therein, or as so advertised. Any violation of the provisions of this section is a misdemeanor punishable by imprisonment in the county jail not exceeding six months, or by a fine not exceeding two thousand five hundred dollars ($2,500), or by both."

2. *Health & Safety Code.* Several sections could be cited. The most pertinent are Sections 26460, 26461, 26534 and 26528.
   "Section 26460. It is unlawful for any person to disseminate any false advertisement

of any food. . . . An advertisement is false if it is false or misleading in any particular."

"Section 26461. It is unlawful for any person to manufacture, sell, deliver, hold or offer for sale any food . . . that is falsely advertised."

"Section 26534. It is unlawful for any person to manufacture, sell, deliver, hold or offer for sale any food . . . that is adulterated."

"Section 26528. Any food is adulterated if any one of the following conditions exists:

"(a) If any valuable constituent has been in whole or in part omitted or abstracted therefrom.

"(b) If any substance has been substituted wholly or in part therefor.

"(c) If damage or inferiority has been concealed in any manner.

"(d) If any substance has been added thereto or mixed or packed therewith so as to increase its bulk or weight or reduce its quality or strength or make it appear better or of greater value than it is."

NOTE: Violations of these sections of the Health & Safety Code are misdemeanors subject to imprisonment in county jail for not more than six months or a fine of not more than $1,000, or both. Subsequent convictions or violations committed with intent to defraud or mislead are subject to one year in jail, or $1,000 fine, or both.

VIOLATIONS

Violations may be referred to the appropriate district or city attorney for criminal prosecution, or the Attorney General's office for civil prosecution, depending on the severity of the situation. Less severe or unintentional violations *may* simply result in order to eliminate the violation, with prosecution following if full compliance is not obtained.

LOS ANGELES COUNTY POLICY

The Los Angeles County Menu Misrepresentation Policy, which has become the basis for most statewide enforcement, describes five broad types of violations:

1. Quality or grade of products misrepresented;
2. Point of origin of food products not as advertised;
3. Size, weight or portion of food not as advertised;
4. Products advertised as fresh which have been frozen, canned or preserved; and
5. Merchandising term(s) of advertised food not accurate.

The first of these categories—Quality or Grade of Products Misrepresented—is further defined by the Department to include violations resulting from:

(a) Adulteration of products (see Section 26528, Health & Safety Code, above),
(b) Substitution of food which is of lesser quality or value or which is different from that advertised (grade or brand names, species of fish or meat, type or cut of meat, etc.),
(c) Hamburger or imitation hamburger being served which does not meet statutory specifications for the products, and
(d) Dairy products not meeting statutory definition specifications.

ILLEGAL SUBSTITUTIONS

Some of the most common violations occur through substitution of one product for another. When restaurants serve food of a lesser quality or value than that represented in the menu *(or orally by employees)*, or one food item is substituted for another without informing the customer (whether the substituted item is of lesser or greater quality or value), the restaurant has engaged in false advertising, a violation of Section 17500 of the California Business & Professions Code and Sections 26460 and 26461 of the California Health & Safety Code. NOTE: In most cases, it is not considered a violation for a restaurateur to substitute a food item of *greater* quality or value than the one specified on the menu; e.g., USDA Prime served for Choice.

Illegal substitutions may occur across a broad range of menu items and statements. The final determination as to what is an illegal substitution, however, almost always boils down to whether or not the menu description or name accurately represents the item that is actually served. In this regard, it is hard to go wrong if the menu description of an item is the same as the description or name on the product label or the package in which it was shipped. Operators may also wish to obtain certification from their suppliers that products delivered are the same as those ordered and/or listed on the menu. In brief, care should be taken to see that purchase orders, invoices and product labels support your menu descriptions.

Federal Standards of Identity. Several products listed on menus must meet state and/or federal standards of identity. Many of these items are dairy, meat and fish products (discussed further below). Others include maple syrup (must be prepared from 100% sap of maple trees), maple flavored syrup (contains at least 10% maple syrup), honey flavored syrup (contains at least 10% honey, and orange juice (must be true juice; orange drink cannot be substituted).

Product Brands and Grades. Illegal substitutions occur whenever any product *brand* is served other than that advertised, or when a different *quality grade* product is served than the one stated on the menu. Examples of such violations include serving other colas for Coca-Cola; other gelatins for Jell-O; other decaffeinated coffees for Sanka; bleu cheese for Roquefort cheese; bar liquor for brand name alcohol beverages; other hams for Swift Premium Ham, etc. Similarly, it is a violation to serve USDA "Good" or nongraded beef for USDA "Choice"; Grade A eggs for Grade AA; nongraded poultry for Grade A; or nongraded fruit for fancy, etc.

Dairy Products Generally. Misrepresentations relative to quality grades or statements may occur with *dairy products.* The California Food and Agricultural Code and Regulations of the Department of Food and Agriculture (Title III, California Administrative Code) outline specific definitions and standards of identity for various dairy products, including milk, cream, and such manufactured dairy products as ice cream, sherbets, ice milk, butter, cheese, sour cream, sour cream dressing, buttermilk.

In addition, the codes provide specific definitions and regulations governing the manufacture and sale of *products resembling dairy products,* including "imitation milk products" (defined as products containing oils or fats other than milk fat in combination with a milk product) and "nondairy products" (defined as products resembling a milk product but which contain no milk or milk solids). The codes also establish standards for oleomargarine, "imitation ice cream," "imitation ice milk," "imitation cheese," "imitation sour cream," etc.

Oleomargarine. Restaurants may serve margarine to customers only if notice is given on the menu or menu board that margarine is served (those requirements must be met even if a customer requests margarine). Although margarine may be used in food *preparation* without meeting the above notice requirements, such use would be an illegal substitution if the menu proclaims food items are prepared with butter.

Cheese. Cheese products also invite misrepresentation violations, with "Cheeseburgers" and pizza the most obvious opportunities for inaccurate use. In order to use the term cheese, an operator must use either "natural cheese" or "processed cheese." If an operator serves "cheese food," "cheese spread," or "cheese product," the term *cheese* may not be used. (The California Administrative Code provides specific standards of identity based on minimum milk fat content for these products.)

"Cream" Products. In addition, whipped topping may not be called whipped *cream,* IMO or other cultured baked potato dressings may not be called "sour *cream,*" and nondairy creamers may not be served as *cream* or half-and-half. It should be emphasized that it is perfectly legal to serve such products, and that there is no requirement that they specifically be labeled as such; however, it is illegal to represent them as the actual dairy product either *orally by employees* or in writing on the menu.

"Fresh" Products. Similarly, frozen or canned products may legitimately be used without specifically calling them frozen or canned; however, meats, fish, vegetables or fruits that have previously been frozen, canned or otherwise processed may not be called "fresh." Specifically, frozen means 32°F.

Species and Cuts of Meats. Also providing many opportunities for misrepresentation are illegal substitutions and inaccurate descriptions of species of fish or meat products and type or cut of meat. Examples of this type of illegal substitution include serving turkey salad as chicken salad; turkey roll (soya or other vegetable protein added) served as "turkey"; turbot as halibut; shark meat for whitefish; another species of sole for "Dover sole"; milk soaked pork as veal; and small chickens for rock cornish game hen. More common are chopped veal patties served as veal cutlets; smoked pork shoulder or "picnic ham" served as ham; and ground beef served in place of ground round or ground sirloin. Inaccurate descriptions occur when beef liver is merchandised as calves' liver or "baby beef" liver, and hot dogs are merchandised as *all* beef" or "*all* meat." Tuna merchandised as "white" must be albacore.

Despite arguments to the contrary by some enforcement agencies, the Association's position regarding "Prime Rib" has been accepted. The enforcement policy is that "prime rib" is a long-established, accepted and understood term for the cut of beef served to customers and does not represent the grade quality unless the term USDA is used in conjunction with the description. The cut of beef is from the rib *primal* area, ribs 6-12 (commonly referred to as a standing rib roast).

One species of fish that has caused considerable concern relative to misrepresentation is rockfish served as Red Snapper. The California Fish and Game Commission has identified 12 species of rockfish that may be called by the common name of "Pacific Red Snapper." The 12 species and their common names are as follows:

1. *Sebastes entomelas* (widow rockfish)
2. *Sebastes flavidus* (yellowtail rockfish)
3. *Sebastes goodei* (chilipepper)
4. *Sebastes levis* (cowcod)
5. *Sebastes melanops* (black rockfish)
6. *Sebastes miniatus* (vermillion rockfish)
7. *Sebastes ovalis* (speckled rockfish)
8. *Sebastes paucispinnis* (bocaccio)
9. *Sebastes pinniger* (canary rockfish)
10. *Sebastes rubberrimus* (yelloweye rockfish)
11. *Sebastes fufus* (bank rockfish)
12. *Sebastes serranoides* (olive rockfish)

If "Pacific Red Snapper" is used on a menu, it is recommended that the restaurateur receive certification from the fish supplier that the product delivered is one or more of the above listed species. Any rockfish other than the 12 species listed should simply be called rockfish rather than "Pacific Red Snapper." NOTE:

The use of the term "Red Snapper" is strictly limited to identify the true "Red Snapper" (*Lutjanus campechanus*).

Enforcement agencies contend that when a menu lists a product simply as "scampi," the product served must be a species of crustacean known as "scampi"—not shrimp or prawns. However, the agencies also recognize that the term "scampi" is used to designate a method of preparation with the product usually cooked or served in a seasoned butter and garlic sauce. Thus, if the species "scampi" is *not* served, the product *served* must also be designated on the menu *along with* the term "scampi." Examples include: "shrimp scampi," "scampi-style shrimp," "lobster scampi," or "scampi-style lobster."

Hamburger Requirements

Closely related to the general prohibition against substitutions are the specific requirements relative to the sale of "hamburger" as provided in Sections 26595 and 26596 of the California Health & Safety Code. These sections read as follows:

"Section 26595. DEFINITIONS. As used in this article, the following definitions shall apply:

"(a) 'Hamburger' means chopped fresh or frozen beef, or a combination of both fresh or frozen beef, with or without the addition of beef fat as such and with or without the addition of seasoning. Hamburger shall not contain more than 30% fat, and shall not contain added water, binders, or extenders. Beef cheek meat (trimmed beef cheeks) may be used in the preparation of hamburger to the extent of 25%, and if in excess of natural proportions, its presence shall be declared on the label in the ingredient statement, if any, and otherwise contiguous to the name of the product.

"(b) 'Imitation hamburger' means chopped fresh or frozen beef, or a combination of both fresh and frozen beef, with or without the addition of seasoning. Imitation hamburger may contain binders and extenders, with or without the addition of partially defatted beef tissue, without added water or with added water only in amounts that the product's characteristics are essentially that of a meat pattie.

"(c) 'Restaurant' means restaurants, itinerant restaurants, vehicles, vending machines or institutions, including hospitals, schools, asylums, eleemosynaries, and all other places where food is served to the public for consumption on the premises of sale which are not included within the definitions of the terms *restaurants, itinerant restaurants, vehicles* and *vending machines.*

"Section 26596. LISTING INGREDIENTS IN MENU, OR POSTING INFORMATION: PROHIBITED AND PERMITTED USE OF TERMS.

"(a) If imitation hamburger is sold or served in restaurants, a list of ingredients thereof shall appear on the menu, or if there is no menu, such information shall be posted as state department shall by rules and regulations require. No list of ingredients, however, shall be required for imitation hamburger which contains not more than 10% added protein and water, and which does not contain other binders and extenders.

"(b) No restaurant shall use the terms 'hamburger,' 'burger,' or any other cognate thereof in any advertisement or menu to refer to any imitation hamburger. A restaurant selling or serving imitation hamburger may refer to such product as imitation hamburger or by any other term which accurately informs the customer of the nature of the food product which he is sold or served."

As indicated in Section 26595, "hamburger" may not contain more than 30% fat or added water, binders or extenders. A chopped beef product containing any binders, extenders or added water, *regardless of percentage to total weight,* is "imitation hamburger." Such a product may be served, but it must be called "imitation hamburger" or any other term accurately describing the product as long as the terms "hamburger" or "burger" are not used.

Section 26596 requires that *if "imitation hamburger" is sold* or served in a restaurant, *a list of ingredients must appear on the menu except* when the "imitation hamburger" contains no more than 10% added protein and water and does not contain binders and extenders. No specific requirements for "menu" listings are included in the law nor will they be spelled out in regulations. However, the California Department of Health has adopted regulations relative to the listing of ingredients of "imitation hamburger" in restaurants without menus as required by Section 26596(a). The regulations (Sections 13620 and 13621 of Title 17, California Administrative Code) are as follows:

"Section 13620. DEFINITIONS.

"(a) 'Wallboard' means any permanent sign used to display or describe food items for sale in a restaurant.

"(b) 'Placard' means any nonpermanent sign used to display or describe food items for sale in a restaurant.

"(c) 'Menu' means any list presented to the patrons stating the food items for sale in a restaurant.

"Section 13621. WALLBOARD AND PLACARD REQUIREMENTS IN RESTAURANTS WITHOUT MENUS.

"Restaurants serving imitation hamburger containing more than 10% added protein and water or other extenders or binders shall post an ingredient statement on a wallboard or placard. (a) The ingredients shall be listed in descending order or predominance by weight. (b) The term 'imitation hamburger' or any other term which accurately informs the customer of nature of the product and its ingredient shall be stated in letters of at least one (1) inch in height (72-point letters) in bold face in colors which contrast with the wallboard or placard. (c) The wallboard or placard shall be posted in a permanent place, conspicuous to the customers, in each room or area where food is served."

POINTS OF ORIGIN/PORTION SIZES AND WEIGHTS

Another type of violation occurs when restaurants advertise food items on the menu as originating from a specific geographic place or area but cannot substantiate that origin. If the point of origin cannot be substantiated by observing the labels, bulk packages or boxes in which the product was shipped, or by the invoice or other means, a false advertising violation may be charged.

Examples of the type of menu items that are potential violations include Colorado trout, Maine lobster, European ham, Lake Superior whitefish, Wisconsin cheese, Louisiana frog legs, Idaho potatoes, Chesapeake Bay oysters, Kansas City beef, etc.

NOTE: Such generic terms as *french fries, french toast, french dip, danish pastries, english muffins,* and *swiss cheese* (unless the menu claims it is imported) are not included in this category. The enforcement agencies have accepted the Association's arguments that geographical terms do not automatically denote the origin of a product but may also indicate a recipe or style of preparation. It is generally accepted that geographical terms used with products prepared with more than one ingredient, such as a Denver sandwich, Boston clam chowder, German potato salad, etc., denote a method of preparation rather than a point of origin. It is *not* necessary to use the word "style" to qualify such products.

Menu items represented to be specific sizes or weights must also be no less than advertised. For example, 12-ounce steaks or quarter-pound hamburgers must weigh no less than those amounts (precooked). "Bowls" of soup should contain more than "cups" of soup; a double martini should be double in comparison to a regular martini; "large" eggs must not be "medium," and the like.

According to federal government standards, the word "jumbo" when used with shrimp applies to commercial counts of 21–25 headless shrimp per pound. (Although no regulation defines "prawns," the Health Department guidelines indicate that headless shrimp meeting or exceeding the size standards for jumbo—25 count per pound or less—may be called prawns.) Government regulations also stipulate that "breaded shrimp" must be at least 50% shrimp.

MERCHANDISING TERMS/GRAPHICS

This aspect of menu misrepresentation is one of the most sensitive parts of the overall enforcement program. It is an emotional issue that sometimes overshadows more serious misrepresentations in the mind of the restaura-

teur. The basic enforcement policy is that merchandising terms relating to the quality, quantity, method of preparation or characteristics of the food product served to the consumer are questionable and misleading unless they can be verified by the owner or by observation, checking the product, label or invoice or discussion with chefs or cooks.

Included in this category are such merchandising statements as "best blend," "our own special sauce," "finest quality," "fresh daily," "homemade," "low calorie," etc. Other merchandising misrepresentations might relate to cooking style (e.g., barbecued, roasted, sauteed, fried, broiled, baked, smoked, etc.) or use of a pictorial representation on the menu that does not accurately represent the quality, quantity, method of preparation or characteristic of the item usually served to the customer.

Special Notes

1. *Homemade.* California law prohibits any restaurant from offering for sale, selling, or giving away any food or beverage products wholly or partially prepared in a private home. However, the term "homemade" does not refer to made-in-the-home products. The terms "homemade," "home style," or "homemade style" may be used for products prepared in a restaurant's kitchen or in a restaurant firm's *own* commissary or bakery.

2. *Low Calorie.* The term "low calorie" may not be used unless a restaurant has obtained a laboratory certification of the calorie count for the product served. Even so, there is no definition or standard of how many calories equal "low calorie." Thus, other terminology, such as "dieter's special," etc., is recommended. CAUTION: The term "Weight Watchers" is registered by Weight Watchers International.

3. *Barbecue.* The term *barbecue,* for purposes of menu misrepresentations, has never really been adequately defined. Instead, the enforcement policy states that "merely cooking and then basting the cooked product with barbecue sauce would not qualify as a barbecued product." This policy would also prohibit calling a beef sandwich with barbecue sauce added a "barbecued beef sandwich."

4. *Advertising Puffery.* After prodding by the Association, the enforcement agencies have acknowledged that certain menu merchandising statements, such as "best" or "finest" are not automatically illegal but are often nothing more than advertising puffery. A statement such as "We serve the best chili in town" would not be considered a misrepresentation because it can be understood by the consumer for what it is—advertising puffery. However, "the best" or "the finest" must be substantiated when the product advertised has an established standard of quality, e.g., "the finest beef" must be USDA Prime, and "the best eggs" must be Grade AA.

FALSE ADVERTISING OTHER THAN MENUS

Another area, besides menus, in which the potential exists for misrepresentations is in general advertising (newspapers, magazines, billboards, radio, etc.), promotions, coupons, two-for-one plans, and the like.

Specifically, false advertising violations may occur on coupon promotions or two-for-one plans when restrictions on usage of the coupons or the plan are not clearly indicated or are misleading. Similarly newspaper advertisements and coupons must clearly indicate the exact nature of what is being offered. If photographs or drawings are used in ads, they should accurately reflect the items being offered. Restrictions placed on how many meals, what type of meals, or when the coupon may be used, must be clearly indicated.

If the advertisement is for the unit of a franchise company or a chain organization but the "special" or coupon is good only for one or specific units, the advertisement must clearly indicate which ones or if too many units would have to be listed, the term "good at participating restaurants only" would be acceptable.

CRA SUMMARY

The basic key to this question is to study your menu and be sure that it tells the truth—not just partial truth but the whole truth. Substitutions of products other than those advertised on the menu remain the largest single type of violation: smoked pork shoulder or "picnic ham" is *not* ham; veal patties are *not* cutlets; frozen or canned is *not* fresh; USDA Good or ungraded beef is *not* Choice; California potatoes are *not* Idaho potatoes; maple flavored corn syrup is *not* maple syrup; turkey salad is *not* chicken salad; and on and on.

If you are not sure about a menu item or description, check with your supplier or with the Association. In addition, most county health departments will, upon request, review your menu and advise you of potential problem areas.

NOTE: MEMBERS ARE URGED TO NOTIFY THE ASSOCIATION IF CONTACTED BY A HEALTH DEPARTMENT OR LAW ENFORCEMENT AGENCY REGARDING MENU MISREPRESENTATIONS AND IF CHARGES ARE FILED. SUCH NOTIFICATION, INCLUDING PARTICULARS, MAY BE USEFUL IN THE OVERALL CRA PROGRAM.

The ultimate responsibility for truthful menus rests with *you.* Creativity and development of appealing merchandise is still possible, though greater care may be necessary in developing the "romance of the menu." There is no question, however, that menu names and descriptions must accurately reflect the items served to avoid costly litigation, fines or adverse publicity and to reduce the prospects of new restrictive legislation.

GLOSSARY

A Cost: The reduction of an asset for the benefit of the company.

Analysis Ratio: A mathematical relationship between any items of operational cost.

As Purchased (AP): Foods as they are received from the vendor.

Average Check (AC): Dollar amount of food sales or beverage divided by total number of checks.

Beverage Cost: Money spent to purchase alcoholic beverages.

Break-Even: The point at which income from sales equals the total cost of operations. There is no profit and no loss.

Check Distribution: The number of persons who purchase at specific price levels.

Closing Point: That point in volume where all variable costs are paid; sometimes referred to as minimum sales point.

Contribution Margin (CM or Gross Profit): The profit or margin after the product cost is subtracted from the selling price.

Controllable Cost: Any cost that is decreased or increased by management actions.

Cost of Food Consumed: The dollar value of food used for all purposes.

Cost of Food Sold: The dollar value of food sold at menu price to only the customers of the establishment.

Daily Actual Food Cost: The food cost determined on a day-to-day basis using one of several different methods.

Edible Portion (EP): Food items ready to serve after preparation and cooking.

Eye Gaze: The direction that the customer's eyes follow when the menu is open.

Fixed Cost: Any cost not responsive to volume.

Internal Sales: Any sales promotion based on point-of-sale advertising or done by the service personnel.

Market Plan: A systematic program to penetrate a market with the products offered on your menu.

Market Share: That portion of the business done in relation to the total amount of business done for a market segment.

Menu Mix (or Sales Mix): The total of the individual sales of each of the menu items in relation to total sales.

Menu Objective: A formal statement of the expectations for an operation based on the marketing plan and the menu policy.

Menu Policy: A statement of the number of items and types of food that will be offered for sale.

Merchandising: Whatever is done in the operation to promote sales.

Overhead: All costs over and above food and labor.

Percentage Cost: The cost of any profit-and-loss item expressed as a percentage of sales:

$$\text{percentage cost} = \frac{\text{cost}}{\text{sales}} \times 100$$

Pricing: The method of establishing the menu prices to be charged to the customers.

Profit: The dollar amount remaining after all expenses have been deducted from income.

Profit-and-Loss Statement: The listing of all income minus all expenses with a resultant profit or loss.

Promotion: Any device used to stimulate the selling of a product or service.

Raw Food Cost: The cost of each ingredient in a recipe; used to determine the exact food cost of a menu.

Secondary Sales: The sales of additional items—i.e., appetizers, drinks, and desserts—in addition to the entrée items.

Shrinkage: Loss of weight or volume during cooking or preparation of a food item.

Standard Food Cost: What the food cost should be, provided that all established standards are adhered to and there is minimal food waste in the operation.

Standards: Established quality and performance as a basis for comparison of an operation's performance.

Uncontrollable Food Costs: Costs that the management cannot control.

Unit Cost: The cost of each recipe portion.

Value Perceived: The customer's belief that there is a value to the items that he is purchasing.

Variable Cost: Any cost that is responsive to volume.

Variances: Differences between actual and the established standard.

Yield: The usable quantity after processing an as-purchased item.

BIBLIOGRAPHY

Bell, Donald, A. *Food and Beverage Cost Control.* Berkeley: McCutchan Publishing Corp., 1984.

Carlson, Howard M., Joseph Brodner and Henry T. Maschal. *Profitable Food and Beverage Operation.* 4th ed. New York: Ahrens Publishing, 1962.

Conducting a Feasibility Study for a New Restaurant. Chicago: National Restaurant Association, 1983.

Dittmer, Paul R., and Gerald C. Griffin. *Principles of Food, Beverage, and Labor Cost Controls for Hotels and Restaurants.* 3rd ed. New York: Van Nostrand Reinhold Company, 1984.

Dukas, Peter, and Donald Lundberg. *How to Plan and Operate a Restaurant.* 2d ed. rev. New York: Hayden, 1972.

Eckstein, Eleanor. *Menu Planning.* 3d ed. Westport, Ct.: AVI, 1983.

Fay, Clifford T., Richard C. Rhoads, and Robert L. Rosenblatt. *Managerial Accounting for the Hospitality Service Industries.* 2nd ed. Dubuque: William C. Brown Company, 1976.

Hayes, David K., and Lynn Huffman. "Menu Analysis: A Better Way." *The Cornell Quarterly,* Feb. 1985:64–70.

Horwath, Laventhol. *Uniform System of Accounts for Restaurants.* Rev. ed. Chicago: National Restaurant Association, 1983.

James, Robert W. *Decision Points in Developing New Products.* Washington, D.C.: U.S. Small Business Management Series, No. 39.

Kasavana, Michael L., and Donald I. Smith. *Menu Engineering: A Practical Guide to Menu Analysis.* Lansing, Mich.: Hospitality Publications, 1982.

Keiser, Ralph J., and Elmer Kallio. *Controlling and Analyzing Costs in Food Service Operations.* New York: John Wiley & Sons, 1974.

Keister, D. C. *Food and Beverage Control.* Englewood Cliffs, N.J.: Prentice-Hall, 1977.

Keister, D. C. *How to Use the Uniform System of Accounts for Hotels and Restaurants.* Chicago: National Restaurant Association, 1977.

Kotschevar, Lendal H. *Management by Menu.* Chicago: National Institute for the Foodservice Industry, 1981.

Kotschevar, Lendal H. and John B. Knight. *Quantity Food Production: Planning & Management.* New York: Van Nostrand Reinhold Company, 1979.

Kreck, Lothar A. *Menu: Analysis & Planning.* 2d ed. New York: Van Nostrand Reinhold Company, 1984.

Kreul, Lee M., and Anna M. Scott. "Magic Numbers: Psychological Aspects of Menu Pricing." *The Cornell Quarterly,* Aug. 1982:70–75.

Lundberg, Donald E. *The Restaurant from Concept to Operations.* New York: John Wiley & Sons, 1985.

"Menu Design for Effective Merchandising." *The Cornell Quarterly,* Nov. 1978.

Ninemeier, J. *Planning and Control for Food and Beverage Operations.* East Lansing, Mich.: The Educational Institute of the American Hotel and Motel Association, 1982.

Pavesic, David V. "Cost-Margin Analysis: A Third Approach to Menu Pricing and Design." *International Journal of Hospitality Management,* 2, no. 3 (1983).

Samuelson, Paul L., and Will D. Nordhaus. *Economics.* 12th ed. New York: McGraw-Hill, 1985.

Schewe, Charles, and Reuben Smith. *Marketing Concepts and Applications.* 2d ed. New York: McGraw-Hill, 1983.

Seaberg, Albin G. *Menu Design: Merchandising and Marketing.* 3rd ed. New York: Van Nostrand Reinhold Company, 1983.

Shugart, Grace S., M. Molt, and M. Wilson. *Food for Fifty.* 7th ed. New York: John Wiley & Sons, 1985.

Stokes, John W. *How to Manage a Restaurant: Or Industrial Food Service.* 4th ed. Dubuque: Wm. C. Brown Co., 1982.

West, B. B., Levelle Wood, Virginia Harper and Grace Shugart. *Food Service in Institutions.* 5th ed. New York: John Wiley & Sons, 1977.

Witzky, Herbert K. *Practical Hotel-Motel Cost Reduction Handbook.* New York: Ahrens Book Co., 1970.

INDEX